RUSSIA'S PROVINCES

STUDIES IN RUSSIAN AND EAST EUROPEAN HISTORY AND SOCIETY

Arup Banerji
MERCHANTS AND MARKETS IN REVOLUTIONARY RUSSIA, 1917–30

Vincent Barnett
KONDRATIEV AND THE DYNAMICS OF ECONOMIC DEVELOPMENT

R.W. Davies
SOVIET HISTORY IN THE YELTSIN ERA

John Dunstan
SOVIET SCHOOLING IN THE SECOND WORLD WAR

Stephen Fortescue
POLICY-MAKING FOR RUSSIAN INDUSTRY

James Hughes
STALINISM IN A RUSSIAN PROVINCE

Peter Kirkow
RUSSIA'S PROVINCES

Taras Kuzio
UKRAINE UNDER KUCHMA

E.A. Rees (*editor*)
DECISION-MAKING IN THE STALINIST COMMAND ECONOMY

Vera Tolz
RUSSIAN ACADEMICIANS AND THE REVOLUTION

Matthew Wyman
PUBLIC OPINION IN POSTCOMMUNIST RUSSIA

Studies in Russian and East European History and Society
Series Standing Order ISBN 0–333–71239–0
(*outside North America only*)

You can receive future titles in this series as they are published by placing a standing order. Please contact your bookseller or, in case of difficulty, write to us at the address below with your name and address, the title of the series and the ISBN quoted above.

Customer Services Department, Macmillan Distribution Ltd
Houndmills, Basingstoke, Hampshire RG21 6XS, England

Russia's Provinces

Authoritarian Transformation *versus* Local Autonomy?

Peter Kirkow
Research Fellow
Centre for Russian and East European Studies
University of Birmingham

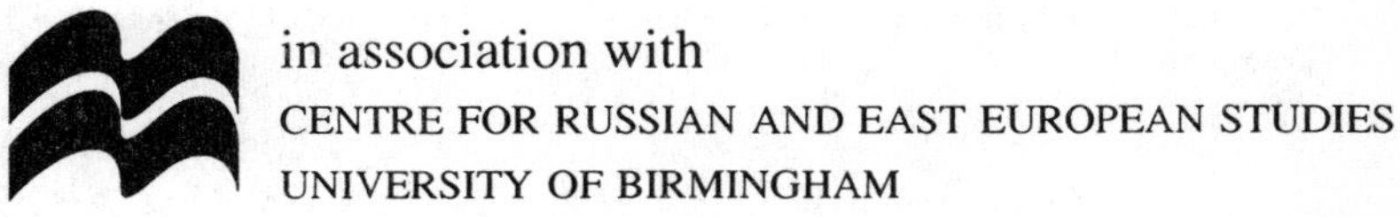

in association with
CENTRE FOR RUSSIAN AND EAST EUROPEAN STUDIES
UNIVERSITY OF BIRMINGHAM

First published in Great Britain 1998 by
MACMILLAN PRESS LTD
Houndmills, Basingstoke, Hampshire RG21 6XS and London
Companies and representatives throughout the world

A catalogue record for this book is available from the British Library.

ISBN 0–333–71789–9

First published in the United States of America 1998 by
ST. MARTIN'S PRESS, INC.,
Scholarly and Reference Division,
175 Fifth Avenue, New York, N.Y. 10010

ISBN 0–312–17595–7

Library of Congress Cataloging-in-Publication Data
Kirkow, Peter, 1966–
Russia's provinces : authoritarian transformation versus local autonomy? / Peter Kirkow.
p. cm. — (Studies in Russian and East European history and society series)
"St. Martin's Press in association with Centre for Russian and East European Studies, University of Birmingham."
Includes bibliographical references and index.
ISBN 0–312–17595–7
1. Regionalism—Russia (Federation) 2. Federal government—Russia (Federation) 3. Russia (Federation)—Economic policy—1991– 4. Russia (Federation)—Politics and government—1991– I. Title. II. Series
JN6693.5.R43K57 1997
320.447'09'049—dc21 97–8880
CIP

This book is printed on paper suitable for recycling and made from fully managed and sustained forest sources.

10 9 8 7 6 5 4 3 2 1
07 06 05 04 03 02 01 00 99 98

Printed in Great Britain by
The Ipswich Book Company Ltd
Ipswich, Suffolk

Contents

List of Tables

List of Figures and Tables in Appendix

Figure

Tables

Preface

This book is the outcome of my PhD research carried out at the Centre for Russian and East European Studies of the University of Birmingham in 1992–5 and it covers events until early 1996. In fact, it is a continuation and extension of work I originally started at this Centre in 1991–2 for a MSocSc degree, when I was analysing the Russian discussion on the viability of setting up free economic zones (FEZs) in different parts of the country for the period 1988–92. This experiment of creating market enclaves within a then still stringent planning system resulted in some of the most conspicuous bids for regional independence, following President Yeltsin's encouragement of regional elites to 'take as much sovereignty as you can'. However, the almost complete failure of the FEZ projects led me to look at more general issues of centre-periphery relations in the context of intended transformation in contemporary Russia.

As a general rule, regional development is characterised by a tension between economic efficiency and social equality. This conflict between allocating resources to those territories where the highest marginal rates of return are expected, and the need for redistribution to problem regions, which are experiencing levels of income and growth below the national average over a period of time, is further aggravated, in the case of Russia, by the simultaneous attempt at building both a market economy and democratic institutions. Moreover, Russian reformers are not only faced with specific pathologies of the former Soviet planning system and its spatial repercussions in terms of excessive metropolitan dominance over peripheral regions and a high degree of urbanization, but also the tradition of a paternalistic, egalitarian regime and patron-client relations with particular strongholds in rural areas.

It is not clear though, whether history books will describe one day the political and economic changes in Eastern Europe and the former Soviet Union more in the light of democratic institution-building or whether pictures of national conflicts, massacres and ethnic cleansing will dominate. Although the latter was also on the political agenda during the transition to democracy in Southern Europe and Latin America, it became in former state socialist countries a horrifying dimension and a characteristic feature of intended systemic transformation. Feelings of national identity and the perception of central state exploitation, which were supressed or marginalised over many decades, unleashed a sudden, dynamic process of finding ethno-spatial identity as well as the desire for national self-determination including the control over territorial resources. The importance of these conflicts motivated my search for further explanation.

While having an early interest in reform attempts in Hungary and former Yugoslavia as a student of Moscow State University during the late *perestroika* period, I had also the chance to travel around the country and to get an idea of the sheer diversity in climatic conditions, natural resource endowment and indigenous traditions and culture. This interest was later further enhanced by reading literature on adjustment programmes and regional development in Latin American countries when I was getting my first degree at Berlin (West) University.

At that time, I had already established contacts with politicians and academics in the Altaiskii *krai* (AK). My choice of the Primorskii *krai* (PK) as a second case study was encouraged by the director of our Centre, Professor Julian Cooper, helping me to get in touch with a former postgraduate student of the Centre, who was based, at that time, in Vladivostok, as well as by another member of staff, Dr Anthony Rimmington, who went to that city a few months before my first visit in summer 1992. These pragmatic considerations are still highly important for choosing places to carry out field work in Russia. Moreover, both regions are well suited to my research approach in terms of their peripheral location (though, admittedly, in a completely different context), having roughly the same size of territory and population, which makes them in some respect comparable, as well as the fact that both provinces embarked on projects of FEZs, so that I was already familiar with one part of the local discussion on market reform.

My primary concern was, after having lived through state socialist authoritarian rule in East Germany, how people in remote regions could take their fate at last in their own hands and start a new life without commands and petty tutelage from above. At the same time, having had the chance to travel to each region three times in the course of my research work, I could also observe how people's attitude towards market and democracy changed from initial euphoria to one of scepticism, disillusionment, and a renewed secretiveness and even suspicion towards foreigners. This set me to thinking of what went wrong during the implementation of reforms and where forces of resistance were located.

Many people joined me on this research journey and there is clearly not enough space to thank all of them appropriately. In fact, my PhD research programme was only made possible by a studentship I received from the School of Social Science of this university, which was granted to an EC citizen for the first time in 1992, and I gratefully acknowledge the strong encouragement I received from the head of the school, Dr Adrian Randall. However, first and foremost, I want to thank my supervisor, Professor Philip Hanson, for all his patience, correctness and professional suggestions whenever doubts arose. His convincing and strong arguments were a fantastic guidance in this labyrinth of events in Russian provinces. I am grateful to the director of the Centre, Professor Julian Cooper, for his great support for young people to carry out research, as well as to Dr Michael Bradshaw, lecturer at the School of Geography of this university, for abundant advice and help with scarce Russian regional statistics. Many members of staff read earlier drafts and gave useful comments. I am thankful to all our librarians and secretaries of the Centre for their technical, informational and moral support.

Among my Russian colleagues, I gratefully acknowledge the help I received from Dr Alexander Loginov, the former head of the Altai Department of the Siberian Branch of the Russian Academy of Sciences, as well as Dr Viktor Savalei, the former director of the Pacific Centre for Economic Development and Cooperation in Vladivostok. I also want to thank Dr Anna Shkuropat and Professor Mikhail Terskii from the Far Eastern Technological Institute, who twice provided me with a safe haven in Vladivostok at a time when not only were typhoons raging but political storms had also started.

However, most of all, I am thankful to my parents in Germany. Without their financial and moral support this book would not have been possible.

List of Abbreviations

Monographs and articles are quoted in brackets right after the information used by indicating the author, year of publication and the page, e.g.: (Hill, 1983, p.29), while listing the complete source in the bibliography at the end. The same applies to important newspaper articles. In the case of more general newspaper information, the source is indicated instead of the author of the article, while using the following abbreviations:

AP	*Altaiskaya pravda*
DM	*Delovoi mir*
DS	*Delovaya Sibir'*
EkiZh	*Ekonomika i zhizn'*
FI	*Finansovye izvestiya*
FT	Financial Times
KD	*Kommersant-daily*
NG	*Nezavisimaya gazeta*
RET	Russian Economic Trends
RFEU	Russian Far East Update
RG	*Rossiiskaya gazeta*
RV	*Rossiiskie vesti*
UR	*Utro Rossii*

Abbreviations of Weight, Statistical and Currency Units

bn	billion
cbm	cubic metre
DM	German Deutschmark
ha	hectare
kg	kilogramme
km	kilometre
kWh	kilowatt hour
l	litre
mn	million
Q	quarter of a year
R	Russian ruble
$	US-dollar
sq	square
t	tonne
trn	trillion

1 The Spatial Context of Intended Transformation

A common historical and ethnographical feature of East European countries and former Soviet republics is the spatially intertwined co-existence of ethnically non-homogeneous nations. This unleashed, after the collapse of the communist system, ethnically motivated conflicts over economic resources, political rights and cultural acknowledgment (Offe, 1994, p.143). While outbreaks of ethnic wars in the Balkans, Caucasus and Central Asia indicated not only the ambiguity of existing or newly drawn state frontiers in a world of increasing globalisation (Beck, 1993, p.121), there started also a process of finding and newly defining ethno-spatial identity (Slovakia, Croatia, Tatarstan, Bashkortostan).

However, the regional impact on intended systemic transformation has a number of other features as well. Particular *actors* at the provincial and local levels are involved in implementing reform policy, while having their own local experience. New democratic *institutions* differed not only between East European countries in dependence on various paths of extrication from state socialism (Stark, 1992, p.20), but even among Russian administrative regions. Moreover, in the case of Russia, the sheer diversity of climatic and time zones, natural resource endowment and indigenous culture has to be taken into account in view of their impact on economic activity, transport and communication. Remnants of the military-industrial complex, which are often concentrated in particular areas and comprise company towns, are under severe strain. Miners' strikes and social unrest in Vorkuta or the Kuzbass remind us of possible hot spots.

It is the intention of this introductory chapter to raise questions about why regions matter in the context of intended transformation and to give some indication on the dimension of social and economic change with which people in these countries (and constituent provinces) are faced. This will be followed by explanations of the structure of the book and the chief hypothesis examined in it. Research methods used in this study will be outlined in a special section, before finally introducing both investigated regions in the national context.

1.1 WHY DO REGIONS MATTER?

At the time of writing, the Russian Federation (RF) is constituted of 89 so-called 'subjects of the federation', the first subnational units in the administrative-territorial hierarchy, which are here frequently referred to as regions or provinces.[1] The Federation Treaty of 31 March 1992 was originally signed by only 86 provinces due to the hold-outs of Tatarstan and Chechnya-Ingushetiya which split up later (Hanson, 1993, p.45–6).[2] In fact, three separate versions were signed, according to different administrative formations, with 20 republics, 10 autonomous *okruga* and one autonomous *oblast'* and 57 ordinary or standard regions (*oblasti*, *kraya* including the cities of Moscow and St Petersburg), a perilous division, which was inherited from Stalin's arbitrary 'divide and rule' along ethnicity lines. The centre in Moscow came to a special agreement with Tatarstan in February 1994,[3] while in Chechnya a bloody war was started by Moscow's military establishment in December 1994 to stop the Chechen leadership's assertion for state independence.

There was some discussion at the beginning whether to change administrative boundaries and to set up larger subnational units, for example, along the lines of former planning regions. However, as Hanson (1994b, p.2) noted, the centre feared that a smaller number of larger provinces could exert stronger power against Moscow and even enforce separation from the RF. Moreover, representative bodies in the provinces had a democratic mandate after the elections in March 1990 in the same way as Yeltsin had, which he could not simply abolish. Nevertheless, such kinds of discussion are still going on,[4] while regional elites are trying to change the administrative status of their province.

These attempts are motivated by regional leaderships[5] through a perceived hierarchy of Russian regions with the republics at the top enjoying exclusive privileges (tax allowances, customs exemptions) and the ordinary provinces at the bottom. Such kind of preferential treatment, however, was neither specified in the Federation Treaties nor in the new Russian Constitution adopted in December 1993, although formulations like the joint use of natural resources or joint foreign trade, which did not apply to republics, left much room for speculation. The only clear difference is that the head of executive power in the republics is not appointed by the President (Wishnevsky, 1994, p.9). This promoted natives to power, who pursued a strong localist policy (Tatarstan, Sakha/Yakutiya, Bashkortostan). The new Russian Constitution specifies merely the right of republics to establish their own languages for use alongside Russian and the right to their own constitutions (Teague, 1994, p.26), although it is not legally clear what difference it really makes to ordinary provinces' 'statutes'.[6]

There seem to be more mundane reasons for the desire to 'enhance' the administrative status (portfolio of minister, travel abroad) and it is not clear whether the economies of all the republics are really performing better. What is clear is that the initial circumstances and prospects of successful adaptation vary enormously across republics – from relatively developed (Komi, Tatarstan) to fairly underdeveloped (Tuva, Dagestan). Lavrov (1994, p.6) argued that about 10–12 regions (mainly standard provinces) provided 60 per cent of total tax revenues in 1993, while a number of republics (North Caucasus, Marii-El, Kalmykiya and Altai) were heavily subsidised. The centre tried undoubtedly to appease the more assertive republics (Tatarstan, Bashkortostan, Sakha/Yakutiya, Kareliya), but *ad hoc* deals were made through bilateral bargaining without a clear formula.

Chapter 2 will analyse more extensively traditional Soviet regional policy and try to show that regional leaders' lobbying and bargaining efforts have been familiar features for a long time. It gives, in the discussed context, a clear sign of how regional elites can influence national economic policy. Yavlinskii (1994, p.4) estimated that state subsidies amounted to 30 per cent of GDP in 1992 and soft credits to another 12 per cent,[7] which had a detrimental effect on macroeconomic stabilisation efforts. Industrial and agrarian lobbies used their channels in conjunction with those of regional leaders to exert pressure on the centre, including levers like the refusal to transfer federal taxes or to deliver grain to the federal food reserve fund. Apart from this traditional way of rent seeking, more sophisticated forms were developed in recent years, capitalising on market imperfections or deficiencies of government regulation as Kuznetsov (1994, p.490–1) showed with respect to defence-related enterprises in Russia.

The peculiar administrative division is one main reason for continuing troubles between Moscow and its constituent provinces, while the central leadership is trying to push through market reforms and to devise democratic institutions in which a new federation could work. The distribution of powers between centre and provinces is blurred, since there is no strong institutional link between the policymakers at different territorial levels; neither through the coherence of national parties with strong representation in the provinces nor through an independent judiciary which would enforce law. The abolition of the industrial branch structure and the disbanding of the CPSU resulted in a loosening of institutional coherence.

Yeltsin tried to impose executive rule by a number of institutional arrangements, which were enacted through clauses in the new Russian Constitution but violated main principles of a federal system:

1) the President has the authority to suspend acts issued by regional executive power if he considers them contradictory to the constitution or international treaties on human and civil rights;
2) the President may act as final arbiter in conflicts between federal and regional bodies or between constituent members of the federation;
3) the institution of presidential envoys or representatives would apply more to a unitary than a federal state;
4) the main power in Russia's regions is concentrated in the hands of governors (heads of administration), who were mainly appointed by the President and, in most of the cases, were not to be popularly elected until 1996 (Tolz, 1994, p.3–4).

While the institutional structure will be discussed in more detail in Chapter 3, it will suffice to stress here that these constitutional devices, though obviously tailored for Yeltsin's authoritarian rule, did not materialise into effective instruments to implement market reforms. Even worse, some of them had a boomerang effect. For example, an association 'Governors of Russia' was created, which is bypassing the President's administration and directly approaching the government (*Izvestiya*, 5 July 1994, p.5).[8]

The Federation Council (the upper house of the federal parliament) elected in December 1993 is also perpetuating the administrative-territorial division inherited from Stalin. At the 1993 elections to the Federation Council, 85 federal subjects elected two deputies each and 54.6 per cent of the 171 deputies held appointed posts in the executive, including 53 chief administrative officers (Hough, 1994, p.13, note 17). Rather than a new federal institution that could help in advancing reforms, the Federation Council was widely expected to become 'a "stock exchange", in which whoever happens to be President seeks to barter favours for the regions in exchange for help staying in power' (Webb, 1994, p.44).

Apart from the focus on institutions in the spatial context of intended systemic transformation, social actors and particular policymakers in the regions have also to be scrutinised. Among those who have an impact on the national policy agenda are mainly regional politicians, the industrial management and the military.[9] While the macroeconomic stabilisation programme was elaborated by technocrats in the centre and decrees were issued by politicians in Moscow, regional elites had to carry out the blueprint. However, as Hanson (1994a, p.21) argued, they have not necessarily an interest in stabilisation ('not in my backyard') and liberalisation (populist 'consumption bias' through local price controls). Insider privatisation (many of them are managers or close associates of managers) may provide opportunities for control and personal acquisition of property as well as in special trading arrangements for their regions; trying to shelter the provincial economy from outside control, while, at the same time, earning revenues from foreign trade under conditions of local prices for primary products (oil, coal, electricity) being far below world market prices.

Stabilisation and price liberalisation are opposed by regional elites. Indirectly, in the case of the former, through their pressure on Moscow for the issue of subsidies and local surrogates (money substitutes) as well as the manipulation of extrabudgetary funds. Directly, in the case of the latter, through price controls, trade barriers and rationing. These are important reasons why regions matter in the context of intended transformation. Hanson (1994a, p.24) pointed to the profound conflict between the objective of a stable currency as a national public good and the interest of regional politicians to favour their electorate due to their desire to gain popular votes at the next ballot box and, consequently, trying to reduce transitional social costs by lobbying for subsidies and soft credits.

Local discretion over particular issues of reform implementation like price controls led to a regional differentiation of levels of prices and real wages as indicated in Tables A.1 and A.2 in the appendix. Given the paternalistic, egalitarian tradition in the former Soviet Union, when a reduction of real income differentials took place between the top 10 per cent and the bottom 10 per cent from more than 7:1 in 1946 to 3:1 in 1970 (Nove, 1986, p.212–13), egalitarian sentiment was used by local elites, in particular in rural areas, to fuel resentments against metropolitan reformers and the *nouveaux riches* in the big cities. The result in terms of voting patterns was a distinct urban-rural cleavage with the rural population predominantly voting more conservatively (Hough, 1994, p.23–7). In fact, free trade could act as a powerful equilibrating mechanism for regional diversity and could be a substitute for migration (Armstrong and Taylor, 1993, p.106) in a country where a proper housing market and an interregional system of job centres have still to be created. But local elites impeded free trade often through trade barriers, tariffs and rationing (Bradshaw and Hanson, 1994). Finally, the existing tax system is also not conducive for reducing regional diversity, since it is not differentiating progressive and regressive tax forms according to various regional real income,[10] but rather drawing along the existing administrative-territorial division. Only institutions which cross regional borders in their economic activity like industrial alliances and new investment funds could currently act as an equilibrating mechanism.

Another reason for the importance of regions for the intended transformation is the regional bias of the Russian privatisation programme, which was elaborated along provincial divisions, and for which regional institutions were set up to carry out the programme and to meet the privatisation targets set by the centre.[11] This led to a 'localisation' of privatisation authority (Radygin, 1994, p.71) with many provincial authorities claiming competences of federal committees. Further complications of this regional approach[12] could be summarised in the following way:

1) The speed of mass privatisation varied considerably between regions due to different attitudes of regional politicians toward market reform and the given variety of industrial structure.[13] This could lead to regional disparities in the microeconomic performance of enterprises.
2) Another complication arose from the difficulty, due to the size of the country and the cost of transfer of vouchers across regions, of affording citizens the opportunity to use their vouchers to acquire property in any part of Russia, regardless of their place of residence (Thomas and Kroll, 1993, p.457).
3) The lack of information (insider privatisation) within and across regions strengthened the tendency to localise ownership, which also further emphasised the importance of management and workers in the enterprise themselves (Clarke *et al.*, 1994).

These complications could only be eliminated, in the medium term, by the proliferation of interregional voucher investment funds, which are currently acting as substitutes for non-existing primary and secondary capital markets (Filatotchev, 1994, p.7), and can promote interregional competition in local privatisation auctions.

Finally, our approach to analyzing the spatial context of intended systemic transformation was also encouraged by recent Western studies of sectoral meso-levels, which claim that 'the most competitive forms of economic coordination are neither market nor statist but new forms whose alternative operations we are only beginning to understand and identify' – like networks, alliances and inter-firm agreements (Stark, 1992, p.53). Russian spatial networks like the Siberian Agreement, alliances of energy-producers or new financial-industrial groups with a distinctive spatial activity (oil production in Tyumen, coal extraction in the Kuzbass) provide some evidence of these phenomena in Russia. Whether they facilitate higher economic competitiveness or are simply remnants of routine behaviour, remains an open question.

1.2 THE DIMENSION OF SOCIAL AND ECONOMIC CHANGE

Post-communist societies are faced with three dimensions of change which Offe (1994, p.19) called a 'magic triangular':

1) national polities have to define identity, civil rights and both historically and culturally legitimated territorial borders;
2) a political constitution[14] and democratic institutions have to be set up;
3) new forms of allocation and redistribution of resources have to be found.

All of these issues of transformation have a spatial component and have to be carried out more or less simultaneously. The latter fact points to an important difference to the transition to democracy in Southern Europe and Latin America. Moreover, both the settlement of rival nationalisms and the creation of market economies in former state socialist countries are further distinguishing features (Friedheim, 1993, p.511).[15]

This is essentially 'political capitalism', in which reform elites represent the common interest of society in setting up an efficient economy, but they cannot rely on capitalist owners. On the contrary, the 'revolutionary installation of an entrepreneurial class … is the task, which in none of the previous transformations had to be fulfilled' (Offe, 1994, p.60).[16] Moreover, decisions taken by reform elites have now to be legitimated. This peculiar relationship between political means and economic ends is at odds with the necessary functional disentanglement of all social spheres (economics, jurisdiction, education, science, family) from the political sphere towards autonomous subsystems in post-communist countries.

One has to keep in mind that the Bolsheviks were originally serious about the fusion of politics and economics and also, following Marx' theory, about taking the state back into society. Moreover, the programme to eliminate commodity production during War Communism was sincere in its original promise to abolish market regulation as a means of so-called 'expropriation of man by man', but it had to be abandoned because it became a serious threat to the political power of the Bolsheviks (Roberts, 1990, p.37), thus leaving the initial vision of the Russian Revolution unfulfilled. Most present authors agree today on the pervading role of the communist political regime through all capillaries of social life.

Roeder (1993) considered the 'constitution of Bolshevism' as the institutionalization of reciprocal accountability and balanced leadership, in which a two-tier authoritarian structure[17] was unable to respond to social change. Kornai described a chain of causality, in which 'a specific political structure and ideology have gained sway, as a result of which specific property forms have developed, which has led to the preponderance of bureaucratic coordination and the typical behaviour patterns of the participants' (1992, p.364). However, this chain of causality is now being subjected to a process of multidimensional differentiation and functional separation between the component parts.

What kept them originally together (hierarchically structured political loyalty and personal dependence) acquires now a new quality of impersonal regulatory instruments (money, power, law) and its own codes of communication (government/opposition or property/non-property). Recent qualitative changes in post-communist societies appeared in the political structure from a one-party system to a developing multi-party system, in the re-established institution of private ownership, the dismissal of the duplication of the party and the state as well as the provision of new incentives to change people's behaviour (private property, democratic participation). The attempt at differentiating politics from other social spheres led, in fact, to a 'restoration of politics' (Sakwa, 1993, p.409) with its own functional autonomy.

As for the *institutional* structure, which was briefly discussed above in its spatial context, two different theoretical explanations[18] could be identified in more general terms. *Modernisation* theories interpret the contemporary changes in post-communist countries as a new shift of modernisation, but this time, in contrast to the Soviet period, not in terms of the intention to develop higher productive forces and to 'catch up' and to 'overtake' Western material rationality, but to modernise in terms of procedural rationality by introducing the Western concepts of market and democracy as more complex and efficient modes of regulating human interaction. There is an 'extension of modernity' over these countries, and this time the 'spirit of the Occident is catching up the East not only with the technical civilisation, but also with its democratic tradition' (Habermas, 1990, p.185). It has been argued that post-communist societies want to project themselves into the spatial sphere of Occidental rationality and that they became, for that reason, an 'object of Western activities and omissions' (Offe, 1994, p.238).[19] Thus, the task of an intended evolutionary result (civil rights, mass participation, private ownership and market) is reduced to a problem of conscious design.

The profound essence of change, according to modernists, is the functional differentiation between politics and economics toward autonomous, self-regulating spheres with their characteristic regulatory instruments and codes of communication. Indeed, there is suddenly more difference than people are used to and which developing institutions can still not regulate. The outcomes are, according to Offe (1994, p.288), two pathological reactions: (a) the rejection of difference and, effectively, the attempt to preserve 'communal' forms of organisation; and (b) the strategic use of difference.

Postmodernist theories accept the notion of functional differentiation, but they also stress functional coordination, networks and synthesis. Beck introduced the metaphor of social transition from a state of 'either or' to one of 'and' (1993, p.12), arguing that differences became increasingly obsolete after the collapse of the communist system. However, Stark found a 'complex reconfiguration of institutional elements rather than their immediate replacement' (1992, p.22) in East European countries.[20] According to his 'path dependence' theory (see note 16), actors who seek to move in new directions find that they are constrained by the existing set of institutional resources (*ibid.*, p.21). Moreover, Bruszt (1992, p.57) argued that there are differences amongst the structural and institutional legacies of post-communist regimes and that one should expect individually distinct capacities to channel conflict into the framework of democratic politics.

Stark's questioning of teleological constructs driven by hypothesized end-states could be one of the main differences from modernist theories, which Beck summarised when he argued that 'the classical dialectic of structure and actors has been reversed' (1993, p.90–1). This means that actors' behaviour is not merely driven by institutions and incentive systems, but that, in fact, a discourse over the rationale of existing institutions started,[21] leaving scope for new input and change.

As for *actors* in the process of intended transformation, there has been a long discussion on the speed of their possible adaptation, knowledge and learning in social change. A number of authors stress the need for gradual change and evolutionary selection of arrangements (Murrell, 1992, p.4–5).[22] The microeconomic analysis of privatisation in four Russian enterprises by Clarke *et al.* (1994, p.179–83) found that social relations at the enterprise level are resistant to change and that a strengthening of authoritarian paternalism between management and workers took place. However, other authors (Fan and Schaffer, 1994, p.163) considered the reason of initially slow adjustment of Russian enterprises in external factors such as incomplete trade and price liberalisation, macro-instability and excessive governmental crediting of loss-making enterprises. They found from their case studies that Russian enterprises do adjust if faced with tough external creditors even under conditions of weak bankruptcy enforcement and vague property rights (*ibid.*, p.162).

There seems to be more agreement among analysts and observers about the current state of disorder in Russian society pronounced in the lack of efficient institutions and weak law enforcement. Authors of a study analysing the results of the referendum for the new Russian Constitution and the parliamentary elections in December 1993 described the majority of voters as apathetic and disoriented (Grishin, 1994, p.53). Pokrovskii summarised the 'new Russian ideology' in a way which reminds one of America in the 1920s:

> It is expressed simply by the old slogan: 'Get rich!' – by whatever means (now everything is allowed), immediately, without fear or reproach. This is all together: ends, principle, moral value and indulgence, in the case of pangs of conscience. After all, everybody is behaving in that way and is even proud of it and plumes on themselves. To live humbly is today considered indecent and disgraceful. In fact, 'if you are clever, why are you so poor then?' There reigns literally a complete intoxication with commerce in our country today. Every scruple has been discarded. It is not only a matter of business as such, but one of philosophy and morale in the new Russia. (NG, 27 September 1994, p.5)

In the words of another Russian author, Russia remained today in many ways 'totalitarian, completely proletarianised with an utterly aggressive, parasitic and lumpen-proletariat attitude ... [while] violence was legalised; there was a ruthless "law of war", which, in the final instance, embraced political and state institutions' (Alekseev, 1994, p.5). Whatever the judgments of Russians about their own society might be, these descriptions clearly indicate that, in their authors' opinions, current institutions are neither constraining people's actions according to rules of the game nor are they providing positive incentives. Levada (1995, p.3) considered the only positive thing in this disorder of Russian society that it would guarantee that the wheels would not turn back toward state authoritarian rule.

But there is also the issue of 'ethnification' of political systems and political conflicts in a particular spatial context as it was discussed above. Under the old regime, egalitarian norms were at odds with ascriptive ethnical codes and identities. However, Offe (1994, p.151–9) considers the strategy of ethnification of political life in post-communist societies as 'rational' due to the attempted 'self-continuation' of old elites, their protectionist economic calculation and a weak state. The lack of structured oppositional relations between social classes and political parties seems to 'justify' this revival of ethnic antagonisms, which appear as the only 'real' conflict.

Finally, Friedheim (1993, p.482–8) criticized the prevailing theoretical concentration on elites in the analysis of East European countries and called for a distinction between political and civil society. He based his argument on mass demonstrations in 1989 and negotiated transition pacts afterwards. In his view (*ibid.*, p.496), civil society (social movements, organisations) has not only tangible resources (money, labour, facilities), but also less tangible resources like time, nationalist or religious symbols and creeds. However, while this might have applied for civil society during extrication from socialism, such alternative formations to the political establishment have now a much lower importance. Apart from a few sporadic strike movements, the main pressure groups in the regions with impact on the national policy agenda are local politicians, the industrial management and the military, on which we will concentrate our focus.

1.3 HYPOTHESIS AND THE STRUCTURE OF THE BOOK

The main question of this study is whether post-communist transformation in its spatial context has to be carried out 'from above' or whether there is any potential for autonomy for regional elites to implement institutional restructuring and economic adjustment. We posit that both investigated regions – due to their industrial structure discussed below, which restricted their economies traditionally to the extraction of natural resources and the supply of raw materials, and military hardware to the centre – will continue to exert pressure on the centre for subsidies and soft credits to cope with problems of social protection and infrastructure investment under conditions of economic crisis. This would not only have a detrimental effect on the national policy agenda of macroeconomic stabilisation and price liberalisation, but it would also limit regional economic autonomy.

We also expect that in some areas of policy the PK and the AK will diverge. New market opportunities through foreign trade could have a multiplier effect on the economy of the PK, but institutional restructuring would have to start right from the beginning to prevent crime and corruption and to define the new rules of the game. The decline of the Pacific Fleet has had a profound impact on the growth of the criminal underworld, and the region's peripheral location could make it to a prime area for drug trafficking, money laundering and arms deals. One has to take into account the considerable flow of foreign cash into the PK due to its geographical location as a transit point for trade in Japanese goods, the importance of cross-border trade with China and the trade of Siberian resources and securities at Vladivostok's commodity and stock market. However, leakages after first injections into the regional economy could have negative income and employment effects (Armstrong and Taylor, 1993, p.23) and one policy implication would be a switch from export orientation to import substitution. Tendencies of political separatism and regional elite's bid for a special economic regime in the PK could become a serious challenge for the viability of Russian federalism. This would enhance the scope of autonomy for the regional elite in the PK.

The AK with its large number of rural areas can still rely on a state commitment to soft credits and subsidies for agricultural production and a process of open-ended lobbying by regional elites in the centre will presumably continue. Due to its remote geographical location and poor conditions of transport and communication, there is no immediate, tangible impact on the AK economy after its opening to the world market. Economic activity has to be oriented towards interregional trade at the meso-level, predominantly in Western Siberia and Kazakhstan. However, the dominance of the former party nomenklatura and the agrarian clan could become a serious impediment for thorough-going institutional changes. One would then have to favour a transformation 'from above'.

The hypothesis is that economic change and institutional restructuring in Russia's provinces imply a scale of different implementation policies, ranging from an imposed form of transformation 'from above' to devolved regional autonomy. Due to its gateway location in proximity to international trade and financial markets, the PK could be at one end of the scale, seeking an independent role in economic change and it could have the potential to become a pilot project in terms of market reform. In contrast, the AK as a predominantly agricultural region will be expected to adopt a slow pace of economic change, while heavily relying on state subsidies. This could place the AK at the other end of the scale, where an assertive and perhaps authoritarian transformation 'from above' would be necessary to induce change. We expect that traditional elites in the AK will have a conservative attitude toward market reform and democratisation.

This hypothesis will be tested through both quantitative and qualitative data. Statistical comparisons of economic performance (output, regional budget, foreign trade), social indicators (real wages, unemployment) and institutional restructuring (privatisation, farming, housing) will be carried out, although with caution due to difficulties with Russian statistics (regional price differences, biased reporting, inflation). The qualitative analysis will rely on observations, interviews and documentary analysis in an attempt to assess the regional elite's attitude toward market reform and democratisation. It is hoped that qualitative data will also help to tackle problems with the reliability of statistical data.

The structure of the book follows a common structure for PhD dissertations. Chapter 2 is a review of literature discussing traditional Soviet regional policy. Chapter 3 discusses in more detail the questions of regional impact on intended transformation in Russia focusing, in particular, on existing institutional arrangements and regional elite's interests, attitudes and types of policy making. This wider range of analysis (including empirical evidence from other regions in Russia) should help to explain the essential conflict between the national policy agenda and regional interests during intended systemic transformation. This chapter will also focus on current fiscal arrangements and investment policy in the RF. Comparative studies of Western federal and unitary states (Canada, Western Europe) will act as a complement for this discussion. Chapters 4 and 5 are the regional case studies of the AK and PK respectively, which mainly focus on the struggle for political power in the regions, issues of policy making and reform implementation. Finally, Chapter 6 compares economic results of institutional restructuring, budgetary and fiscal arrangements and possibilities for mobilising internal financial resources between both regions. The conclusion will either confirm or reject the hypothesis and assess prospects for economic change in Russian regions with a particular focus on the investigated provinces.

1.4. METHODS OF RESEARCH

This analysis has an interdisciplinary approach, the arguments and theoretical concepts of which are located in the fields of political economy, economic geography, political science and sociology. It will cast doubt on modernisation theories of linear rationalisation with hypothesized end-states. It will also treat both qualitative and quantitative data as valuable.[23]

The analysis is also based on case studies. Experience shows that extensive empirical work at grassroots level can reveal an entire microcosm of transformational issues, with a unique, inside view. On the basis of both local specifics and generalisable problems, a theoretical discourse can make progress. The limitations arising from the uniqueness of local conditions has been tackled by choosing, for our case studies, two regions of a completely different geographical location and by discussing their problems in a wider meso-territorial (former planning regions) and national context.

Secondary data

Chapters 1–3 are based on extensive reading of Western and Russian (former Soviet) academic literature. This provides the necessary background for a study of the regional impact on intended transformation and of the regional problems the former Soviet leadership was already faced with. Comparative studies on centre-periphery relations in other Western countries (Canada, Italy) as well as transformation economies (Poland, Bulgaria, China) were a useful complement in terms of analysing democratic institution-building and fiscal arrangements. Russian central press was used to follow up the events in other regions and to compare transformational problems in a wider national context.

Primary data

Chapters 4 and 5 are two regional case studies on the AK and PK which are based on empirical research carried out through frequent travelling to both provinces in the period 1992–5. Three trips were made to each region (one to each per year), which resulted in about 100 structured and semi-structured (open-ended) interviews with representatives of the regional political establishment (administration, parliament, committees, political parties) and the industrial management (state and private-owned enterprises). These interviews were organized in a standard sequence (biography, activity, institutional affiliation, structural reform, attitude toward the centre) and about 50 per cent of them were recorded.[24] Discussions with people from the academic sphere provided broader background knowledge and they helped in collecting scarce statistical material and analysing sociological surveys. Two local newspapers (*Altaiskaya pravda* and *Utro Rossii*) were subscribed to in the UK and turned out to be a unique source for first-hand information from the ground, although the delivery had its up-and-downs not only because of technical difficulties, but also due to changing local political situations.[25]

Qualitative data

These consist chiefly of opinions and accounts of developments collected from local informants. They were assembled through techniques of observation and documentary analysis. They are not open to quantitative analysis because they were not derived from representative samples, either of the regions' populations or even of regional policymakers. The interpretation of statements published in articles of local newspapers and close analysis of the language used by respondents in our interviews gave a unique inside view of the attitude of regional policymakers toward market reform and democratisation. It revealed not only their mistrust of central policies, but also internal institutional frictions and power struggles. There was also a notable change of attitude of Russian interviewees from open-minded, independent replies in 1992–3 to one of secretiveness, suspicion of Westerners and even deliberate attempts to mislead in 1994–5. The rise of authoritarian power in many Russian regions, in particular in the PK, revived people's fear and subservient spirit.

Quantitative data

These included the collection of statistical data, their processing and analysis, especially in comparison with national data. In view of the above-mentioned questions of regional leaders' impact on macroeconomic stabilisation and price liberalisation, statistical material of the regional economic structure, budgets and extra-budgetary funds, price levels and real wages were of particular interest and are presented in regional comparative perspective. Results of small and large-scale privatisation as well as the set up of private farms give an idea of the progress of institutional restructuring. Statistical data are mainly provided for the period 1992–4, in some cases for 1995.

However, there are serious limitations on the use of Russian statistics.[26] The above discussed price controls by local authorities, in conjunction with wage indexations, lead to price distortions and make regional cross-border comparisons difficult. This is further aggravated by subsidised inputs (coal, energy) and agricultural products, which are still considerably below world market prices and could lead, under conditions of price adjustment, to value-subtracting production in other branches. In fact, price subsidies differ substantially between regions and are overlapped by wage indexations for Siberia and the Far North, which are decided in the centre and are remnants of the old Soviet system of price formation. There is also a great deal of biased reporting[27] involved and a lot of adjustment to account for high inflation and wage indexations are made afterwards. For example, budgetary figures can differ substantially between local and central reports, because transfers from both the local and federal budgets to the regional budget are made with a considerable time delay. For that reason, inflation-adjusted local data for the previous year is used. Tables with relevant statistical data are included in the main text, while a summary of more comprehensive data, in particular comparing the territories studied with the macro-regions of Western Siberia and the Far East, is presented in the appendix.

How to approach Russian interviewees?

This is a very delicate problem and requires a great deal of flexibility, since backlashes and disappointments can always be expected. It is useful to prepare some material in advance for exchange, to give the sense of not only to going there to take, but also to give. There is not only a huge demand for information on Western companies operating and registered in Russia, but also on Western local legislation (fiscal arrangements, issue of bonds or bank credits to local authorities) and mortgage or insurance schemes. Corruption among officials seems to have become the norm in Russia (*Izvestiya*, 22 July 1994, p.5) and managers want to have a certain interest in the interview as well. Nevertheless, one has to be insistent and convincing in gaining information by other means, since the aim of this study was not to buy information by hard currency.[28]

The best way to approach interviewees in Russia is to introduce yourself correctly, explaining what you are doing, what your interest is, and why you are approaching them. In most of the cases, this worked excellently and, in the course of the interview, the interviewees developed even more trust and open-mindedness. Those who really don't want to meet you, will tell you this right from the beginning. A lot are sceptical and don't like being recorded, but most of them are interested in the outcome of this research and want to have copies of publications. In one case only, the head of the foreign economic department of the Altai administration, V. Antropov, told me after we had finished our interview in April 1993, that although he respects my research, 'it would have been better if you had brought a suitcase of hard currency with you instead'.

The situation worsened though in the course of 1994 with the rise of authoritarian power in many Russian regions. People holding office in the PK administration, for example, were intimidated and reverted to old Soviet habits of quoting their governor, and even tried to mislead. This just proved how long and stony the road to democracy in Russia still is.

1.5 THE INVESTIGATED REGIONS IN THE NATIONAL CONTEXT

This section will introduce specific demographical, economic and social features of the AK and PK in the national context. It will mainly use reliable statistics for 1993 as a starting point (more recent statistical data for 1994–5 are provided in Chapter 6).

Both regions have not only a location peripheral to the centre in Moscow, but also within their appropriate macro region; they are territories which embrace the Southern tip of Western Siberia and of the Russian Far East respectively. The AK has a state border with Kazakhstan and a customs frontier with the recently established Republic of Altai (former

Gorno-Altaiskaya autonomous *oblast'*). The set up of this customs frontier was a unilateral decision by the new authorities of the republic, which separates the single economic space of Russia.

The PK has a state border with China and North Korea as well as an open exit to the Sea of Japan. While both are *kraya* (standard provinces) in terms of administrative status, the AK contains a higher territorial subdivision into 77 (60 rural) *raiony*, compared with merely 25 (14 rural) in the PK. However, both regions are characterised by a high concentration of urban settlements, with the PK having an industrial agglomeration of more than one million people in the South (Vladivostok-Nakhodka) and the AK one of 600 000 in the North (Barnaul-Novoaltaisk).

Table 1.1 indicates a considerably higher density of population in both the AK and PK than the Russian average. (A broader comparison of demographic features in their corresponding macroregion is given in Table A.3 in the appendix.)

Table 1.1 Physical and demographic features of the Altaiskii and Primorskii *Kraya* in comparison with Russia, 1 January 1994

Indicators	Russia	AK	% of Russia	PK	% of Russia
Territory ('000 sq km)	17 075.4	169.1	1.0	165.9	0.9
Population ('000)	148 400.0	2 684.3	1.8	2 287.0	1.5
Density (people per sq km)	8.7	15.8	–	13.8	–
Natural increase (compared with 1992, '000)	–300.0	2.3	–	–7.8	–

Source: Compiled from Goskomstat RSFSR, *Narodnoe khozyaistvo RSFSR v 1990g*. (Moscow: 1991); EkiZh, no.6, February 1994, p.9; Mel'nik and Rodionova (1994, p.27); AP (10 February 1994, p.2) and UR (3 February 1994, p.2)

Moreover, both peripheral regions are major junctions for migrants and refugees. The AK had an in-migration of 27 200 people in 1993 (down from 34 760 the year before). These were mainly refugees from Central Asia. In contrast, out-migration was continuously increasing: 4421 people in 1991, 9600 in 1992 and 10 100 in 1993.[29] Besides the dominant Russian population, there is a considerable national minority of 127 000 Russian Germans in the AK.

The 1162 km border of the PK with China had become a very sensitive issue. About 74 mn people live in the two Chinese provinces adjoining the PK, and these mountainous areas have a relatively high rate of unemployment. This caused, after the Russian government introduced visa-free entry in late 1992, a mass-influx of Chinese people. Estimates range up to 200 000 Chinese citizens who have crossed one of the five checkpoints of the PK alone in 1993 and a lot of them have remained in Russia (UR, 16 November 1993, p.1). A report in *Kommersant-daily* (26 May 1994, p.3) claimed that there were 150 000 Chinese citizens resident in the PK at that time. This has to be compared with an annual average of 10 000 Chinese people who are officially under labour contract in construction and logging businesses in the region since the late 1980s.[30]

Apart from timber and, in the case of the PK, fish and precious metals, both regions have no other particular raw materials which could be traded on a mass scale on the world market, as is possible with products like oil, gas or coal. Traditionally, the PK accounted for 17 per cent of the all-union food production by value (as a result of the dominant fishing industry – most of the home ports of the Pacific fishing fleet are here – with 80 per cent of the catch being exported from the region); and the territory delivered nine per cent of the rice and 15 per cent of the soybean production in the RF (Savalei, 1991, p.73). The PK also produced 80 per cent of all fluoride concentrates and 90 per cent of boron in the former USSR (Osipov, 1992, p.13). There are substantial deposits of ferrous and precious metals (tin, lead and silver); timber, copper and furs were exported. The AK has some resources for the construction industry (building materials, sandstone) and a few deposits of mineral salts. The main natural asset for the AK remains the 7.3 mn ha of arable land, which include the considerable extension of arable land at the end of the 1950s as a result of Khrushchev's virgin soil campaign (Kurakin, 1960, p.41).

The economic structure inherited from the former Soviet system of industrial branch planning was characterised by the dominance of union branch specialisation and the central ministries' perception of Siberia and the Far East as an enormous treasure trove and supplier of raw materials. Table 1.2 compares the structure of the industrial sector of the two regions and Russia as a whole.

Unfortunately, comparable data for the same year or years are not available, and substantial relative price and output changes between the 1980s and 1993 blur the comparison. For example, the weight of the machine-building and metalworking-sector has been falling in Russia as a whole. However, some features of comparable structures are clear. The substantial difference between the two regions, on the one hand, and Russia in the

Table 1.2 Branch structure of industry by volume of production in the Altaiskii and Primorskii *Kraya* in 1985 and 1990 in comparison with Russia in 1993 (percentage share of sector in gross value of industrial output; AK and PK in constant 1982 prices, Russia in current 1993 prices)

Sector	AK		PK		Russia
	1985	1990	1985	1990	1993
Total	100.0	100.0	100.0	100.0	100.0
Fuel and energy sector	2.7	3.0	7.7	6.6	26.7
Metallurgical industry	2.4	3.2	3.6	3.8	17.2
Machine-building and metalworking	40.9	37.8	24.3	23.7	20.3
Chemical and forestry industries	21.2	20.9	8.2	8.1	11.4
Construction materials industry	2.4	3.0	6.7	6.3	3.3
Light industry	13.2	13.0	4.4	4.3	5.2
Food industry	15.9	18.4	41.6	42.9	12.4
Other	1.3	0.7	3.5	4.3	3.5

Note: The appropriate figures for Russia in 1985 and 1990 were not available from Goskomstat RSFSR statistical yearbooks. The percentage figures for 1993 were calculated by the author from a 1994 source which indicated industrial output in current prices.

Source: Compiled from Loginov (1993, p.14); Goskomstat RSFSR (Vladivostok: 1991, p.131) and Goskomstat Rossii (Moscow: 1994, p.63)

fuel and energy sector is due to the fact that it includes, by definition, oil, gas, coal and electricity production, while only the last of them is relevant for the AK and PK apart from coal production in the PK. While metallurgical industries had a relatively lower share than the Russian average, that of machine-building and metalworking was considerably higher due to huge production complexes for the defence industry in both regions. The relatively heavy weight of non-fuel primary industries is indicated by higher percentage figures for the food industry. This applies still more strongly to the PK, where fisheries and fish-processing alone amounted to more than 30 per cent of the gross value of industrial output in 1985–90 (Goskomstat RSFSR, 1991, p.131). Finally, chemical and forestry industries had a higher relative importance than the Russian average in both regions.

This distinctive industrial structure, which traditionally restricted the AK and PK to the extraction of natural resources and the supply of raw materials and military hardware to the centre, is today – under conditions of high inflation and the disruption of the system of centrally allocated resources and material supply – limiting opportunities for economic restructuring and for autonomous development. Moreover, both regions lost a substantial amount of formerly provided state subsidies as a previously closed military district in the case of the PK and state compensations for the difference between wholesale and retail prices of agricultural products in the case of the AK. Table 1.3 analyses the economic performance in both regions in comparison with Russia in 1993. (Table A.4 extends this analysis for some economic indicators to the corresponding macro-regions of Western Siberia and the Far East.)

Apart from higher consumer goods production and more investment activities in the PK, the difference in retail trade and services between both regions is striking. However, one has to bear in mind that there are substantial price differences between the two regions, which make comparisons difficult. The fact that the AK with 1.8 per cent of Russia's population had less than 0.1 per cent of Russia's retail turnover suggests a considerable lower per capita consumption in comparison with the Russian average. There could be three reasons for this:

1) people in the AK are really poorer;
2) retail prices in the AK are lower;

Table 1.3 Economic indicators for the Altaiskii and Primorskii *Kraya* in comparison with Russia, 1993 (current prices of late 1993)

Indicator	Russia	AK	% of Russia	PK	% of Russia
Population ('000)	148 400	2684.3	1.8	2287.0	1.5
Industrial output (Rbn)	109 400	1258.9	1.1	1165.1	1.0
Production of consumer goods (Rbn)	36 500	488.1	1.3	705.3	1.9
Capital investment (Rbn)	25 200	254.6	1.0	354.8	1.4
Retail trade (Rbn)	58 800	48.3	0.1	603.6	1.0
Services (Rbn)	6 400	54.8	0.8	102.6	1.6

Source: Compiled from EkiZh, no.6, February 1994, p.7; Sidorov (1994, p.4); AP, 9 February 1994, p.1–2 and UR, 3 February 1994, p.2

3) people in the AK rely much more than the Russian average on subsistence farming and/or informal, unreported trade for their consumption.

Probably some combination of the three explains this bizarre figure.[31] Moreover, the relatively low figure of 1.0 per cent of Russia's retail turnover in the PK, which has a population of 1.5 per cent of the Russian total, has clearly not taken into consideration informal, cross-border trade with China. The 1.6 per cent of Russian total services in the PK could also be an understatement.

This becomes particularly clear if one compares figures for average monthly income, as indicated in Table 1.4 (For a broader analysis within the corresponding macroregions see: appendix, Table A.4).

There was a striking difference in monthly money income in December 1993 between the AK and PK at a rate of 1:2.1, while cumulative savings as an end-year stock of cash and deposits were quite high and similar in absolute figures in both regions, which is due to the fact that money income in 1993 exceeded the increase of prices. However, while the PK had apparently higher prices, higher money incomes, but also a relatively more important informal economy, the AK population faced lower prices in the formal economy and relied probably much more on unreported subsistence agriculture. Moreover, official unemployment in the PK was less

Table 1.4 Social indicators for the Altaiskii and Primorskii *Kraya* in comparison with Russia, December 1993

Indicator	Russia	%	AK	%	PK	%
Average money income (R'000, % of Russia)	141 200	100.0	118 000	83.6	244 400	173.1
Personal savings as end-year stock (cash and deposits in Rbn and percentage of total income)	19 300	24.3	317.9	29.7	303.3	25.3
Official unemployment ('000 people and % of total workforce)	800	1.1	15.8	1.1	6.9	0.5

Source: Compiled from EkiZh, no.6, February 1994, p.9; AP, 10 February 1994, p.1–2 and UR, 3 February 1994, p.2

than half that in the AK in December 1993, which is probably due to more job opportunities in new commercial structures of the PK.

The results of this comparative analysis, which was used as a starting point for this study, could be summarised as follows. Although the AK had a higher total industrial output than the PK in 1993, its retail turnover was less than one-tenth and its services were less than half those in the latter. This, combined with the fact that PK workforce earned officially, on average, twice as much as their counterparts in the AK, give reason to conclude, at this stage of investigation, that PK enterprises were much more involved in barter trade of consumer goods with neighbouring China and other Asian countries; revenues of which were partly used for wage payments and the value of which does not appear in industrial output statistics. Moreover, new commercial structures have probably developed faster than in the AK. Finally, exports of fish resources[32] and precious metals have counterbalanced the general decline of production in the PK (Savalei, 1994, p.2).

This could indicate a greater potential for autonomous development in the PK than in the AK. However, whether there is any indication of radical *institutional* restructuring in terms of ownership, material supply and sales networks or in economic behaviour of *actors* remains to be investigated.

2 Traditional Soviet Regional Policy

The aim of this chapter is to examine, in the form of a literature review, the legacy of Soviet regional policy and its implications for the analysis of new centre-periphery relations in contemporary Russia. The main characteristics of this legacy are the dominance of branch over territorial planning, the small independent income base of local budgets and a distinctive core-periphery relation between the European part of Russia and Siberia, based on underpayment for the extraction of Siberian resources. These features will be analysed in sequence, while focusing on both the institutional setting as well as policymakers in traditional Soviet regional policy.

2.1 BRANCH VERSUS TERRITORIAL PLANNING

In general, there are three aspects of regional policy, which will be discussed in turn in this section:

1) the goals of regional policy;
2) the instruments or means;
3) the implementation and results.

While goals mainly consist of the planned development of all regions and the reconciliation of regional and national interests, methods of implementing these aims through state policy could be the transfer of capital or measures to enhance the mobility of the labour force (Dellenbrant, 1986, p.19–20).

However, in the Soviet context, these three aspects aquired specific features due to the conflict between sectoral (*vedomstvennost'*) and local interests (*mestnichestvo*). The dominance of the industrial branch structure will be analysed here with regard to its implications for Soviet regional policy.

The geographical pattern and locational principles

In its geographical context, the Soviet Union had a very uneven distribution of capital and labour relative to land, which resulted in a West-East-South trichotomy:[1] a well-populated, economically developed and largely Slavic core in the West; an underdeveloped, largely agrarian and labour-surplus region of non-Slavic population in the South; and a largely Slavic, resource-rich East, which still has potential for development but is constrained both by harsh environmental conditions and shortages of manpower (Panel, 1991, p.364). In this spatial configuration, the European USSR formed the core of political and economic power, where over 70 per cent of the population and three-fourths of the Soviet state's economic potential were concentrated (Dienes, 1987).

The distinguishing feature of Soviet central planning and state ownership had a profound impact on regional resource allocation. Moreover, the influence of Marxist ideology with its obsession with industry led to the Soviet decisionmaker's perception of the physical environment in terms of potential productivity rather than potential habitability (Hamilton, 1973, p.256). The assumption that man can entirely control and use nature for planned human needs resulted in unconstrained operation of industrial ministries with an unprecedented waste and exhaustion of human and physical resources.

In accordance with the Soviet perception of developing a harmonious society, the administrative-territorial hierarchy was subdivided and classified according to ethnicity, urbanisation and population size (Hahn, 1988, p.81–3), with largely the same size in territory, population and economic capacity (measured in per capita gross output). By March 1980, subnational, administrative units amounted to six *kraya*, 121 *oblasti*, eight autonomous *oblasti* and ten autonomous *okruga*, which were further subdivided into a total of 3075 *raiony*, 3719 workers' settlements and 41 374 villages in the entire USSR (Jacobs, 1983, p.4). However, for economic planning purposes, 18 macroregions were used, each of which included several administrative territories (for example Western Siberia, Far East and so on).

The initial Soviet effort in the field of integrated regional planning was connected with the GOELRO plan of 1920, which was based on a series of power-oriented industrial complexes and provided the foundation for dividing the country into economic regions.[2] A model scheme for economic macroregions to be developed in the first Five-Year Plan (FYP) envisaged four different types of regions: industrial, agricultural, mixed and wood-processing. These were later further differentiated by the famous Soviet economic geographer, N. Kolosovskii, who divided regions according to 'energy-production processes which are being repeated on a massive scale' (1969, p.144): ferrous and non-ferrous metallurgy, oil extraction and processing, wood-cutting and processing, mechanised agriculture and land improvement as well as electric power production. The

24 economic macroregions of the first FYP were further divided into 32 during the second FYP and their number changed frequently until 1961, when the territory of the Soviet Union was finally divided into 18 planning regions (Minakir, 1988, p.29).

However, since the late 1960s, these macroregions were used by Gosplan merely for statistical and accounting purposes, as they lacked the planning institutional structure of union republics (Shaw, 1986, p.478). Since then, the relationship between the centre and the republics was the prime determinant of regional policy. Later proposals to divide Western and Eastern Siberia each into three and the Far East into four latitude zones (Granberg, 1985, p.3), could not change the dominant planning procedure any more. However, discussions on the creation of economic macroregions marked an early attempt at finding a synthesis between branch and territorial planning, including the organisation of a whole *oblast'* as one combine (Kolosovskii, 1969, p.186).

The theoretical basis for Soviet locational principles was provided, as commonly agreed among Western scholars (Dellenbrant, 1986, p.40–1; Dyker, 1983, p.114–15), by Engels' notion in his *Anti-Dühring* that location in socialism can be in the most suitable places, contributing, in this way, to evening–out differences between the city and the countryside, and in Lenin's remark in his *Draft Plan of Scientific and Technical Work* in 1918 that industry should be located near raw materials so as to minimise transport costs. While the Bolsheviks initially paid considerable attention to the necessity of equalisation among different regions, three basic and conflicting elements in Soviet location theory were already discernible in the period before World War II (Dellenbrant, 1986, p.42): the striving for economic effectiveness, regional equality and location in accordance with military strategy.

As Soviet society grew more complex, these original elements were further developed to a whole set of locational principles (Hamilton, 1973, p.237–9; Schiffer, 1989, p.4–8):

1) production should be developed in proximity to major raw material and energy sources, so as to minimise unnecessary transport of weight-losing or bulky material inputs;
2) production (especially the finishing or assembly stages of manufacturing) and services should be located near consumption centres, so as to minimise transport of bulky but this time weight-gaining products;
3) to achieve some planned balance between specialisation and complex development within each region;

4) economic activity should be evenly distributed throughout the union so as to ensure maximum utilisation of infrastructure, natural and labour resources;
5) the aim of equalising the levels of economic development and living standards between republics and regions;
6) to eliminate social and economic differences between urban and rural areas;
7) the choices of locations for production must be consistent with the need to strengthen the defensive capacities of the USSR;
8) economic activity should no longer be concentrated in large cities, but rather in small and medium-sized cities, primarily to take advantage of underemployed labour resources in the labour-deficit (European) part of the USSR;
9) recognition of the advantages of international specialisation of production between CMEA-countries. Donna Bahry (1987, p.106) added to these principles the objectives of environmental protection and the increase of employment among the able-bodied.

It is evident from this list of locational principles that many of these elements were mutually contradictory, thus making it impossible to carry them all out at once. However, it was more important to find a balance between regional specialisation and complex development and, closely related to this, that of economic efficiency and regional equalisation. Regional equality could clearly be only a long-term goal, while, over the short term, economic efficiency and military security were dominant (Dellenbrant, 1986, p.175).

Wagener considered these principles to be part of an evolutionary process and argued that 'the priority of an individual criterion is determined by the actual historical and political situation' (1973, p.66). His distinction between 'complex development' as the *result* of economic development in Soviet interpretation and 'specialisation', which reflects different natural and social *conditions* of production that favour preferential treatment of certain branches of industry (*ibid.*, p.68), appears particularly useful for the understanding of these Soviet perceptions. In Wagener's words, 'in a dynamic setting a movement towards unity must be interpreted as complex development while all movements away from unity represent specialisation'.[3]

Finally, system-specific deficiencies in Soviet allocational and locational theory could be summarised in the following way (Holubnychy, 1973, p.29–30):

1) the neglect of external economies and diseconomies and joint economic feedbacks arising from differences in development level of various regions (which hindered also the understanding of urban agglomeration);
2) the utter disregard of investment and trade multiplier effects;
3) the insufficient appreciation of the time factor (interest was not included as part of the alternative or comparative costs in practice).

Moreover, as Dienes (1982, p.233) outlined, locational criteria for 'most efficient use' implied not profitability, but an oversimplified yardstick of least production cost, which neglected accessibility, demand linkages and the market factor in general in favour of volume and low production costs at mine and factory sites.

Instruments of regional policy

In order to understand the means of implementation of Soviet regional policy, one has first to analyse the *institutional* structure of nationwide decision making on regional investment. The two most important parts of the institutional setting were individual branch ministries and their project design organisations, on the one hand, and various all-union and territorial planning organs and research institutes, on the other. They not only had unequal access to central government funding, but also, as Schiffer (1989, p.42) argued, operated with different (planning) time horizons and utilised contending criteria in assessing locational problems and spatial development strategies. This resulted in a 'patchwork of investment policies' (Bahry, 1987, p.122) with no comprehensive and internally consistent plan for regional development in the USSR. Moreover, the key *actors'* decision-making on spatial resource allocation could be influenced both by the central party leadership through congress resolutions and directives and by lobbying efforts of the regional party organs.

The three main *instruments* of Soviet regional policy (abstracting from the regional effects of price controls and subsidies, including the pricing of most transport below cost) were capital investment, transfers from union to republic budgets and wage coefficients, which included a supplement added to the basic wage of those employed in certain areas where it is difficult to recruit labour, in particular, in Siberia and the Far East (Dellenbrant, 1986, p.143–50). The means of capital investment is here of primary concern for the understanding of the dominance of branch over territorial planning.

The starting point of the nationwide decision-making investment sequence was first to determine the share of total investment which goes to each individual economic sector and industrial branch and then to direct this investment to that region (and site) in which its productivity is highest in return (Schiffer, 1989, p.181). Due to the early Soviet industrialisation drive, which implied maximising the total output of a definite structure and defining the sphere of producer goods as 'priority sectors', the energy, fuel and raw material extraction branches were, apart from the defence sector, the most important investment spheres. The industrial ministries thus deemed to be 'important' turned out to be the most powerful ones in terms of funds and staff, and their microeconomic ministerial behaviour was in operational conflict with national economic efficiency criteria. This was further aggravated by basic characteristics of the Soviet economic system (the predominance of output success-indicators, prevalent supply uncertainty and ineffectiveness of cost constraints), which led to distortions in the investment process (Dyker, 1983, p.50).

Investment decisions were mainly distorted by the use of non-market (arbitrary) prices, in particular, for raw materials and energy, controlled land rents (Hamilton, 1973, pp.249–50) and by the fact that no rate of interest was imputed (Dyker, 1983, p.101). The above-mentioned impact of Marxist ideology loosened, in fact, the constraints put on location choice by space through transportation costs and the influence of land values or economic rent. Apart from the dominant output maximisation approach and ineffective cost constraints, supply uncertainties led to the attempt by each industrial ministry to become self-sufficient, which resulted in a duplication of production capacity, crosshauling and a lack of interbranch and interregional coordination (Billon, 1973, pp.219–25).

Various elements in Soviet cost calculation turned out to be rather inefficient in reconciling sectoral and territorial interests and to provide an equal regional development. Rates of turnover taxes were differentiated by product, region of consumption, method of procurement for agricultural products, type of producer and according to their ultimate use for personal or industrial consumption (Schiffer, 1989, p.102). This way of setting differentials between the level of industrial wholesale (including purchase) and retail prices or between the level of enterprise wholesale prices and industrial wholesale prices was devised to redistribute funds from better-off regions to underdeveloped ones. However, as Hutchings (1983, p.37) pointed out, turnover taxes were paid by the consumer goods industry, not by producer goods or by agriculture. Consequently, regions characteristically were either predominantly payers or predominantly receivers of turnover tax.

Moreover, indirect rental payments were to be carried out through a complicated system of zonal pricing for both agricultural and industrial products, which was to substitute for non-existent rent payments. Finally, prices for construction materials were an important element of overall cost considerations for individual ministries which, together with higher norms and regional wage coefficients, left 'pioneer regions' in Siberia and the Far East disadvantaged (Schiffer, 1989, p.102–12). Dienes (1982, p.213) added to this list of unfavourable factors of Soviet cost calculation for Siberian regions those of relatively low depreciation rates, which created disadvantages for regions with more rapid wear and tear, as well as hidden cost increases of productive capacity (for investment goods and construction).

Ministerial efficiency versus regional equality

It is commonly agreed among Western scholars that there was only a partial success in the fields of regional equalisation and social justice, whether in terms of per capita indicators of consumption and output or the structural composition of the economy (Dienes, 1982, p.129). Due to a lack of statistical material, the results of Soviet regional policy could, over a long period of time, only be compared among union republics. However, even this sparse material revealed that there was already, in the 1960s and 1970s, a trend towards greater interrepublic inequality in terms of NMP per capita. According to Koropeckyj's study (1982, p.99–100), investment per capita in the more developed republics was, on average, greater than in the less developed republics in 1960–75. He estimated that the share of industry in total fixed capital increased from 44.7 to 48.5 per cent during that period. Koropeckyj explained this development by the Soviet planners' emphasis on efficiency in the allocation of capital rather than of labour, which is, according to him (*ibid.*, p.102), due to their relatively weak control over interrepublic flows of labour and the fact that the growth of output in the entire economy was more closely correlated with the growth of capital than with that of labour.

Concerning the central government policies of redistributing national income among republics through the state budget, it was primarily the less developed republics of Central Asia, and to some extent Kazakhstan and the Transcaucasus, that benefited during the 1960s and the first half of the 1970s, while the major net outflow of national income throughout this period was from the Ukraine (Gillula, 1981, p.166). However, while the non-Slavic republics received some more fixed capital in the chemicals and light industry branches, that in the fuels and ferrous metallurgy branches was even more concentrated in only a few republics in the 1970s and 1980s, in particular, the large investments in the oil and gas complex in Tyumen. Hutchings (1983, p.45) came through his extensive study of the Soviet budget to the conclusion that the budget was used only to a slight extent to counteract inequalities in the living standards of the various republics. In his words, 'the various republics are ... left clustering in groups, characterised by socio-cultural indices, which are very similar to their groupings according to nationality and language' (*ibid.*).

The hierarchy in importance of industrial ministries with 'priority sectors' in fuel and raw materials extraction and other producer goods industries resulted in a hierarchy of regions (de Souza, 1989, p.65), which was in accordance with the sequence of technological processes (Granberg, 1987, p.36) and territorial planning (Minakir, 1988, p.169). Within this hierarchy of branch and territorial planning, the two main goals of Soviet regional policy (maximisation of the nation's economic growth and equalisation among the regions) were in conflict between sectoral (vertical) and territorial (horizontal) interests. The dilemma of Soviet centre-regional relations lay, as Bahry (1987, p.32–3) outlined, in maintaining central control while assuring at least some degree of responsiveness to local needs.

However, as was shown above, the very structure of Soviet central planning worked against territorial interests. In 1967, for example, only two per cent of the personnel of *Gosplan* worked in its territorial planning department, and their role was minimal (Hough, 1969, p.269). Moreover, out of 203 steps in compiling a ministry's plan, the regional dimension was introduced only at step 179 (Bahry, 1987, p.35), after the most important decisions had already been taken; also the regional part of the plan was not binding on the ministry. Finally, there was also a natural conflict between the macro- and micro-level: while the centre was not able to digest enough information in order to grasp a specific situation on a micro-level in all necessary aspects, territorial units were unable to put their micro-level situation and decisions in a macro-level perspective (de Souza, 1989, p.156).

Several consequences of the poor coordination of branch and territorial planning began to appear: the unplanned build-up of cities as a result of the uncontrolled expansion of enterprises; a lag in the development of the infrastructure behind that of industrial production; and wide differences in the provision of housing and social-cultural funds, depending on the relative importance of enterprises and their ministerial affiliation (Ross, 1987, p.124). With the predominance of branch over territorial planning, officials on the periphery found themselves responsible for correcting these problems, while being denied the authority, funding and even information necessary to mitigate all the imbalance. As a consequence, republic and provincial authorities developed distinctive lobbying efforts for additional funding by central institutions.[4]

The Sovnarkhozy period (1957–65)

The *sovnarkhozy* experiment was probably the most serious attempt at decentralisation and reduction of the power of industrial ministries in the former Soviet Union, while that of TPCs entailed sophisticated academic discussions, starting in the late 1960s with Kolosovskii's concept of energy-production cycles (1969, p.143), on how to link branch and territorial planning by synthesising a range of technological, spatial economic and development ideas and to operationalise that linkage in the development of pioneer areas (Dienes, 1987a, p.293), whereas that of FEZs had already a clear orientation toward opening the economy in the late 1980s (see below). For that reason, the *sovnarkhozy* concept will be discussed, at this stage, in more detail.

By a decree of the Central Committee of the CPSU of February 1957, the territorial decentralisation of the Soviet economy was announced, which included the dismantling of central ministries and the setting up of regional economic councils (*sovnarkhozy*). A new State Economic Commission (*Gosek*) was originally created, which was to coordinate the annual plans of the new territorial economic authorities, although its functions very soon became absorbed by *Gosplan*, and a Ministry of State Auditing (*Goskontrol*) was to fight localism (Miller, 1957–8, p.67–8). The decree of the USSR Supreme Soviet of 10 May 1957 established 105 *sovnarkhozy*, covering the territory of a single *oblast'* in the RSFSR as well as that of other union republics and Central Asia as a whole, but its number had decreased to 100 by mid-1962 and was further reduced to 47 in November 1962 (Mieczkowski, 1965, p.481).

The two main objectives of the 1957 reform were that industries of purely local concern were to be handed over to local government and that local soviets and *sovnarkhozy* were expected to work in close cooperation. However, there remained a lot of confusion about the division of responsibilities. While republics were to become the primary administrative and planning units for the entire economy, *oblast'* party units were to become the basic control and policy organs (Cattell, 1964, p.430). A *sovnarkhoz* was declared to be independent of any local authority lower than the government of the union republic in which it was situated (Miller, 1957–8, p.67) and they were, as agencies of republic administration, subordinated to both the republican and USSR Councils of Ministers (Trofimenko, 1973, p.334).

The decentralisation of 1957 clearly gave the republics greater powers. Sectoral ministries were re-established at the republic level and republic authorities were also granted greater powers with regard to budget allocations, the regulation of retail trade, and so on (Dellenbrant, 1986, p.82). While republic governments had accounted for only six per cent of budgetary expenditure on industry in 1950, their share had increased to 76 per cent by 1958. In agriculture, they provided only 26 per cent of expenditure in 1950, but by 1958 they accounted for 95 per cent (Bahry, 1987, p.47).

One major question of the *sovnarkhozy* period was whether the party officials should be more passive arbitrators or whether they should direct the distribution of local suppliers systematically. Jerry Hough (1969, p.56 and 190) indicated two different tendencies. On the one hand, highly experienced industrial administrators came to the provinces to represent the interest of the branch ministries. This caused severe problems for the local party organs in maintaining their authority over the industrial establishment they were required to supervise. On the other hand, the creation of the *sovnarkhozy* increased the effectiveness of the intervention of party committees at the *oblast'* level (*obkomy*) in the planning process. Since the plans of the individual enterprise were, for the first time, integrated into an *oblast'*-wide plan, the *obkomy* and republic central committees had their first real opportunity to engage in effective regional planning. However, this was complicated by the split of the party and the soviets into industrial and agricultural branches at the local level (Friedgut, 1979, p.57).

Another contentious issue was the role of the local soviets. Officially, city soviets were to be given more responsibility for ensuring balanced urban growth and more resources to carry out their mandate, which included the transfer of industries from ministerial to local control (Taubman, 1973, p.28–9). However, there were no significant changes in the distribution of industry in favour of local government (Cattell, 1964, p.434) and *sovnarkhozy* continued to construct more housing and welfare buildings than did the local soviets. According to Taubman (1973, p.41), only 32 per cent of all state-owned housing in the USSR belonged to local soviets in 1960, which was still fairly close to the average figure of 35–41 per cent for most of the Soviet period. Much was complicated by the fact that there was no clear division and responsibilities between *sovnarkhozy* and local soviets and influence was mostly in one direction, since a good part of the income of local soviets came from turnover taxes, profits and land rent of *sovnarkhozy* industries (Cattell, 1964, p.439).

The 1962 reforms consolidated not only the *sovnarkhozy* into larger units, but made them also stronger in terms of population and economic capacity (Mieczkowski, 1965, p.482). Localism and autarkic tendencies such as preferential treatment to customers in the plant's own region (Billon, 1973, p.226) was cited as one of the main reasons for recentralisation. As a result, the stature of local government was further reduced by transferring the major portion of local industry to the new *sovnarkhozy* and removing all control over agriculture from urban communities (Cattell, 1964, p.441). Moreover, construction was removed from the control of the *sovnarkhozy* system to special republic administrations, a USSR Supreme Council of the National Economy was established and USSR State Production Committees were set up in November 1962 which contained 'camouflaged ministries in all the important fields of the national economy' (Mieczkowski, 1965, p.492–3).

Besides the discussed confusions in rights and responsibilities between different institutions, one of the main reasons for the malfunctioning of the *sovnarkhozy* system was the fact that the centre never disengaged itself from detailed planning and did not relinquish control over the physical allocation of resources or over large parts of the state budget. In fact, not only the defence industry, but transport and the bulk of the service sector were never put under the control of the regional councils (Dienes, 1987a, p.289). With Brezhnev and Kosygin coming to power in 1965, the last remainders of the *sovnarkhozy* system were dismantled and a stringent system of industrial branch planning was re-established.

2.2 LOCAL GOVERNMENT AND LOCAL BUDGETS

While the first part of this chapter focused primarily on Soviet regional policy from the centre's position, this section will be concerned with the situation of local governments, the provision of local budgets and the impact of regional and local activism on national policy choices. However, it starts with a theoretical discussion of the nature of the Soviet system, since a number of regional studies in the West have provided a somewhat more accurate picture of Soviet society over the last three decades.

The challenge of the totalitarian schema

The totalitarian model, which dominated the Western discussion in the 1950s and 1960s,[5] had an almost exclusive focus on national politics and ignored governments at the subnational level. Since the decision-making process was considered to be extremely centralised, subordinates in the provinces were acting, according to this schema, in conformity and unquestioned compliance with their national leaders and were hence perceived to be merely administrative instruments of the centre. This widely accepted picture of Soviet society was increasingly questioned among Western scholars after Khrushchev's attempts at decentralisation in the late 1950s and early 1960s. Academic discussions centred around both the structural-institutional aspects of local government and the input and output side of policy making at the subnational level.

The main thrust of the challenge to the totalitarian model was provided by the argument that Soviet society was more *pluralist* than it appeared to the outside world, with more complex party-state relations and a considerable involvement of the ordinary citizen in governmental affairs. The 'mobilising and socialising aspects of participation' were the main subject of Friedgut's study (1979), although he clearly discerned the ambiguities of a simultaneously 'growing intrusion of government into the lives of citizens' and stressed that this broad participation is at the implementation stage rather than at the stage of influencing decision making (*ibid.*, p.13–22). Hill analysed the local elite in a city in Soviet Moldavia, coming to the conclusion that a main feature of the Soviet system is its mobilising potential and that it is at the local level that 'the ordinary citizen has the greatest opportunities for experiencing the social and political benefits of membership of a political elite' (1977, p.187). A more recent study by Hahn (1988, p.258) suggested that even the rank and file were not wholly without opportunities to influence policy and the deputy of the local soviet did have the ability to obtain attention for constituency problems and to resolve them successfully.

Another approach was in considering the Soviet system as a huge *bureaucratic* machine, where at all spheres of administration bureaus compete, bargain and negotiate. Soviet local politics was characterised, according to Taubman (1973, p.18–19), by the competition of local institutions (industrial, soviet, party), the fact that organisations act incrementally,[6] the great size of the bureaucracy and scarce resources. In order to implement party policy, special organisations outside the normal bureaucracy had to be set up and special campaigns had to be launched. Hough perceived the local party organs not only as prefects of the Soviet system, but also as arbitrators in conflicts of interests which 'would be resolved through the bargaining and accommodative political action' (1969, p.282). With the rising level of professional competence among industrial managers and of technical competence of local party officials, 'the rational-technical society comes to predominate over the totalitarian one' (*ibid.*, p.50–1 and 280).

A third mainstream approach, which was closer to the classical totalitarian model, emphasised the importance of the *implementation* stage and claimed that, since the early 1970s, there has been 'a concerted movement by the central leadership to reassert its control over policy execution' (Ross, 1987, p.3). Ross considered party organs as the political boss of their territory, as the chief policy-making body as well as the chief control agent for the centre. However, although there was a clear dominance of provincial committee (*obkom*) first secretaries in their territories, Moses' extensive empirical study (1974, p.154) showed that their independent (from higher authorities) impact upon regional policy was only limited.

Another empirical analysis by Harasymiw (1983, p.105) suggested that the higher the proportion of communists in local soviets, the lower the level of services in the localities. Rutland (1993, p.22), who examined Hough's concept of the local party organs for the period of the 1970s and the first half of the 1980s, came to a similar conclusion in relation to the whole economy, arguing that the party had seriously to be blamed for the economic stagnation of the 1960s and 1970s. He argued that 'the more the party sphere encroached on the economic sphere, the worse it was for the economy' (*ibid.*, p.23), which he illustrated by extensive studies of local party intervention in energy, transport and agriculture, suggesting that there was, in fact, a post-totalitarian system throughout the 1953–88 period.[7]

The structure of local budgets

As a result of the dominance of branch over territorial planning, the industrial structure of subnational administrative units[8] appeared to be the most important single factor in determining their budget. The number, size and jurisdiction of enterprises situated in an area appeared to be crucial, since turnover tax and payment from profits were directly related to the industrial base of the soviets and composed the main income sources of local budgets. Soviets with a considerable number of enterprises of higher subordination and a simultaneously poor local industrial base under their jurisdiction were not only heavily dependent on the goodwill of higher authorities, but also of local managers of those enterprises. Thus, there were wide variations in the structure of local budgets from area to area and over a period of time, which did not only depend on the industrial structure of the territory, but also on the political status of subnational party and soviet officials and their relationship with the all-union and republic leadership as well as the directors of local enterprises with higher subordination (Ross, 1987, p.66).

Local budgetary *incomes* consisted of two main parts:

1) secured (*zakreplennyi*) income–made up of payments of profits of enterprises of local subordination, including services and municipally operated industries, local taxes and charges (transport, collective farm markets), income tax on cooperatives and public organisations (trade unions, sports societies, clubs) and state duties on legal administrative services (notary public);
2) regulated (*regulirovannyi*) income–consisting of federal revenues handed down to local soviets as a percentage of the total sum of turnover tax, taxes from the population and profits of enterprises of republic subordination collected in the territory of the soviet each year.[9]

Although there was a widening of the income base of local budgets, in particular, after the 1959–61 legislation, most of the increase came from central sources, while the percentage of independent income had actually declined. According to Taubman (1973, p.39), there was a decline of income from local sources from 64.8 per cent of the total in 1946 to merely 37.1 per cent in 1962. He explained this mainly by the abolition of the tax on buildings and rents of state enterprises and public organisations in June 1959. Ross (1987, p.79–80) found for the period 1964–80 also a reduction in the local soviets' *secured* income due to the insignificant growth of local services, unprofitable local enterprises and the loss by local soviets of a number of enterprises after the formation of production associations at the beginning of the 1970s. Concerning *regulated* income, there was also a lot of instability with turnover taxes, since this source was mainly beyond the control of local soviets – unstable from year to year (see Table A.5 in the appendix) and dependent on the production activities of enterprises of higher subordination. This process of 'sharing upwards' was followed by arbitrary redistribution of percentage shares of regulated income for each subnational administrative unit, which was not subject to clear and transparent rules (Solyannikova, 1993, p.32).

Moreover, local budgets could benefit from three types of federal transfers to help meet additional expenditure needs, which were all open for bargaining by regional and local elites with higher authorities:

1) 'subventions' or grants-in-aid to cover operating expenditures;
2) categorical grants (*dotatsii*) to finance specific projects such as public buildings or roads;

3) 'means' (*sredstva*) to cover programmes jointly financed by the centre and the republics (for example elections) and to cover funding needs unforeseen at the start of the fiscal year (Bahry, 1987, p.59).

Lewis (1983, p.52–4) described different opportunities and strategies for local administrators to increase the flow of financial resources in their territories:

1) they can attempt some minor manipulation of budget estimates or bargain straightforwardly with members of their finance and planning departments (*local* options);
2) they can go *outside* and seek project approvals from higher party and state authorities;
3) considerable *off-budget* funds were available locally.

The latter resources went not through the state budget but rather through the ministries and enterprises in the form of social and cultural funds, incentive funds and others for the construction of housing, clinics, kindergartens or clubs. Ross (1987, p.63) assumed that these funds had actually increased, since in 1976 only 40.8 per cent of investment flowed through the state budget compared with 66 per cent in 1966. They accounted for 65–80 per cent of infrastructural projects in the late Soviet period (Rutland, 1993, p.104).

On the *expenditure* side, regional and local budgets were predominantly used for spending in the social and cultural spheres as shown in Table A.6, which indicates also a considerable amount of spending by *oblast'* and city budgets in the territorial economies. Hahn (1988, p.129–32) estimated that about 70 per cent of the total local expenditure was on housing repairs, while the remaining part went on public works, street cleaning, park maintenance, pothole repair and rubbish collection. However, local soviets were responsible for only about one-third of the urban housing stock, since, in the USSR as a whole, 61 per cent, and in the RSFSR 72 per cent, belonged to ministries and other production organisations at the end of the 1970s (Dienes, 1987a, p.303).[10]

A large part of services and cultural amenities was not only financed by enterprises of higher subordination, but, as Lewis (1983, p.56) argued, both siting and service volume were subject to norms and indices developed and implemented by sectoral and functional ministries (number of hospital beds, seats in dining facilities, square meters of housing and so on). Local budget spending in territorial industry and agriculture represented only five and 10 per cent respectively (Bahry, 1987, p.135). If one includes the figure for construction, which received a growing share of local budgets, the total figure for local financing of industry and construction increased steadily from 24.4 per cent in 1950 to 36.2 per cent in 1965, comprising 40.7 per cent in 1975 (Ross, 1987, p.76).

According to Aksenova (1992, p.122), regional and local budgets in the USSR comprised in 1989 only 18 per cent of the combined (*konsolidirovannyi*) state budget, while other countries had an average of 29.7 per cent. The appropriate figure for 1990 was 19.3 per cent as can be seen in the more comprehensive statistical analysis in Table A.7. Table A.8 shows the disaggregation of regional and local budgets according to the administrative unit. It indicates a fairly stable percentage share of expenditure among different local budgets in the administrative hierarchy for the period 1960–75.

The weak financial base of most subnational units and the fact that the budget-planning process was entirely separate from that for the city were the main reasons for the ineffectiveness of local planning (Dienes, 1987a, p.302). Hutchings (1983, p.178) found that the Soviet budget had been structured to exert a damping-down effect on competing expenditures, without which it would not have been possible to concentrate spending in what were perceived as strategically vital spheres. Moreover, another means to exert power at the local level was the industrial ministries' ownership and control of infrastructural and service facilities which left local officials often at the mercy of enterprise directors.

The organisation of local government

The dominance of the territorial CPSU committees in the localities, which provided not only a link to the centre, but also the control over the implementation of national policies, was a distinctive feature of Soviet local government. In practice, local governments had virtually no autonomy from party supervision and intervention into the details of its functioning. In fact, the XXIV Party Congress enacted the formal extension to local party organisations of the right to control or scrutinise the work of the state apparatus (Hill, 1983, p.29). While the Soviet system differed from the classical Western idea of functionally dividing legislative and executive power, principles of 'democratic centralism' and 'dual subordination' were applied in Soviet *administration* which ensured a high degree of centralisation of decision making.

However, after Khrushchev's attempt at decentralising territorially and involving state administration into policy making, there were, apart from the reassertion of CPSU power under Brezhnev, other changes in the process of local government after 1964, which comprised four main features (Churchward, 1983, p.39–44). Firstly, there was a renewed emphasis on professionalism, which included the administrative expansion in the replacement of non-staff (unpaid, volunteer) departments in city and city borough soviets by staff (paid, professional) departments, the abandonment of compulsory retirement at each election of one-third of all current deputies which had been introduced by Khrushchev earlier, the improved security of tenure and the rising educational standards of chief executive officials of local soviets. Secondly, there was an increased emphasis on formal procedures and rule observance. Thirdly, the Brezhnev years witnessed also a rapid rise to prominence of certain new agencies and practices (village committees, deputies' groups and electors' mandates). Finally, there was an increased role of public discussion of policy in the Soviet Union.

In contrast to parliamentary representation, *participation* in the Soviet Union was perceived to be administration of community affairs and it had also to involve unpaid, volunteer work in addition to the basic employment of the citizen (Friedgut, 1979, p.22). This perception led to a dilemma of Soviet local politics: how to combine expertise and professional administration with broad participation and the involvement of the masses in local government (Hill, 1977, p.82), who could not choose between competing candidates in local elections.[11]

In general, the party bodies duplicated the soviets at each level of the territorial hierarchy and had a strong control over policy implementation in their locality. Moreover, deputies were also dominated by their executive committees which formulated, in consultation with higher state and party bodies, policies at the local level (Ross, 1987, p.11–12). All three elements of local government (party, soviets, executive committee) were composed of a common leadership pool, which formed, in the positions of decisive power, a smaller core of nomenklatura cadres across the party-state divide. This core of members of the party and executive committees as well as industrial managers could be considered as the local elite, while elected deputies and public activists formed a 'sub-elite' (Friedgut, 1979, p.322).

Functions of local *party* organs were, in practice, mainly organisational-political work, industrial and construction questions as well as ideological matters (Hough, 1969, p.22). They were primarily engaged in the implementation and enforcement of national policies in the localities. Through party groups in the soviets and primary party organisations in the executive committees, it ensured a high degree of control and even *podmena*, that is the substitution of state functions by party intervention. Moreover, as Rutland (1993, p.26) outlined, the structure of the CPSU was well suited to the supervision of the Soviet economy according to the territorial-production principle.

However, local party organs were not able to coordinate and control actions of the ministries in their territory, which Ross (1987, p.18) called a 'control gap' between top party supervision over the ministries and local party control of enterprises subordinate to those ministries. But party supervision could all too often obstruct economic reform within the enterprises, since it was primarily concerned with the imperative of plan fulfillment in their territory expressed in gross output success indicators. Moses (1974, p.250) found in his empirical study that subnational party committees in the Soviet Union were granted at least some autonomy to direct their concerns selectively to local problems (cadre-organisational problems, social welfare, substantive industrial and agricultural problems), but they had much less autonomy in deciding what occupational sectors could participate in policy making.

Local *soviets* had, according to Lewis (1983, p.51–61), allocation, distribution, control and production functions. The role they played in the first two functions was relatively small, since, as outlined above, budgetary allocation and distribution were heavily dominated by central institutions and ministries. Control and production functions were of far more importance. Control was carried out by exercising supervisory, monitoring and reporting reponsibilities over a wide range of activities and transactions, particularly through their deputies, standing committees and finance departments (*ibid.*, p.58). However, there was only a formal authority in controlling non-subordinate enterprises, which varied with the soviet, the power of the sectoral ministry and the issue in question. Local soviets' production function comprised the management of retail trade, dining, educational, housing, entertainment and cultural facilities. They delivered a wide range of services including shoe and road repair, medical care and day care (*ibid.*, p.61).

However, their regulatory duties (regional planning, labour planning) and the provision of a wide range of goods and services were also part of the local enterprises' responsibility which led to an uncoordinated territorial planning, where local soviets were in a disadvantageous position *vis-à-vis* industrial ministries. Friedgut (1979, p.46–7) considered their importance primarily in normative, long-range educational and short-range operative functions, which clearly indicated Soviet mass participation at the input side, while the stage of implementation was left with the party and executive committees. In practice, the main duty of a local soviet was to give legitimacy to the work of the executive committee by conferring legal status on executive decisions (Jacobs, 1983, p.11).

The window-dressing element of 'socialist democracy' appeared also in the composition of local soviets which was supposed to ensure the representation of certain demographic and socioeconomic groups in proportion to national or regional criteria, although, as Hahn's study (1988, p.109) showed, deputies at the regional level were more likely to have higher education, to be party members and to work in non-manual jobs, compared with those at the village and settlement level. Thus, the pretense at representativeness was more likely to disappear, the higher the level of the soviet, and also among executive personnel. Jacobs (1983a, p.87), who analysed the hierarchy of political-demographic and social-occupational characteristics in the selection of deputies for all soviets, found that there was a great variation between the republics, suggesting that the norms were tailored to each republic.

Since the 1936 Constitution, the *executive* committee was subordinated both to its counterpart at the next highest level of government as well as to its territorial soviet. Its functions were, by contents, closely related to those of the soviet, but with a clear responsibility for policy implementation (Hahn, 1988, p.117–18):

1) administrative activity (including, for example, implementing the economic plan and overseeing the work of enterprises within the soviet's jurisdiction as well as those subordinated to higher ministries);
2) organisational matters (for example convening sessions of the soviet, coordinating the work of the standing commissions and preparing elections).

Members of the executive committees were also more likely to be male, a party member, older and better educated. Their advantage in professional expertise, skills and information gave them a clear dominance in sessions of the local soviet, where they prepared the majority of reports and draft decisions. Membership of the executive committee was clearly geared toward maximising the administrative efficiency of the soviet (Jacobs, 1983, p.12).

Finally, as Bahry (1987, p.12) observed, the impact of regional activism on Soviet policy choices was stronger at the republic than at the local level under Khrushchev and Brezhnev. This was primarily due to republic leaders' growing responsibility for managing their own affairs, more seats in the Politburo and the fact that issues of republic development received more national attention. However, her extensive study of republic leaders' requests to the central leadership showed a lack of attention to major industry (*ibid.*, p.81), which provides further evidence for the continuing dominance of industrial branch over territorial planning.

2.3 SPECIFIC FEATURES OF SIBERIAN DEVELOPMENT

Siberia represents a striking example of the conflict between national growth maximisation and regional equalisation as the two main goals of Soviet regional policy. In a distinctive core-periphery constellation, it was treated as a raw materials appendage of the centre over many decades. Natural resources were extracted in its regions, processed in the European part of the country or exported and the proceeds used in large part to buy capital goods for investment in other regions. Since the two case studies that form the core of this study focus on regions in Siberia and the Far East, this literature review includes also some discussions on the traditional centre-Siberian relationship.

The core-periphery dichotomy

Siberia covers a territory of about 13mn km^2 which comprises 7.5 per cent of the total territory on earth (Bobrick, 1993, p.14). Siberia's topographic structure is characterised by three different belts: a treeless *tundra* in the North, the broad forest landscape of the *taiga* in the middle and arable land (2.3 per cent of the total) in the South which merges into steppes and deserts. Besides sheer size, the most striking feature of Siberia is its environmental harshness (permafrost, seismic activity, low temperature over most of the year), resulting in low population densities, lack of infrastructure as well as high investment requirements for economic development (Dienes, 1982, p.207).

Siberia's traditional relationship to Russia west of the Urals was that of a mercantile colony to a colonial metropolis. However, while the economic resources of Siberia were under the tight control of the central government, it had enjoyed a considerable degree of political autonomy in pre-revolutionary Russia (Panel, 1991, p.367). During the Soviet period, there was a three-part strategy in the region which partly reinvigorated regionalist impulses:

1) a massive programme of economic development based on resource extraction;
2) the continued use of Siberia by Stalin as a place of exile or forced labour for political prisoners and ordinary criminals;

3) the creation of nationality-based units, which diverted attention from regional issues to ethnic ones and provided a pretext for ignoring regional challenges to Soviet legitimacy in Siberia (*ibid.*, p.370).

Prior to the *perestroika* period, there were three distinctive periods of changing investment priorities in Siberian development:

1) the prewar eastward movement focused on the Urals-Kuznetsk Combine, followed by the eastward evacuation of manufacturing plants during World War II;
2) a downward trend in Siberian development during the early postwar period until the mid-1950s;
3) the new resource-based focus in the 1960s and 1970s, shifting successively from East Siberian hydroelectric development to the oil and gas programme of Western Siberia, the Kansk-Achinsk lignite and power development and to the Baikal-Amur Mainline project in the Far East (Shabad, 1977, p.4).

This indicated a shift of priorities in Siberian development strategy from an earlier effort to endow Siberia with an integrated economy and settlement, to one where the influx of population was encouraged only to the extent that workers were needed to operate resource industries and power-intensive activities.

Moreover, it perpetuated a dichotomy, in which 75 to 80 per cent of the population and economic activity continued to be concentrated in the European part of the USSR, while about 80 per cent of gas and coal reserves, 75 per cent of water resources and a large part of nonferrous metals were found in Siberia (Mozhin, 1980, p.7). Table A.9 in the appendix shows the traditional industrial structure of Siberia and the Far East in comparison between 1960 and 1970. It clearly indicates the dominance of basic resource and first-stage processing industries, with fuel industries being particularly strong in Western Siberia, nonferrous metals in Eastern Siberia and food industry in the Far East where fishing accounted for about a fifth of the region's industrial output (Dienes, 1982, p.234).

Favourable factors of Siberian development such as good natural geological conditions for extraction of oil, gas, coal and certain ores, large timber reserves and cheap electricity costs in terms of unit capital costs, were, over the long period, counterweighted by such negative factors as higher capital-output ratios and labour costs as well as large capital investment requirements per unit of output and increased transport costs relative to the European USSR (Schiffer, 1989, p.143). The relative underpricing of energy and raw materials (in comparison with what a market would generate) entailed a systemic bias against fuel-and-raw-material-producing regions with respect to revenue distribution. Texas and Aberdeen are relatively rich provinces while Tyumen is not. Table A.10 indicates the 'labour intensity' (the reciprocal of labour productivity) of different industrial branches in the European RSFSR and Siberia in 1977, according to which not only the figures for light and food industries were much higher, but also crucial industries like electric power and nonferrous metals branches.

Apart from Siberia's inhospitable climate, poor transportation links and a badly developed physical and social infrastructure, the region was also faced with problems of high labour turnover and low capital efficiency. Moreover, Siberian scholars frequently pointed out that the Soviet relative pricing of Siberian resources was far below world market prices, in particular, those for oil, gas and coal (Granberg, 1991, p.12). However, if all the costs for transport, construction, technology and wages were to be reassessed at world market prices, there would be a different picture with clear disadvantages for Siberia. Finally, beside the higher depreciation rates and hidden cost increases of productive capacity, the device of official normative investment efficiency coefficients (10 belts for new industrial construction, four climatic zones and different coefficients for the installation of equipment) simply meant that costs were permitted to be higher (Holubnychy, 1973, p.26). Some of the consequences for social infrastructure can be seen in Table A.11 which shows, paradoxically, that less services were provided in those spheres where the share of industrial ministries in financing them was higher.

Two opposing strategies during perestroika

Gorbachev's economic reform raised again the issue of regional specialisation versus complex development and provoked a discussion about the role and significance of Siberia's development for future geopolitical structures and tendencies. Some authors argued that Gorbachev's general approach to economic growth and his emphasis on intensification and modernisation (especially in the machine-building industry) focused primarily on the development of Western regions of the former USSR. This 'European oriented strategy' would have a negative impact on Siberia and make economic growth in this region highly selective and distorted both in the sectoral and regional dimensions (Dienes, 1987). Others outlined the beginning of decentralisation and economic autonomy and with it the expansion of Siberia's sovereignty in the framework of ongoing economic and political reforms (Granberg, 1989).

The most likely scenario was drawn by de Souza (1990–1), taking into account a hierarchy of policies related to Siberian development. In the short-term, economic exploitation within high-priority sectors (oil and gas in Western Siberia) would continue and with it the one-sidedness of Siberia's production structure. But by medium and long-term investment (BAM railwayline, long-distance container handling), the participation of Siberia's regions in Pacific basin activities would possibly result in more economic diversification and self-sufficiency. De Souza anticipated a 'new economic-geographical map' for Siberia.

However, despite frequently changing investment priorities and attempts to integrate the Siberian economy in a more complex way (for example through TPCs[12]), Siberia remained, over the whole Soviet period, strongly dependent on the European core west of the Urals (capital, technology and workforce), and the dominance of branch over territorial planning was particularly evident for this region. The resource-based industrialisation in Siberia, a non-diversified industrial structure and the lack of intraregional-interbranch exchanges were the outcome of prevailing microeconomic efficiency criteria of industrial branch ministries. For the late *perestroika* period, Dienes (1989, p.257–8) observed not only a growing polarisation between metropolis and periphery, but also a 'dead circle' in the centre-periphery relationship, in which natural resources shipped in from the latter were mostly converted to capital goods (machines, drilling towers) and later shipped back to the periphery, which became a sterile circulation, benefiting neither centre nor periphery.

At present, the bulk of Siberia will continue to be more an obstacle than an attraction to development (Dienes, 1991, p.455), while a more autonomous and self-sufficient development requires a stabilisation of the economy and institutional restructuring. It is likely that regions and resources west of Lake Baikal will be oriented westward toward the European part of Russia, while those east of Lake Baikal could become increasingly integrated into the Asian Pacific basin. Political and economic changes will serve to differentiate numerous separate and distinct regions within Siberia. In particular, price liberalisation, by raising energy prices relative to other prices, will tend to favour income in energy-rich parts of Siberia, relative to incomes elsewhere. This is one of the main subjects of our case studies.

3 Russian Regional Roulette: Asymmetric Federalism and Economic Reform

The simultaneous attempt at building a new democratic society and pushing through economic reform in Russia is complicated by the current turmoil of intragovernmental relations. This is partly due, as discussed in Chapter 1, to the Soviet legacy of an intended assimilation and arbitrary territorialisation of ethnic groups, which had suppressed their feeling of national belonging and regional identity over many decades. Much of the turmoil of intragovernmental relations in Russia, however, is a result of the fact that institutional arrangements remain blurred, administrative competences are not clearly defined and that Moscow did not draw a clear line between central and provincial/local property and taxes which left the struggle for control over economic resources open-ended.

This chapter will first scrutinise the policy of creating a new federation in Russia with a particular focus on both regional elites and institutions, while turning later to fiscal arrangements and changing patterns of investment in the course of institutional restructuring. This discussion will be followed by a selective analysis of intragovernmental relations in other countries (both unitary and federal states) to draw from their experiences some lessons for Russia.[1]

3.1 IN SEARCH OF NEW FEDERAL RELATIONS

It could be argued that contemporary Russia is characterised by an asymmetrical federalism which has resulted from holding on to the former administrative-territorial division and continuing constitutional disputes. But it also contains features of a unitary state as a result of the formally strong power of provincial governors, the ubiquitous representation of federal structures in the regions and executive institutional arrangements down to the lowest level of government. At the same time, however, in 1994–5, Russian federalism was particularly shaped by regional and local elections as well as the attempt at setting up local self-government.

Administrative-territorial division

Chapter 1 discussed the difficulties for thorough market reform as a consequence of holding on to the inherited administrative structure. As on several previous occasions in Russian history, state formation preceded nation-building after the break-up of the Soviet Union in late 1991, which made the fostering of collective values and the building of social cohesiveness an imperative (Wagstaff, 1994, p.4). Not surprisingly, it unleashed a war of sovereignty in which ethnically-based territories took the lead. Consequently, the Russian concept of 'region' with its arbitrary administrative definition became amorphous.

Ethnic minorities in Russia claim a cultural and historical individuality as characterised by common values, traditions, language and regional identity, which does not necessarily correspond to existing administrative boundaries. While nationality-based administrative units (namely, all republics and autonomous *okruga*) cover about half of the territory of the RF, the population of these ethnic territories amounts only to about 20 per cent of the Russian total (Wallich, 1994, p.21–2). Moreover, at the time of the 1989 census, the titular nationality formed a *majority* of the population in only five of the 21 republics, while in three other republics it made up a *plurality*, which meant that most of the indigenous nationalities were heavily outnumbered by ethnic Russians.[2]

However, the signing of the Federation Treaty in March 1992 meant a juridical petrification of the arbitrary territorialisation of ethnic groups that was inherited from Stalin's policy of 'divide and rule' along and across ethnicity lines. According to this treaty, republics claimed state sovereignty including the recognition of their own language and citizenship as well as more rights for the control of natural resources in their territories, fiscal autonomy and independent foreign trade. To the two republics (Tatarstan, Chechnya-Ingushetiya), which held back from signing the treaty, Moscow responded in a different way.[3]

By signing a bilateral agreement with Tatarstan in February 1994, which until then considered itself as merely associated with the RF, the central authorities wanted to establish a precedence in terms of solving intragovernmental conflicts with resistant republics.[4] According to the census in 1989, only 27 per cent of all Tatars had their residence in Tatarstan, while about five million Tatars were living somewhere else in the former USSR (Henze, 1994, p.14). At that time, Tatars amounted to 48.6 per cent of the total population in their republic compared with 43.4 per cent ethnic Russians (Perepelkin, 1992, p.92). But they enjoyed an improvement of their social status in the Tatar ASSR in the 1970s and

1980s, which was reflected not only in numbers entering higher education but also in the fact that they increasingly took over leading positions in the economy and administration (see appendix, Tables A.12 and A.13). Relying on these positions as well as a relatively developed economy (oil, defence industry), the Tatar political leadership acquired the necessary confidence for declarations of sovereignty.

But the bilateral agreement between the centre and Tatarstan defined, at least for the time being, the limits to this drive of independence. Although Tatarstan was granted the right to exploit independently its natural resources, including oil and gas, Moscow kept control of the annual total amount of oil production (Tatarstan is completely dependent on the Russian pipeline network). According to this agreement, Tatarstan can keep all duties accruing from the sale and production of hard liquor, oil and gas and those arising from privatisation and the sale of land. But it lost a considerable amount of its former fiscal autonomy. Moscow again collects federal taxes on Tatar territory and the emission of money remains the exclusive preserve of the Russian Central Bank (Teague, 1994, p.23).[5] Tatarstan also provides a good example of the fact that, in the ethnically-tinged competition for scarce resources, a minimum of economic strength and political power is necessary in order to take on the struggle for national self-determination (von Beyme, 1994, p.138).

The Russian administratively defined concept of 'region' also became amorphous as a result of conflicts between republics as well as of conflicts between standard provinces and republics in the RF. On 31 October 1992, a military conflict between Osetiya and Ingushetiya broke out which cost the lives of about 800 people in the period up to October 1994 (*Segodnya*, 11 October 1994, p.2), and as a result of which an estimated 46–60 000 Ingush people had to flee from the Prigorodnii *raion*, territory disputed by both sides until mid-1995 (*Segodnya*, 8 July 1995, p.2). Moscow denounced martial law in early 1995 (KD, 18 February 1995, p.3), but, at the time of writing, the provisional administration appointed by the centre is still in power. Political leaders of the Cherkesy and Abasiny nations declared their intention to separate from the Karachaevo-Cherkesiya republic in December 1994 claiming an underrepresentation in leading administrative positions (*Segodnya*, 14 January 1995, p.3).[6] In this article it was also reported that Russian Cossacks in the Naurskii and Shelkovskii *raiony* of Chechnya want to return these territories to the Stavropol *krai*, which were taken away from that province in 1957. The republic of Adygeya, which separated from Krasnodar *krai* and has a 68 per cent share of ethnic Russians compared with only 22 per cent of the titular nationality (Teague, 1995, p.17), adopted a constitution which grants legal preferences to the Adygeitsy including residency and citizenship (RG, 2 November 1994, p.2) as well as a minimum of 50 per cent representation of the titular nationality in the parliament (*Segodnya*, 15 February 1995, p.2).

Another contentious issue is the fact that Russian Cossacks required to be recognised as a 'special nation' (*Segodnya*, 22 October 1994, p.3) and that they want to transform from a social movement into a 'state structure' of national importance (RV, 27 October 1994, p.2). Although in pre-revolutionary Russia Cossack movements were traditionally organised in border regions, they are today not satisfied with local self-government including the control of local budgets (RV, 10 February 1995, p.2), but aspire to a strong political representation in the future State Duma as was proposed at the founding conference of the nationwide Cossack movement in February 1995 (*Segodnya*, 15 February 1995, p.2). This was an attempt at consolidating three different Cossack groupings (*Izvestiya*, 2 June 1995, p.5), but their reputation is often in question as a result of criminal activities by Cossack members (RG, 23 May 1995, p.1–2).

Finally, Russian regions could considerably change their features in the next few years as a result of migration and depopulation. The number of refugees in North Osetiya amounted to 41 900 people in October 1994 which then accounted reportedly for 17 per cent of the total population (KD, 13 October 1994, p.3). This led not only to inter-ethnic tensions due to a general shortage of housing and jobs in the Caucasus, but could also result in new political alliances and a change of the potential electorate for political leaders in office. It was aggravated during the war in Chechnya when 50 000 people from the Chechen republic reportedly sought refuge in Krasnodar *krai* alone (*Segodnya*, 7 June 1995, p.2). However, the main flows of migration into heartland Russia are expected by central officials, according to the former Vice-Prime Minister Sergei Shakhrai, from the Russian Far North and Central Asia (DS, 20–26 April 1995, p.1).

Many parts of Russia – which played under the Soviet rule a mere military-strategic role or from which only a few natural resources were extracted – are today threatened by depopulation. According to a survey among the population of the Kurile islands carried out after the devastating earthquake in October 1994, only three per cent of them intend to stay there (*Segodnya*, 3 November 1994, p.3). About 80 settlements in Tomsk *oblast'* (with an estimated population of 100 000 people) specialise in wood-processing, but with the break-up of the USSR they have lost their traditional markets in Kazakhstan and Central Asia, at least so long as payment arrangements remain problematic, remaining without any new orders (DM, 14 January 1995, p.4). Even worse is the situation in the

Russian Far North which could lead to an irreversible decline in population there.[7] In many settlements in the Yamalo-Nenetskii *okrug* post offices, schools and other parts of the social infrastructure (clubs, museums) are closing (RG, 9 February 1995, p.3), which could accelerate people's decision to migrate. About 10 000 people in the Nenetskii autonomous *okrug* intend to move out from their provisional housing (DM, 24 February 1995, p.8); they have little reason to stay, with the harsh climatic and poor social conditions (they were presumably employed in the oil industry).

Constitutional issues

It is not only the case that the Russian concept of 'region' became amorphous; the concept of federalism was also obscured by an ambivalent delegation of sovereignty between the different administrative levels. Joint functions between the centre and standard provinces, as they were defined in the Federal Treaty (use of natural resources, foreign trade), left much room for speculation. Teague (1995, p.16) argued that these ambiguities could be, in fact, a valuable tool by which politicians could concentrate, in the short-term, more on mutual interests instead of competing claims. However, in order to set up proper federal relations, regional governments will have, in the medium- and long-term, to be equipped with 'consequential power' (Litvack, 1994, p.229–30), including legal and revenue powers as well as an institutionalised influence on central policy making.

After Moscow loosened its grip on the provinces and more centres of power appeared, territorial jurisdiction acquired a new meaning in which local authority could be extended, rather than the territory being subject only to central jurisdiction (Mitchneck, 1994, p.74). Under emergency conditions, federalism appeared as the only viable form of state-building in Russia to accommodate regional demands for more sovereignty. But to make federalism workable Russian authorities will have to constitute at least two levels of institutional political autonomy and to grant a minimal degree of economic self-sufficiency (fiscal autonomy) for all administrative levels, while not denying differences in cultural identity, traditions, values and religion.

Federalism is an important source of innovation and adaptability in many other countries (see below). However, as Putnam (1993, p.47) pointed out, the distinction between centralised and federal systems is not necessarily a clear dichotomy, but rather a continuum in which many centralised countries (in this case Italy) have moved recently to a more decentralised system of intragovernmental relations. In the case of Russia, where many provinces claim their own statehood, the pendulum could easily swing towards a confederation (RG, 15 February 1995, p.2). Moscow will certainly keep its special relations with ethnically-based territories. Shakhrai as one of the most influential advocates of a strong regional policy called publicly for a distinction between 'universal' and strategically important, 'specific' (border regions, enclaves and territories in military conflict) provinces (RG, 4 February 1995, p.4).[8]

To make federalism workable in Russia, conflicts in legislation at both the central and regional levels will have to be smoothed out. The former head of the President's administration, Sergei Filatov, has argued that the following are serious infringements of the Russian Constitution: the fact that many republics (Ingushetiya, Tyva, Sakha) claim the primacy of their constitution over the federal one;[9] the attempt by a number of republics (Komi, Bashkortostan, Sakha and Tyva) to claim full responsibility for matters which were defined as joint functions in the Russian Constitution (federal taxes, customs duties, defence) and the independent appointment of a general procurator in Bashkortostan, Tatarstan, Tyva and Chechnya (RV, 31 August 1994, p.2).[10] Another contentious issue is the right to control natural resources in the territories. Komi republic wanted to reconsider *Gazprom's* exclusive right of resource extraction in the province, which its constitution reserved as its own (*Segodnya*, 27 October 1994, p.3).

Finally, a study carried out by the President's administration on constitutional law found violations of human rights in a number of regional legislations including the denial of citizenship, the ban on officials in leading administrative positions taking an active part in political parties and associations, the violation of national equality, the use of a non-Russian official state language in regions where the majority of the population are ethnic Russians, as well as the formation of state organs staffed only by particular nationalities and the setting of an age limit for heads of administration (RV, 16 February 1995, p.3). Officials in the republic of Sakha (Yakutiya) set restrictions on free entrance into 11 cities and *raiony* in its territory, while Kalmykia's authorities reserved the right to declare martial law (RG, 30 June 1995, p.4).

However, the most sensitive issues remain those of the change of the legal status of a province and territorial separation. The Federation Council proposed a new draft in November 1994 which would considerably complicate the procedure of changing the legal status, or even separating from the RF despite public approval expressed in a referendum in the region (KD, 12 November 1994, p.2). However, through its military intervention in the civil war in Chechnya, Moscow showed also that it is prepared to preserve the territorial integrity of the RF by military means, ignoring federal legislation and human rights.

Regional elites

Recent Western studies have shown that the widespread view on elites in the provinces as the strongholds of resistance to market reform has to be partly reconsidered. Hahn (1994, p.231) argued that 'the struggle is not over reform *per se* so much as it is over who will get to decide who gets what, when and how ...'. Regional elites in Russia have, compared with other federal states, a considerable influence on the outcome of national economic policy and they decide on the rules of the game for companies operating in their territory, which makes them responsible to a great extent for the turmoil and resistance against economic change. This is mainly due to their attempt at tailoring central policy to local interests, trying to keep a firm grip on pricing, property and investment policy (Young, 1994, p.146). Provincial politicians are now faced with the ballot box, which makes them more likely to turn to populist policies and to favour a particular electorate. McAuley (1992, p.87) concluded from this conflict that the fate of the national economic reform would depend on where members of the provincial elite perceived their interests lie: in 'exercising their ownership rights through market mechanisms or by operating state concerns'.

There was not only more of a 'circulation of elites' instead of a 'change of elites' (Wollmann, 1994, p.336), but also a 'commercialisation of the nomenklatura' in which former party and state leaders poured into new commercial structures and used their insider knowledge to transform state property into private property. Even in the reform model of Nizhnii Novgorod 80 per cent of the employees in the regional administration were reportedly former party officials (Magomedov, 1994, p.74). However, two different prototypes of regional elites can be discerned from a comparison of Nizhnii Novgorod and Ul'yanovsk regions. While the former consisted, in leading positions, of young, technocratic politicians who involved local intellectuals and international advisers to carry out market experiments and democratic reform, the latter was characterised by local corporatism of the former nomenklatura, the authoritarian and populist leadership of its governor, Yurii Goryachev, and patron-client relations (*Segodnya*, 31 December 1994, p.10).[11]

There was a consensus among Western researchers that the political context of 1989–90 was an important factor in regional differences (Moses, 1994, p.129–30). Hahn (1994, p.230) found that the greatest support for reform was in those regions (Yaroslavl, Saratov), where there had been major personnel changes in the provincial leadership. However, a review of the Russian central press in 1994–5 gives the impression that patron-client relations, populist price controls and the autocratic rule by governors was a widespread phenomenon even among new politicians. Apart from McAuley's (1992, p.87) observed shift 'from elections and assemblies to a struggle within the elite [in each region] for control over economic resources' in 1992, there was also a growing local corporatism in political decision making, which effectively marginalised former democratic movements, and a new entanglement of politics and economics at the provincial level was witnessed in the more recent period.

This is particularly evident in Moscow city, where the so-called 'Moscow group' represents a combination of members of the former nomenklatura, the new business and new apparatchiks, who came to power during the democratic wave of 1989–91. They can rely on a powerful network of banks, mass media, political parties and deputies in the city Duma (RV, 26 May 1995, p.2). Bryansk *oblast'* provides a conspicuous example of how the criminal underworld undermined the provincial administration, where the business tycoon, Oleg Kibal'chich, arranged the appointment of his own business partners in leading positions, for which he was granted tax exemptions and the right to acquire municipal buildings (*Izvestiya*, 26 July 1995, p.5).[12]

In Volgograd region, which was presented in Western literature as a reformist province (Moses, 1994), the creation of the holding company *Sfera* was set up by the regional administration to organise a network of public services (bakeries, production of textiles and medicine) using 20 per cent of shares reserved for state property from privatisation of other enterprises for its founding capital (DM, 28 February 1995, p.5). In April 1991, Leonid Polezhaev, the later governor of Omsk *oblast'*, became a founding member of a new conglomerate of large industries and commercial enterprises in the region known as *Omskii Torgovyi Dom* (OTD), which started buying up profitable local enterprises (Young, 1994, p.147).[13] The former governor of Sakhalin *oblast'*, E. Krasnoyarov, transferred R100mn from the regional budget in November 1993 as his own share as a founding member of a new commercial bank. He lobbied for the issue of soft credits from the Central Bank, assigned to the bank a role in the finance of regional export quotas and included a paragraph in the bank's founding document which said that an amount of R1bn (late 1993 prices) and $2.5mn should be transferred from the regional budget annually (RV, 31 March 1994, p.2).[14]

The most notorious example of a Brezhnev-style dynasty in political office, patron-client relations and an autarkical regional economy can be found in Ul'yanovsk *oblast'*. The governor of the province, Yurii Goryachev, who was the first CPSU secretary in the region from 1973, has a firm grip on the agrarian lobby, appoints officials of federal structures in the province, controls the creation of political parties and the lowest consumer prices in Russia in recent times (see below). To keep prices down, an off-budgetary fund for the stabilisation of the economy was set up, which is derived from 30 different sources of revenues and amounted to R1bn in 1993 (*Izvestiya*, 3 December 1994, p.5). This populist 'consumption bias' (Berkowitz, 1994, p.198), through which provincial governments believe that an increase in consumer surplus attracts more votes than an increase in state profits, was also a widespread phenomenon in other regions.[15]

Institutions

One of the main reasons for the turmoil in the RF is the fact that the separate roles of federal and provincial institutions remain blurred and administrative competences are not clearly defined. Executive and legislative power at both levels of government have their own institutional arrangements, which compete for control over resources and the means of coercion. National parties have a generally weak representation in the provinces and can not provide a coherent institutional structure for central policy implementation. This led to a mushrooming of committees and associations dealing with regional policy at both the federal and provincial levels as documented in the appendix (Figure A.1).

In the centre, President Yeltsin tried to overcome the perceived resistance of regional elites to market reform by asking the Supreme Soviet in November 1991 for special powers including the appointment of heads of administration (governors) in each province. However, after Yeltsin sacked the governor of Bryansk *oblast'*, the Russian parliament announced new legislation ending Yeltsin's right to appoint or dismiss heads of administration. In early 1993, a number of provinces appointed their own new governors. Several of these later came into conflict with the President over his showdown with the Supreme Soviet in September-October 1993 (Teague, 1993). Yeltsin reasserted his special power afterwards, but several provinces challenged this again in summer 1994 by announcing elections of governors.[16]

The President issued a new decree on 3 October 1994 (RG, 7 October 1994, p.1–2) in which he delayed the elections of governors until 1996. In fact, the 'Union of Governors' had elaborated this decree which included social benefits for the governors (life insurance, increase of salary) as well as political concessions like the governors' right of veto against the appointment of officials of federal structures in their territories (KD, 8 October 1994, p.2). However, Yeltsin's decree became ineffective after he allowed, in exceptional cases, the election of the governor in Nizhnii Novgorod (*Segodnya*, 27 April 1995, p.3) and Sverdlovsk *oblasti* (*Izvestiya*, 16 May 1995, p.2). This started a new and perilous development of granting preferential treatment to particular provinces where the central leadership perceived, as in the case of Nizhnii Novgorod, 'the economic and political situation to be stable' (RG, 23 June 1995, p.4). However, why Yeltsin acceded to the demands of Eduard Rossel', who was sacked by him earlier as governor of Sverdlovsk *oblast'* for threatening to declare an independent Urals republic and who was, in fact, the main advocate of new elections of the governor (*Segodnya*, 18 May 1995, p.2), remains an open question.

In the course of 1994, governors had concentrated more power in their hands. Apart from authoritarian rule in some standard regions discussed above, presidents in ethnically-based republics showed a particular bias towards Byzantine executive relations. The Bashkir President, Murtaza Rakhimov, set up in his presidential apparatus structures paralleling federal institutions (army, police), thus effectively establishing Presidential rule (RG, 7 September 1994, p.2). Punitive measures were created in the Bashkir Ministry of Interior intimidating all oppositional forces (RG, 11 February 1995, p.3). A ruthless struggle for control over oil and energy resources broke out in this republic.[17] Moreover, the Bashkir leadership keeps the trade in real estate under central control (KD, 30 May 1995, p.2). The Tatar President, Mintimer Shaimiev, required his appointed heads of *raiony* administration to gain 'legitimacy' in local elections, as a result of which almost half of all deputies in the new republic parliament are representatives of the executive branch (KD, 7 May 1995, p.3). Finally, the President of Sakha (Yakutiya), Mikhail Nikolaev, arranged reportedly an unlimited extension of his presidency through the republic parliament (*Segodnya*, 27 July 1995, p.2).

To keep an additional control over regional elites, Yeltsin appointed his representatives in each province, who have to check how the President's decrees are carried out and report to central institutions on the progress of reforms in the region. They came originally mostly from the democratic fraction of the former Supreme Soviet and could only make recommendations to provincial officials, as a result of which they were widely considered to be 'toothless commissars' (Webb, 1994, p.36).[18]

An important issue for a viable federation was the institutional integration of regional perspectives into central policy making. One way in which this might be facilitated is the movement of leading personnel between posts at the regional and federal levels. To some extent, this has happened. Regional leaders were appointed to higher office in central institutions like the governor of Krasnodar *krai*, Evgenii Egorov, who became the Minister for Nationalities and Interregional Relations (RV, 16 August 1994, p.2) or the governor of Amurskaya *oblast'*, V. Polevanov, who took over briefly as Minister of Privatisation. Figure A.1 documents the growing number of committees and associations dealing with regional policy at both the federal and regional levels. A particular feature of the central leadership's regional policy making is the setting up of intersectoral commissions to solve a particular regional problem, like the supply of foodstuffs to the Russian Far North (RG, 11 April 1995, p.2). Apart from regular visits of the provinces by central politicians, more recent techniques and institutional arrangements include the set up of intragovernmental legal committees to check on the legality of provincial statutes (*Segodnya*, 4 July 1995, p.2).

The Muscovite bureaucracy had forced regional authorities to create corresponding structures in the provinces (RV, 15 July 1994, p.3), but with the growing number of federal structures the administrative apparatus in the regions was also extended. In Rostov *oblast'*, 255 people were employed in the governor's apparatus and another 200 in the department of agriculture in late 1994 (RV, 23 November 1994, p.1). St Petersburg's former mayor, Anatolii Sobchak, complained that in his city 64 different federal structures were operating in early 1995 employing 11 000 people, compared with 280 employees in his apparatus (DM, 9 February 1995, p.1).[19] In Voronezh *oblast'*, 5400 people employed in the regional state apparatus compare with almost 7000 in federal structures operating in the territory. In early 1995, the Voronezh provincial administration (excluding lower-level bodies) consisted reportedly of 1096 employees, while, during the late Soviet period, 1100 people worked in the regional party and state apparatus (DM, 30 March 1995, p.4). This could simply indicate a fusion of former structures within the new executive branch.

In the regions, different institutions represented distinct constituencies. Young (1994, p.150) found in Omsk *oblast'* that the former regional soviet represented rural and agricultural interests, while the provincial administration had close ties to large-scale industry in Omsk. Moreover, whereas the administration in Omsk city advanced a small business agenda, the city soviet represented varied and disparate urban constituencies. In the meantime, central institutions competed for different regional alliances. While the President's administration did not get on very well with interregional associations (North-West, Central Russia, 'Siberian

Agreement' and others),[20] the Federation Council granted a higher legal status to regional associations in summer 1994 (KD, 15 July 1994, p.3).

Finally, the development of both national and regional parties is only in its infancy. While national parties with a strong representation in the provinces could provide for more institutional coherence in the implementation of central policy, regional parties could more effectively articulate their specific interests and influence national policy making. But there are either too many small parties and associations in Russia's provinces[21] or national parties are simply too weakly represented to have any significant influence on regional policy making. Among democratic parties, it was reported that Gaidar's 'Democratic Russia's Choice' had regional representation in more than 60 provinces in late 1994 compared with 35 of Yavlinskii's '*Yabloko*' (Petrov, 1994a, p.3). Due to the lack of a clear social base, the set up of national party structures took bizarre forms in many places.[22]

An exception in the run-up to the election of the federal parliament in December 1995 was supposed to be Prime Minister Chernomyrdin's movement 'Our Home Russia' which previously witnessed a mushrooming of regional branches composed of alliances of leading politicians, businessmen and military officers in the provinces, as a result of which it was widely considered as the new 'party of power'.[23] However, it performed badly compared with the Communist Party and Zhirinovskii's 'Liberal Democratic Party', both of which managed to gain most of the votes in rural areas and small towns (RG, 6 January 1996). While the left-centrist bloc of the speaker of the State Duma, Ivan Rybkin, had hardly gathered momentum, the chairman of the Sverdlovsk provincial Duma, Eduard Rossel', tried to set up his own movement 'Transformation in the Urals' as a counterbalance to the Moscow-based blocs of Chernomyrdin and Rybkin (RV, 9 June 1995, p.3). Parties with a particular thrust on regional policy like Shakhrai's PRES party or Skokov's 'Congress of Russian Communities' play a rather marginal role.[24]

Regional and local elections

Procedures of the voting system, the size of voting districts, the financing of election campaigns and the required quorum and amount of signatures for registration of candidates differed widely in Russian provincial elections in 1994, since federal legislation on elections was not clearly defined or simply ignored and these procedures were subject to the power struggle among regional elites to favour their potential electorate. Two distinctive features appeared in the Russian regional elections in 1994. Apart from a political revitalisation of former nomenklatura members ('neosovietisation'), there was also a 'ruralisation of political life' (Petrov, 1994a, p.12). Voters in rural areas acquired a stronger political voice through their higher participation rates at provincial elections compared with cities, where the turnout was generally low, together with the frequent redrawing of constituency boundaries to raise the 'weight' of the rural electorate in the election of regional assemblies. The election of many local heads of administration to regional parliaments meant also a strengthening of the position of governors,[25] since they appoint or dismiss the former, which became effectively a fusion of executive and legislative power and a new tool for local corporatism.

The *urban-rural cleavage* of voting patterns became particularly apparent in Yaroslavl *oblast'*, which has a predominantly urban population, but where 18 per cent of the rural population had a decisive say in the election of the majority of new deputies (RV, 24 February 19994, p.2). Two-thirds of the deputies in the Bashkir Supreme Soviet were elected by the rural population in early 1995, which amounts to only one third of the total population (KD, 4 March 1995, p.3). The same applies to the Tatar republic, where two-thirds of the eligible voters in rural areas went to the ballot box compared with only 30 per cent in the capital Kazan' (*Segodnya*, 7 March 1995, p.2).

The required *quorum* was achieved in spring 1994 in only 58 regions (Petrov, 1994a, p.8) and re-elections had to take place in summer/autumn 1994. The quorum varied between 25 and 50 per cent and was a subject of political struggle.[26] The President of Chuvashiya, Nikolai Fedorov, even went to the Constitutional Court in Moscow after the Chuvash parliament abolished the 25 per cent quorum following low election turnout in the republic (*Segodnya*, 1 July 1995, p.2). An even more contentious issue was the *procedure* of elections. Most of the regions chose a majority system, while about one-fourth of them voted in multi-mandate districts (Petrov, 1994a, p.9). Most of the voting districts simply conformed with the local administrative subdivision of the region.

The *timing* of regional elections appeared also to be an important issue. Officials in Krasnodar *krai* delayed the elections from 25 September to 20 November 1994, because it was feared that too many people would still work at their private plots, which would give the oppositional movement of *Otechestvo* with its potential electorate of pensioners and unemployed people an advantage (KD, 11 August 1994, p.3). Tatarstan established extremly arbitrary procedures for its parliamentary elections on 5 March 1995. No voting according to *party lists* was allowed, the *size of voting districts* varied between 20 000 and 200 000 people and oppositional forces were deprived of *finance* for their election campaign (*Segodnya*, 23 February 1995, p.2). There were also reported cases of manipulated counting of votes, the refusal of access to polling stations for election observers and the rejection of registration of candidates for the Tatar parliament (*Segodnya*, 10 March 1995, p.2). At the elections of local heads of administration in Khakasiya, techniques of manipulating votes included several-voting by one person, voting by non-eligible voters like teenagers and the early opening of ballot boxes (*Segodnya*, 28 March 1995, p.3).

Even the amount of necessary *signatures* for registration of candidates became an issue of political struggle. Only nine of the 17 political associations in St Petersburg could collect the required 35 000 signatures for the re-election of the remaining 25 seats in the city parliament (*Segodnya*, 6 October 1994, p.3). The results of the election in what was then Leningrad in 1990 were extensively analysed in Western literature showing a clear division between supporters of the movement 'Democratic Elections 90' and Communist Party members still being in power (Andrews and Vacroux, 1994, p.59–65).[27] But there was a growing political apathy among ordinary voters in 1994. According to a telephone survey among 1055 people, 75 per cent did not even know that re-elections would take place on 30 October 1994 (RV, 7 October 1994, p.2). In fact, a second round of the re-elections was necessary, in which the turnout varied between 10 and 18 per cent (*Segodnya*, 22 November 1994, p.1). Where the democratic opposition was most advanced in 1990 (St Petersburg, Moscow), locally-based political organisations like 'Favourite City' in St Petersburg appear to be now the most influential groups, while strongholds of support for Zhirinovskii's ultra-national LDPR and the Communist parties are reported to be in provincial capitals, small factory towns and rural areas.[28]

Local self-government

The concept of local self-government, in the sense of lower-tier (town, *raion*) elected government, as a building block for Russian federalism became a very popular issue in late 1994 and early 1995 with a national conference being held in Moscow on 17 February 1995. However, central and provincial leaders had a rather different view of what it should be like and, not surprisingly, this concept became a subject of political struggle among different levels of government. The most contentious issues were those of whether elected representatives of the organs of local self-government should be members of the local administration, whether they should be financially independent, which functional competences different to those of the local administration they should have and which territory local self-government should embrace.

In many provinces it was proposed to return to the pre-revolutionary *zemstvo* territorial subdivisions. The leader of the Russian *zemstvo* movement, Elena Panina, proposed three different levels of local self-government:

1) at the territorial level of former village soviets *volost'* assemblies should be created;
2) in rural settlements *raiony* assemblies would gather;
3) in urban settlements, city *dumy* and *upravy* would be elected.

However, it is not clear to what extent this would differ from the existing administrative-territorial structure and, as it was claimed, whether national or political considerations would really play no role (RG, 19 November 1994, p.9).

Many provincial activists, supporters of local self-government, complained about the centre trying to impose its concept from above (*ibid.*, p.15). In the centre, the elaboration of the law on local self-government became an issue of institutional competition as a result of which five different versions were originally prepared and suggested to the regions (RV, 10 February 1995, p.2). However, only three of them, including the drafts of two deputy groups in the State Duma headed by I. Murav'ev and A. Dolgopolov respectively, came under closer scrutiny (DM, 20–26 March 1995, p.45). As with the new Russian constitution, the government tried first to push its own version through. In his speech at the national conference on local self-government in February 1995 Prime Minister, Viktor Chernomyrdin, left unclear what the division of administrative competences at the local level would be. He declared that organs of local self-government would not be part of the state administration, but they could own, use and dispose of municipal property, collect taxes and share responsibility for law and order (RG, 21 February 1995, p.1). Some outside observers interpreted the government's approach of strengthening local power as an attempt to undermine the growing executive power at the provincial level (Kuznechevskii, 1995, p.2).

A new law on self-government could only be adopted in late August 1995 (RG, 1 September 1995, p.4–6). This followed a long parliamentary debate when a compromise draft approved by the State Duma was first turned down by the Federation Council in early July 1995 (RV, 21 July 1995, p.2). For most of the time, provincial leaders were left to read between the lines of different drafts and the process took on its own dynamic. In the 56 provinces, where elections to local self-government were reportedly held in the period from late 1993 to February 1995, a total of 21 000 heads and 14 000 *starosta* of local self-government (this presumably distinguished between *raiony* and villages) took on their new responsibilities (RG, 2 March 1995, p.2).[29] However, many provincial authorities were stuck in deadlock between executive and legislative power over the legislation on local self-government, as in Krasnoyarsk (*Segodnya*, 6 October 1994, p.2), and a particularly contentious issue was that of *raiony*, which were created as an intermediate territorial level during the Soviet time to exert party control over *kolkhozy* and *sovkhozy* (*Segodnya*, 21 October 1994, p.9).

Thus, the concept of local self-government still remains very much in flux, state administrative officials can easily intervene in the operation of local government, and financial independence seems not to be sufficiently provided. In a survey among 331 representatives of local power in Astrakhan *oblast'*, for example, 87 per cent of the respondants thought that organs of local self-government should be staffed by state employees (RG, 23 June 1995, p.5). In villages and settlements of Tula *oblast'*, local self-government organs are responsible together with the local administrations for water and gas supply, medical treatment and other social services (RV, 3 February 1995, p.2). Whether this could lead to a growing bureaucratic apparatus, remains an open question.

3.2 FISCAL ARRANGEMENTS BETWEEN CENTRE AND PROVINCES

The viability of a federal system in Russia is, to a considerable extent, in question due to the turmoil of fiscal arrangements which have no transparent, fair and consensus-based intragovernmental financial framework, but consist of a series of bilaterally bargained, *ad hoc* deals and are based on no clear grant equalisation formula. Despite some modifications in 1994, the budgetary system as it was inherited from the Soviet Union in 1991 has not been substantially reformed and a basic correspondence between revenues and expenditures could not be ensured for each region. This was complicated by the frequent use of extrabudgetary funds, while federal subsidies and transfers also appear in the budgetary equation.

The legacy of the Soviet tax system

Russian fiscal arrangements are characterised by dual subordination; that is revenues are shared upward from the local to the regional and then to the federal budget. Main taxes (VAT, profits tax) which are collected at the territorial levels, are first shared in fixed percentages with the federal budget, while central authorities redistribute a part of them afterwards. This not only entails a considerable time lag and therefore, under conditions of high inflation, effective devaluation, but it is also subject to non-transparent, bargained, *ad hoc* deals and open for regional lobbying. The latter has no normative basis, but rather indicates political strength and bargaining skills of regional politicians. Table A.15 shows the sharing rates for revenues and expenditures between the centre and the regions in 1992–4.

Another legacy of the Soviet budgetary system is that subnational governments have not been assigned any major taxes, but only their revenue, and they have no significant rate- or base-setting authority (Wallich, 1992, p.7). There is also a dual subordination in terms of employment, since finance departments in the provinces are accountable to both the Ministry of Finance and the regional administration. Although the federal state tax inspections have been institutionally separated from subnational government, it is not clear yet whether proper disentanglement has taken place. Finally, the practice of distinguishing between 'guaranteed' and 'regulated' taxes continued (DM, 26 December 1994–1 January 1995, p.17), in which the assignment of tax shares for regions was fixed in the case of the former, while the latter left the provinces at the mercy of central authorities.

The legacy of the Soviet tax system also appears in particular methods of tax collection. For example, there is still a double licencing of trade at both the place of registration and the place of sale. Moreover, taxes on profits are also collected at both the place of registration of the main company and the places of operation of its subsidiaries (KD, 10 February 1995, p.8).

Correspondence of revenues and expenditures

The key challenge for Russia's fiscal federalism, as Wallich (1994, p.2) stressed, is to ensure revenue-expenditure correspondence by which central authorities would first have to determine the cost of public expenditure and then to design a system of tax assignments, shared taxes and intragovernmental transfers that provides regions with sufficient revenues to meet necessary expenditure. Revenue-sharing, equalisation and financing programmes of national interest in the provinces appear as main principles of fiscal federalism. This also includes both budgetary discretion for local officials and a mechanism to make them accountable.

However, in the case of Russia, there are no specific assignments of expenditure responsibilities between levels of government. In Russia it is the other way around: the availability of revenue is dictating the distribution of expenditure responsibilities between different administrative levels (Wallich, 1992, p.4–5). A correspondence between revenues and expenditures would be ensured by a more decentralised system of intragovernmental relations. Fiscal decentralisation would increase economic efficiency through direct linkages between costs and benefits as well as political responsibility for the provision of social services in the region. Heavy reliance on grants goes hand in hand with central intrusion into expenditure decisions and destroys the incentives for responsible local decisions (Oates, 1992, p.241). Provincial authorities would also have a much higher interest in the efficiency of their tax collection.

In Russia, the lack of local budgetary discretion and transparency are still major obstacles to a correspondence between revenues and expenditures. In 1992–4, almost every region came to special arrangements with Moscow, which included preferential treatment like tax allowances and additional subsidies, effectively undermining the goal of macroeconomic stabilisation. These arrangements differed from one region to the other and depended on the strategic importance of the provinces for the centre, the value of their natural resources and the political assertiveness of regional politicians. Export regions even seemed to receive hidden subsidies. The assigned share of revenues from VAT increased in Tyumen *oblast'* in 1992 from originally 30 per cent to 43 per cent, in Udmurtiya from 20 per cent to 56 per cent and in Tatarstan and Bashkortostan from 20 per cent to 100 per cent, while those for St Petersburg decreased in the same year from 20 per cent to 14 per cent and in Moscow city from 20 per cent to 13 per cent (Dmitrieva, 1994, p.115). On the basis of the bilateral agreements between the centre and particular republics, as discussed above, numerous tax exemptions were granted, which denied Moscow an estimated R2trn of federal tax revenues from Tatarstan, Bashkiriya, Kareliya and Sakha (Yakutiya) alone in 1994 or 2.3 per cent of total federal budget income in that year (Lavrov, 1995, p.5).

Expenditures

Seeking fiscal austerity in early 1992, the central government shifted formerly federal outlays to the subnational level including social expenditures (price subsidies, social benefits) and capital investment in the spheres of infrastructure, utilities and military housing. In most countries, income redistribution would be an expenditure responsibility of central authorities.

Moreover, subnational funds are not the proper financial source for infrastructure and investment projects whose benefits go beyond provincial boundaries (Wallich, 1992, p.69). This naturally caused additional expenditure pressures on subnational governments.

The provincial authorities' response to these pressures was to accumulate arrears, to borrow from local banks and public enterprises, to use extrabudgetary funds, to arrange new tax deals with the centre or simply to retain unilaterally federal taxes and to rely on local state enterprises to provide social services (Wallich, 1992 and 1994). This kind of response, though rational from the point of view of provincial politicians who are now faced with the ballot box, had a detrimental effect on macroeconomic stabilisation.[30]

Most of the Russian regions have, according to the statistics of their accounts departments, considerable budget deficits. Apart from the fact that Moscow helped in most of the cases to bail out provincial authorities from their financial troubles (soft credits, subsidies), the latter cannot cover the budget deficit by increasing money supply and the issue of municipal bonds to provide for additional revenues was only in its infancy (Hanson, 1994, p.26); some of them devised, nevertheless, some new methods to smooth out fiscal pressure. St Petersburg officials managed to decrease the budget deficit from 40 per cent in early 1994 to eight per cent by the end of the year through selling real estate to commercial banks and selling land (*Segodnya*, 17 November 1994, p.3).[31] The selling of municipal bonds would be another way of financing a deficit in the form of borrowing. The administration in Nizhnii Novgorod *oblast'* started reportedly the issue of bills of exchange to cover the budget deficit (KD, 18 October 1994, p.5).

However, the turbulence of current fiscal arrangements can only be overcome by a thorough fiscal reform, which would probably include the reassignment of some expenditures to the federal government (income redistribution, capital investment). Martinez-Vazquez (1994, p.102) stressed the necessity of drawing a clear distinction between the provision, production and financing of services, since many functions may be provided subnationally but need to be financed centrally (social welfare) and the production of goods and services may be contracted to the private sector.

Revenues

Due to the absence of any significant rate- or base-setting authority, subnational governments were, for most of the time, vulnerable to changes in central tax policy and were not able to pursue a discretionary policy of their own. Through the erosion of the corporate income tax base due to the reduction of enterprise subsidies and their decline of profitability, provincial authorities were denied major revenues (Wallich, 1992, p.49). Moreover, the existing tax regime applied to natural resources in Russia appears to be ill-suited to the extraction of economic rents (McLure, 1994, p.186).[32]

More than half of the total federal revenues in 1993 came from 14 of the 89 regions, while Moscow city provided for 13 per cent alone in that year (Bell, 1994, p.10).[33] On the other hand, 85 per cent of all provinces received subsidies from the federal budget in 1994 which amounted, on average, to 20 per cent of regional budgets in that year (Semenov, 1994, p.42). A few republics (Bashkortostan, Ingushetiya, Sakha, Tatarstan and Chechnya) are reportedly exempted from the transfer of the federal share of VAT, while companies operating in Kaliningrad do not have to pay profits taxes (Bell, 1994, p.14). However, preferential treatment for the latter ended with Yeltsin's decree in March 1995, according to which all former exemptions from customs payments were abolished (KD, 16 March 1995, p.2). Ingushetiya and Kalmykiya declared their republics as 'offshore zones'.[34] In the first nine months after Ingush territory was declared an offshore tax haven in June 1994, 2000 enterprises registered reportedly in the republic and the provincial budget received additional R90bn in revenues (DM, 6 April 1995, p.4). In Kareliya, 90 per cent of all collected taxes in the territory remained there in the form of a soft credit from the federal government (FI, 16 February 1995, p.11), but this ended in late 1994 (*Segodnya*, 16 March 1995, p.2).

Despite the abolition in 1994–5 of some anomalies, there is no evidence for an efficient tax rate- or base-setting authority for subnational governments. Local taxes provided for only between one and two per cent of total regional revenues in 1994 (Leksin *et al.*, 1994, p.27). Revenues from territorial taxes on land amounted to less than one per cent of the federal budget in 1993 (Leksin and Shvetsov, 1994, p.44–5). The small town of Polyarnye Zory with a population of 25 000 people was reported to have a budget of only R4000 at the end of 1994 (RG, 19 November 1994, p.1). This shows that most of the 23 local taxes as assigned by the centre turned out to be 'nuisance taxes' (resort tax, dog and gambling taxes, fee on trading wine and liquor and others).[35] However, a more recent study by Mildner (1995, p.7) showed that there was, at least in some provinces (St Petersburg, Leningrad and Voronezh), a growing importance of local taxes as a share of the total of regional budgetary income in 1994.

These problems led to a new debate on fiscal reform in Russia, in which three different approaches were proposed (Semenov, 1994, p.39):

1) particular taxes could be assigned to different administrative-territorial levels;
2) fixed percentage shares of taxes could be assigned to the appropriate administrative levels;
3) one could agree on a percentage share of the total regional revenues which would have to be transferred to the federal budget.

Panskov (1994, p.23) suggested adding a particular percentage share for local taxes on federal and regional taxes to end the practice of complete fiscal dependency of local administrations on higher authorities.

A few minor modifications of fiscal arrangements were undertaken in 1994. Profits taxes and corporate income taxes were changed from 'regulated' to 'guaranteed' taxes; that is provincial administrations could rely more confidently on these taxes in their budget. This was a first step towards ending the practice of dual subordination since regional authorities got assigned a fixed percentage share of these major taxes. While the tax rate for profits taxes was changed to 38 per cent in 1994, regional governments had some discretion above a 13 per cent federal tax yield (Mildner, 1994, p.22). There were also other changes in percentage tax assignments to federal and provincial budgets like 50 per cent excise duties on alcohol and a 25 per cent assignment of VAT to the regions (Leksin and Shvetsov, 1994a, p.38). Moreover, there was a consensus that personal income taxes should be completely retained at the territorial level (DM, 12–18 December 1994, p.23).

However, major deficiencies of intragovernmental budgetary relations appeared in 1994 in the form of non-transparent mutual payment settlements between different administrative levels and hidden subsidies handed down by the centre, which were estimated at R9trn in that year (Lavrov, 1995, p.5). The transfer of federal tax shares was also considered to have worsened in 1994 (Shirobokova, 1995, p.18). As a result, a new governmental programme on fiscal and budgetary reform was announced in June 1995, including a reduction of the amount of taxes at all administrative levels, measures to improve fiscal discipline and the ending of preferential tax treatment for particular provinces (*Izvestiya*, 22 June 1995, p.4).

Equalisation formula

The regional differences in industrial output, natural resource endowment, population and price levels led to a differentiation of the costs of consumer baskets in the Russian provinces of 1:3.5 in early 1994,[36] per capita income of 1:4, while per capita nominal expenditures varied in mid-1993 from a lowest level of R97 000 in Ingushetiya to a highest one of R510 000 in Magadan (Bell, 1994, p.16), that is more than 1:5. The decision as to which territories needed federal support was a problematic issue in Russia, since per capita expenditures for the last three quarters of the previous year were taken as a basic indicator of the level of income. However, this does not reflect the real purchasing power due to substantial differences in real income and widespread price controls, which resulted, as Bell (*ibid.*, p.13) outlined, in a new reproduction of branch-based redistribution.

An equalisation formula should first estimate subnational spending needs, then assess the local revenues available for financing these needs adjusted by local tax effort and also take into account how far equalisation should go. Expenditure norms should not only be calculated from some basic variables like population density, city size, per-capita income, poverty rates and the quality of infrastructure (Wallich, 1992, p.10), but also from the costs of providing basic social services, which is a particularly sensitive issue for the Russian Far North.

In 1994, a special 'Fund for the Financial Support of Regions' was set up in Russia with the aim of redistributing finances from relatively highly developed regions to poorer parts of the country. This fund originally consisted of 22 per cent of the federal share of VAT which was increased to 27 per cent in 1995 (RG, 21 February 1995, p.2). However, local budgets ended up even less independent than before, since the share of 'regulated' as against 'guaranteed' taxes in their tax base was increased in order to redistribute finances to regional budgets afterwards. Panskov (1994, p.21) estimated that only 89 (mostly regional) of the total of about 3000 territorial budgets (including local) gained from this new form of redistribution in 1994. Other tax assignments to the regions for 1995 including 25 per cent of VAT, up to 12 per cent of profits taxes (as part of the reduced federal rate of 25 per cent) and 84.5 per cent of personal income taxes (FI, 20 December 1994, p.II) appear, compared with much higher rates the years before, as a new attempt at concentrating revenues in the federal budget.[37]

However, the share of total revenue and spending in the consolidated budget (total of federal and regional budgets) accounted for by the regions has tended to rise, if allowance is made for a change in method of reporting in the first quarter of 1994. The problem of assessing equalisation efforts in Russia is complicated by the widespread practice of granting budgetary loans, tax and customs preferences as well as credits by different central institutions and ministries to particular provinces (FI, 27 July–3 August 1994, p.VIII). Regions also gain from federal programmes and central investments directed to their territories. A critical issue is that of hidden transfers including parts of the federal budget with a clear regional objective and subsidies for industrial sectors concentrated in particular regions.[38] For Kemerovo *oblast'*, for example, R330bn were planned as official federal transfers for the region and another R1.5–2.0trn for the coal industry in 1995 (DM, 12–18 December 1994, p.23).

Equalisation measures were also used as a political tool by the centre to appease oppositional leaderships in the provinces. As Lavrov (1995, p.5) showed, 55 per cent of those regions which opposed the new Russian Constitution at the December 1993 referendum received higher budgetary transfers afterwards compared with only 40 per cent of those which approved it. In terms of federal subsidies, as the author pointed out in the same article, provinces in the Russian Far North and Far East ended up worse off in 1994, receiving only 10 per cent of the Russian total in that year compared with 21 per cent the year before. This could indicate a new setting of regional priorities by central authorities in recent times.

Finally, the use of extrabudgetary funds also obscures the picture of equalisation efforts. These are channelled through the vertical of central institutions down to the local level (pension fund, social insurance fund, employment fund and others) and their finances are redistributed through enterprises' tax and wage payments. This appeared to be an ideal opportunity for withholding money from the state budget, since extrabudgetary funds can be spent fully at the discretion of the respective level of government and they need not be shared with higher levels (Wallich, 1992, p.54). Apart from federal extrabudgetary funds, subnational authorities did also set up their own off-budget funds, but they are estimated to have lower total amounts than the federal ones (Mildner, 1995, p.13).

In 1992 alone, 45.5 per cent of total payments for extrabudgetary funds were reportedly not used, of which R600bn remained on accounts of federal institutions, while R900bn were retained on the accounts of enterprises (Delyagin and Freinkman, 1993, p.51). Both sums taken together amounted to 30 per cent of total bank deposits in Russia by the end of 1992. In practice, they turned out to be preferential credits for enterprises on low interest rates. In 1993, the total amount of all 18 extrabudgetary funds counted for 10 per cent of the federal budget, while about R8bn were retained on the accounts of provincial enterprises which equalled five per cent of GDP in that year (Leksin and Shvetsov, 1994a, p.40).

Although there was a tendency towards a decline of the surplus of federal off-budget funds in 1993–4 (*Segodnya*, 19 July 1995, p.5), the amount of extrabudgetary funds relative to regional budgets was still substantial in many regions.[39] The attempt at seriously restructuring extrabudgetary funds, as a result of which they would be consolidated with the state budget, was strongly resisted by ministries in Moscow, among which the majority wanted to control their own extrabudgetary fund, as well as provincial authorities, for whom this was a good opportunity to escape from hard budget constraints.

Viability of fiscal federalism

To establish workable fiscal federal relations, Moscow has to set up a transparent and fair system of revenue-sharing, grant equalisation and financing of national programmes in the provinces. Moreover, intragovernmental dimensions of fiscal reform play a crucial role in the success of Russia's macroeconomic stabilisation effort and the extent of tax assignments and expenditure responsibilities at each administrative-territorial level will determine the cohesiveness of the RF. Finally, the equity and incentive aspects of tax and decentralisation policies are crucial for structural reforms (Wallich, 1994, p.19–20).

The lack of transparency and the turbulence of fiscal arrangements posed a major threat to the viability of the RF. Better-off regions do not only resist equalisation efforts, but the inherited system of dual subordination makes the centre dependent on provincial compliance and vulnerable in case of their unilateral tax retention. 'Single channel systems', in which regional authorities decide unilaterally which amount of taxes they transfer to the federal budget, became a widespread practice in Russia. Moscow's threatened (and used) sanctions, like halting all central expenditure on the territory, withholding export and import licences or denying central bank credits (Wallich, 1992, p.35) apparently did not change provincial leaders' attitudes substantially.

One recent technical device to make the operation of fiscal arrangements more efficient was the setting up of treasury offices in the regions in order to concentrate the flow of federal finances in one institution and to separate federal from regional taxes.[40] Officials of the treasury office have also the right to control budgetary expenditures and to issue sanctions and penalties, but it remains to be seen what difference they really make to state tax inspections and which new kinds of local corporatism could evolve.

3.3 FEDERAL AND REGIONAL INVESTMENT POLICY

In Russia's search for new forms of resource allocation and institutional restructuring, the investment policy has to acquire new patterns in which the overwhelming dominance of the state will have to decline if the aim of a more efficient and competitive economy is to be pursued. Nevertheless, central investment and state programmes play still a major role for primary (fuel and energy, agriculture) and secondary (military production) sectors of the economy and state monopolies have a specific regional pattern of activity. This will lead to regional differentiation in terms of institutional restructuring and the mobilisation of internal resources by provincial governments.

Central investment

In the centrally planned economy, there was a strict centralisation of capital investments and resource transfers through the system of industrial branch ministries. With the collapse of this economic system, central investments were mainly reduced to the fuel and energy sector, agriculture and the defence industry, while machine-building and metalworking enterprises, which were used to central material supply and financial support by sectoral ministries, were suffering a tremendous cut of their working capital. In 1992, central capital investment as a share of total investment in the national economy declined to 38 per cent, while 46 per cent were provided for so-called 'productive investments' in the fuel and energy sector alone in that year (Maevskaya, 1994, p.73).[41] This sector has the highest priority in state investment policy and it receives most of its finances from the state budget, soft credits and subsidies for the provinces. More than half of total central investments in 1994 went to three macro-regions (Central, Urals and Western Siberia), which have a particular specialisation in fuel and energy production and the defence industry, compared with only 46 per cent in 1990 (Guseva, 1995, p.131).

In 1994, the centre continued with the practice of selective financial help for particular industrial sectors. The agricultural sector received R11trn and the fund for conversion in the defence industry R755bn from the federal budget in 1994, while R300bn were provided for compensations after mine closures. The coal industry had already received a total of R2.2trn as budgetary subsidies in the year before (Leksin and Shvetsov, 1994a, p.44).

These sectors had established strong industrial and regional lobbies and managed to get the biggest slices of the budgetary cake. During the adoption of the 1994 federal budget, the agrarian lobby in the State Duma insisted on a cut in the share of regions in the section on 'support of the national economy' from an initially proposed 40.2 per cent to 34.5 per cent, which led naturally to additional expenditures of the state budget (Semenov, 1994, p.45). Regional lobbies in the lower house of parliament pushed a clause through according to which 20 per cent of the special tax paid by enterprises and institutions for the financial support of 'vital spheres of the national economy' (about R1.8trn) was to be transferred to provincial budgets in 1994 (*ibid.*, p.46).

The agrarian lobby led by the former Vice-Prime Minister, Alexander Zaveryukha, required a budgetary share of R31trn for 1995 compared with a planned budgetary deficit of R97trn for that year (*Segodnya*, 19 October 1994, p.2). The then newly appointed Minister for Agriculture, Alexander Nazarchuk, the former head of *Agropromsoyuz* in the AK, clearly strengthened the positions of the agrarian lobby, promising to control prices for state suppliers and to provide tax allowances, subsidies and hard currency assignments from the state budget (*Segodnya*, 28 October 1994, p.2). He demanded a 10 per cent share for agriculture from the 1995 federal budget (RG, 3 December 1994, p.2). As a result of his pressure tactics, the Russian government decided to lower interest rates for credits for producers of agricultural products from a regular rate of 170–180 per cent at the end of 1994 to a mere 30–50 per cent (*Segodnya*, 6 December 1994, p.2).

Other forms of central allocation of resources in Russian provinces include the issue of regional export quotas, various preferential treatments for export and import operations (customs, taxes), soft credits and federal programmes. Examples of the latter are the programme for national minorities in the Far North, compensation for victims of the Chernobyl' nuclear reactor accident as well as for the nuclear fall-out from the Semipalatinsk testing facility. State support for the provinces of the Far North, which embrace 60 per cent of the total RF territory and where about 10mn people live, was promised to amount to 3.5 per cent of the total federal budget in 1994, but it is questionable whether this amount was really transferred, since in 1993 only 20 per cent of the promised finances were provided (Leksin and Shvetsov, 1994a, p.40).[42]

In 1992–3, 43 regional administrations (among them 19 out of the 21 republics) received special economic support from the centre by decrees from the President or the Russian government (*ibid.*, p.42). These decisions were not subject to any clear principles and the choice was made for depressed regions (Tyva, Gornyi Altai, Ingushetiya) as well as relatively highly-developed industrial areas (Volgograd, Saratov). These decrees followed, in most cases, visits to particular regions by the President or the Prime Minister. Central subsidies of R30bn were made available for completing the construction of two power stations in Amurskaya *oblast'* after Yeltsin visited this region in summer 1994 (RV, 15 July 1994, p.3). The President continued his trip through Siberia to Krasnoyarskii *krai*, where he promised to lower transport tariffs (EkiZh, no.34, August 1994, p.20). Table A.16 shows planned federal investment programmes by industrial and social sectors for 1995.

Sectoral and regional distribution of national monopolies

An unequal regional distribution of national monopoly production was a characteristic feature of the centrally planned economy and it has a detrimental effect on macroeconomic stabilisation efforts today. In 1993, two per cent of the industrial enterprises employing more than 5000 people produced more than 40 per cent of the total industrial output with a particular concentration in Samarskaya and Nizhegorodskaya *oblasti* and Komi republic (Novikov, 1994a, p.5–6). Russian national monopolists tried typically to control prices, market access and sales networks.

The fuel and energy sector was in a particularly favoured position due to central price controls, subsidies and soft credits. *Magadanenergo*, which is a regional subsidiary of the national monopolist *EES Rossii* and controls the entire energy grid in Magadanskaya *oblast'*, reportedly in August 1994 bought cheap energy for R29 per kWh from the Kolymskaya hydroelectric power station and sold it to enterprises for R129 (DM, 12 August 1994, p.4). *Chuvashenergo* doubled prices for household electricity after its privatisation started, although the price of R12 per kWh in autumn 1994 was still extremely low compared with world market prices (DM, 18 October 1994, p.4). The Bashkir authorities keep 63 per cent of the shares of *Bashneft'* under their control, since this regional monopoly of oil production provided about half of the republic's budgetary revenues in 1994 (KD, 10 February 1995, p.9).

Under current conditions of high inter-enterprise arrears and high refinancing rates, national monopolies try to expand into the banking and insurance sectors. The national coal company *Rosugol'* set up its own pension fund, investment and insurance companies as well as commercial subsidiaries (*Izvestiya*, 20 January 1995, p.5). The national gas company *Gazprom* is a major shareholder in one of the leading Russian commercial banks, *Imperialbank*, and one of its provincial subsidiaries, *Astrakhan'gazprom*, took over two bankrupt *kolkhozy* and *sovkhozy* providing its own employees with foodstuffs (DM, 4 November 1994, p.4).

In contrast, regional concentration of national monopolies led also to substantial drops in output and high rates of unemployment in specific territories as a result of the fall in domestic demand following foreign trade liberalisation. This is particularly evident in Ivanovo *oblast'*, where about half of the Russian cotton textile industries' output was produced in 1994

(DM, 3 March 1995, p.4). The Cherepovets steel combine provided reportedly 80 per cent of total tax revenues in Vologda *oblast'* in 1994 (RV, 24 March 1995, p.2), which could result in major regional hardships in the case of bankruptcy of this combine, but industries of ferrous and non-ferrous metallurgy did generally better on the foreign market.

Finally, new financial-industrial groups (FIG) were created from scratch which have a specific regional thrust. For example, the FIG *Sokol* in Voronezh comprises companies operating in the regional car and electronics industries, the fuel and energy sector, construction and insurance (DM, 10 September 1994, p.4). This is a worring development so long as inter-regional competition has not properly started, since it gives them an almost complete control over the regional market (prices, credits, subsidies).[43] In July 1995, the Federation Council adopted special legislation on FIG including exemptions from customs duties, the free handing over of state shares of enterprises to FIG, the writing-off of debts and the provision of state guarantees for commercial credits (KD, 21 July 1995, p.2).

Regional differentiation

Together with regional authorities' differing attitudes towards institutional restructuring, their capability either to lobby for central investments or to mobilise internal resources and the common use of price controls, as well as past history, economic development varies widely among Russian regions. Prices for fuel oil differed 1:2.8 between economic macro regions in September 1994, those for lubricating oils and electric power 1:2.5 (DM, 28 September 1994, p.2). The costs for the consumer basket varied between a lowest level of R37 300 in Ul'yanovsk and a highest one of R178 600 in Magadan by the end of August 1994 (DM, special issue *Region*, no.1, September 1994, p.4), that is a difference of 1:5.[44]

These differentials, which are very high by international standards, are due to a considerable extent, to populist price controls, trade barriers, limits on 'exports' (from regions) of locally produced products and the setting of quotas for food supply to regional funds like that in Voronezh *oblast'* (*Segodnya*, 29 October 1994, p.3). The republic of Marii-El created a special fund for price regulation based on a one per cent local tax to 'keep prices at the same level in all parts of the republic' (*Segodnya*, 29 December 1994, p.4).

Institutional restructuring also differed widely across regions, in particular, results in privatisation. Table A.17 shows the results for privatisation by macroregion as of 1 August 1994 compared with the concentration of banking capital and insurance payments. Due to the strong concentration of Russia's bank and insurance savings in a few financial centres, the administrations of some of which tried to control or even to stop privatisation (Moscow, Novosibirsk), these variables show no strong correlation.[45] It is another indication of financial-industrial corporatism with a particular regional thrust, in which regional administrations, managers of formerly state-owned enterprises and new banks and insurance companies play their part. This could lead to regional clusters of industrial and financial monopolists.

Moreover, official statistics on privatisation do not reveal the whole story. By 1 May 1994, 68.8 per cent of all industrial enterprises in St Petersburg were reported to be privatised compared with 74.7 per cent in Leningradskaya *oblast'*, but the control package of shares was mostly acquired by working collectives between January and August 1994: 64 and 73 per cent respectively (Bolz and Polkowski, 1994, p.30–1). In neighbouring Kareliya, 60.5 per cent of all industrial enterprises were reportedly privatised by December 1994, but 62.3 per cent of them were acquired by the working collectives (DM, 13–19 February 1995, p.18). While the North-West macro region ranks among the first in our Table A.16 on privatisation results, this gives no evidence of substantial micro-economic restructuring, since savings of employees are generally too low for significant investments and they normally put additional pressure on the management for higher wages and social benefits.

Despite these ambiguities, one can, nevertheless, come to some conclusions from these official statistics. First and foremost, regional authorities have a major influence on institutional restructuring which contributes to substantial regional differences in economic development. Only two per cent of industrial enterprises (by value of industrial assets) and eight per cent in the sphere of small-scale privatisation were reportedly privatised in the republic of Mordoviya by early 1995 (DM, 22 February 1995, p.15). This republic is, at the same time, one of the main recipients of federal subsidies in the RF. The regional administration of Kostromskaya *oblast'* reportedly spent R2bn in 1994 for de-privatisation (*Izvestiya*, 22 December 1994, p.5), which increased not only the authorities' liabilities, but could seriously erode their own tax base.

Tatar authorities introduced 'individual privatisation cheques' for every resident in Tatarstan in August 1993, which differed from national privatisation vouchers in the RF and were supposed to 'shield' the republic economy from outside investors (KD, 26 April 1995, p.3). As a result of this limit on their tradability, they turned out to be economically unattractive, evidenced in the fact that only half of the residents had invested their cheque in one of the Tatar enterprises a few months before voucher privatisation came to an end on 1 August 1995 in this republic (*Segodnya*, 27 April 1995, p.3).

Secondly, the form of local corporatism currently prevailing in Russia concentrates economic activity in particular clusters of regions with a detrimental effect on free interregional trade. This is often associated with serious cases of corruption by leading officials, as in Perm' *oblast'* (RV, 26 February 1995, p.2) and arbitrary changes of ownership rights like that undertaken by Bashkir President, Murtaza Rakhimov, in the case of the Uchalinsk mining company (KD, 7 February 1995, p.5).

Mobilization of internal resources

While the central government off-loaded responsibilities for social services and capital investment to provincial authorities in 1992, the latters' response was to get involved in economic ventures, to manipulate extra-budgetary funds, to increase foreign economic activity, to devise mortgage schemes and bills of exchange and to issue municipal bonds. This attempt at mobilizing internal resources evidenced a new entanglement of politics and economics at the regional level and has not proved yet to provide more efficient institutional changes. It did show that at least some of the Russian provinces enjoyed a considerable autonomy in terms of economic policy making.

Subnational governments' involvement in economic activity does not foster a competitive environment, since their owned businesses will almost certainly compete unfairly with newly created private companies, while, at the same time, exerting pressures to keep their enterprises afloat and maintaining employment through subsidies (Wallich, 1992, p.4). Moreover, it could lead to a new monopolisation of the Russian industry within regional boundaries. In Sverdlovsk *oblast'*, for example, a state investment corporation was set up which gained the right to use extrabudgetary funds and revenues from export quotas for investment and the licence to import foodstuffs on preferential terms (KD, 1 November 1994, p.3). However, cases of corruption by export producers in this region were reported, denying the provincial budget of $40mn in 1992–3 alone (KD, 9 March 1995, p.2).

There was not only an unpredictability of subnational budgetary resources, but provincial authorities' budgetary autonomy was additionally constrained through bargained tax-sharing rates, unfunded central mandates like wage ceilings for public employees and other ceilings on local tax rates and on tariffs on public transport and utilities (Wallich, 1994, p.44). As Mitchnek (1994, p.77) found from her case study in Yaroslavl, regional officials' response was to try to maximise carryover and extrabudgetary revenues, since the central government has no control over these resources. A few republics simply refused to transfer the federal shares of extrabudgetary funds as Sakha, Bashkiriya and Marii-El did in the case of the social insurance fund in 1994 (RG, 10 December 1994, p.2).

A very popular practice used by regional authorities in their attempt at mobilising internal resources was to grant their territories a special status including tax holidays and customs allowances (FEZ or 'offshore zones').[46] Kaliningrad *oblast'* was the most frequently discussed region in the Russian central press in 1994 in connection with the setting up of a FEZ. Due to its exclave location, this region is in a very special situation, being almost completely dependent on electricity from neighbouring Lithuania (RG, 3 December 1994, p.2) and not even having its own construction base (NG, 27 August 1994, p.4).[47]

St Petersburg's mayor's office suggested the creation of a FEZ in Kronshtadt, but one third of the territory belongs to the army (KD, 10 September 1994, p.2). However, many earlier announcements about the formation of FEZs never produced results, for a variety of reasons, including the selection of too large territories like the entire Chita *oblast'* (DM, 31 January 1995, p.4) and the lack of a law on FEZs (DM, 17–23 October 1994). Yeltsin's new decree in spring 1995 stopped all earlier granted preferential treatments for particular regions in conducting foreign economic activity (KD, 16 March 1995, p.2).

At the moment, more viable projects seem to be the set up of free customs zones like that proposed for Sheremet'evo airport in Moscow (KD, 28 October 1994, p.3). Three defence-related enterprises in Nizhegorodskaya *oblast'* were declared territorial production zones in spring 1995 (RV, 21 April 1995, p.3). But there are still legal conflicts since the Russian constitution (paragraph 74, article 1) does not allow for extraterritoriality of customs zones (KD, 16 June 1995, p.3 and 1 July 1995, p.2).

Many regional authorities tried to set up their own regulations on foreign economic activities which is, according to the Russian constitution, an exclusive function of federal authorities. Moscow city officials wanted to retain 20 per cent of state customs duties in late 1994 (KD, 9 November 1994, p.2). Sakha authorities came to a deal with an Austrian oil-processing company according to which the former receive 40 per cent of all profits (*Segodnya*, 3 November 1994, p.3). Tatarstan announced a special regime of tax exemptions for foreign investors in November 1994 (KD, 12 November 1994, p.2).

As Table A.18 shows, resource-rich republics were not necessarily among the leading regions in terms of foreign investment in mid-1994. This is probably the result chiefly of the local business and (often overlapping) political elites being opposed to any loss of control over such resources to outsiders. In some cases, however, they have been trying to provide new and more attractive regulations. However, the general political situation and the existing infrastructure in Russian regions seem currently to be more important issues for foreign investment than untapped natural resources.

Many subnational governments tried to tackle the problem of non-payment and to cover the budget deficit by introducing bill-of-exchange-schemes and municipal bonds.[48] However, this development is, at the time of writing, at too early a stage to judge its effectiveness. The lack of guarantees for bill-of-exchange-schemes was often critised; they tended to resemble pyramid schemes (needing constant expansion of new issues to pay off past issues) and could easily break down (*Segodnya*, 27 June 1995, p.8). Moreover, the issue of municipal bonds by subnational governments has reportedly been opposed by officials of the Ministry of Finance, who saw in them not only a competitor, but also claimed that they had all too often been asked to provide the collateral (RG, 12 November 1994, p.10).

An important question for subnational authorities seeking to issue bonds is whether they can get a government (presumably *Minfin*) declaration that these are government securities. If they can, the bonds then have the backing (implicit guarantee) of the state, and are safer and more attractive to financial institutions. In at least some cases this status has been refused. So far, only nine commercial banks in Russia have obtained licences to operate *Minfin* issued bonds (*Segodnya*, 17 November 1994, p.2).

Since it was reported that people's savings as part of their income increased to 23 per cent in 1994 compared with about 12 per cent in 1993 (*Segodnya*, 3 December 1994, p.2), another possible option for mobilising internal resources and improving housing appeared to be devising mortgage schemes.[49] The collateral for the introduction of municipal housing loans in Nizhnii Novgorod city was provided to the extent of 40 per cent by the city budget and property and 60 per cent by the Gor'kovskii Car Factory (KD, 31 August 1994, p.2).

It is too early to judge the success of subnational governments' efforts to mobilise internal resources and, due to their involvement in economic ventures, to what extent this actually prevented thorough institutional restructuring. Their economic role has certainly increased over recent years, and they still have more functions than simply the provision of public services as in most other countries.

3.4 LESSONS FROM OTHER COUNTRIES

Many issues, which Russia is currently faced with in building a viable federal state, are also serious problems for other countries, both federal and unitary states. These include issues of the territorialisation of national minorities, constitutional problems, particularly citizenship, education and the use of minorities' languages. Both federal and unitary states have been confronted in the period since World War II with regional challenges for more fiscal autonomy and had to take a differentiated approach and to find special arrangements. A particularly difficult task has been to establish a workable institutional setting. However, there has been a strong tendency towards devolution and decentralisation in a lot of countries over recent years, which could provide some lessons for Russia's regional turmoil. Canada with its territorial concentration of both national minorities and natural resources had particularly intriguing experiences of what kind of problems can arise for the coherence of a federal state.

National minorities and natural resources

Francophone Quebec in Canada has long demanded a special relationship with Ottawa, a demand which was conditioned by both a strong political stance on the part of its national leadership and the relative weakness of its business community. More importantly, in the national context, was that a further regionalisation of major social cleavages and collective identities took place after World War II, which was expressed, apart from Quebec nationalism, in the fact that the agrarian movement became largely a matter of western mobilisation against central Canadian interests, while a strong Maritime Rights movement developed in the east (Simeon and Robinson, 1990, p.57). The agrarian movement, for example, managed to keep most of the original features of the Crow's Nest Pass Rate intact, according to which the formula for prices for transporting western grain to the eastern ports had been fixed since 1897 and which also included a paragraph on partial compensation for the higher prices farmers had to pay for tariff-protected manufactured goods from central Canada (*ibid.*, p.232–4).

The division of powers in Canada (provincial ownership and federal regulation) inevitably caused intragovernmental conflicts. Under the constitution of Canada, natural resources belong to the provinces; they have access to royalties as well as to tax revenue (Wallich, 1992, p.109). Simeon and Robinson (1990, p.236) argued that energy divided Canada regionally more than any other issue. This was not only a result of uneven territorial distribution of energy resources, but also that of the allocation of ownership, taxing and trade powers, which maximised interregional and intragovernmental divisions.[50] Canadian provinces strengthened and protected their uneven economic bases through discriminatory purchasing policies and provincial barriers to trade, transportation and labour mobility (Hueglin, 1988, p.26).

Due to the discrepancy between domestic and world oil prices in the 1970s, the federal government was confronted with conflicting demands by provincial authorities:

1) if world prices exceeded domestic prices, the federal treasury had to provide more subsidies for the east coast, which depended on imported oil;
2) if this discrepancy were reduced, Ottawa's commitments under the existing equalisation system would have increased (Simeon and Robinson, 1990, p.237).

Alberta's lobby was too strong to free domestic prices for oil and gas to world market levels. Only after the oil shocks in 1973 and 1979 hit Alberta, was a new pricing and taxing regime introduced, which ensured a more equal national distribution of oil and gas revenues.

Other social cleavages

The regionalisation of social cleavages and collective identities has also caused problems in some unitary states. In Belgium, southern labour militancy in the Walloon coalfield was a distinctive feature compared with industrial peace in the Flemish North (Wagstaff, 1994, p.45). Putnam *et al.* (1993, p.61) found that the regional reform which was started in Italy in the early 1970s exacerbated, rather than mitigated, the existing disparities between the North and the South, which the authors explained by an historically rooted social capital of networks of civic engagement in the North compared with patron-client networks in the South.

Constitutional issues

Apart from the division between regional ownership and federal economic regulation, intragovernmental conflicts in Canada were also caused by the representative asymmetry compounded by the majoritarian, winner-take-all electoral system, which typically does not translate regional percentage shares of the vote into parliamentary seats (Hueglin, 1988, p.22). This was a major criticism voiced by Quebec national leaders, who were at the forefront of the provincial autonomy movement, trying not only to block federal intrusions into areas of provincial jurisdiction, but also to expand both the scope of provincial responsibility in most policy sectors and the provincial share of fiscal resources.

Quebec's political leaders set five conditions for constitutional reform as the basis of negotiations with central authorities in 1987 (Gagnon and Garcia, 1988, p.314):

1) the constitutional recognition of Quebec as a 'distinct society', homeland of the francophone element of Canada's duality;
2) constitutional rights for recruitment and selection of immigrants to Quebec;
3) Quebec officials should have a voice in the appointment of the three Supreme Court Judges with expertise in Quebec civil law;
4) the federal government's spending power should be limited in areas of provincial jurisdiction;
5) a full veto on constitutional reform, entrenched in the amending formula, was demanded.

This put the constitutional principle of citizen equality at odds with that of equality of provinces. The latter principle was no longer tenable if Quebec was constitutionally to be recognised as a different province from the rest of Canada and major asymmetries in jurisdictional status could appear (Cairns, 1991, p.15–16). Quebec has held a number of referendums on sovereignty in recent years,[51] which further destabilised intragovernmental relations, while major constitutional disputes are still not solved.

Special fiscal arrangements

Provincial leaders' economic interests challenged existing fiscal arrangements and shared-cost programmes. Canada has a long history of intragovernmental struggle over revenue-sharing and spending powers. The opting-out provision for Quebec in fiscal arrangements is probably a unique feature of Canadian federalism, which, as was argued by Courchene (1988a, p.384), makes the fiscal structure of the remaining nine provinces more coherent than would otherwise be possible.

By 1979–80, a consensus was reached about shares of various types of revenues between Canadian jurisdictions (Stevenson, 1988, p.45):

1) the central government monopolised those related to international movements of capital and goods;

2) provincial governments have a monopoly on health insurance premiums and a virtual monopoly on natural resource revenues and licence and permit fees;
3) local governments control the field of real estate taxes.

Over the last three decades, provincial revenues have not only increased relative to GNP, but the scope of provincial public policy has also widened.[52] Since differences among Canadian provinces are closely linked with the resource sector, provincial autonomy is most pronounced where the resource-exporting sector has grown most. However, resource industries account for a very small percentage of revenues in most provinces and this proportion has been declining steadily (Young *et al.*, 1988, p.149).[53]

The goal of the Canadian equalisation formula is to ensure that all provinces receive the equivalent of at least the national average tax rate applied to the national average revenue base. The provincial entitlement is defined as the difference between the national and provincial per-capita yields, times the province's population (Wallich, 1992, p.87). Major shared-cost programmes in Canada include medical care, hospital care, welfare assistance and post-secondary education (Barker, 1988, p.195).

In Spain, the Basque Country and Catalonia have the right to collect all taxes within their territories, except customs, petrol and tobacco levies, even though most of the tax rates are dictated by Madrid (Williams, 1994, p.92). Other regions receive up to 98 per cent of their revenues from the centre. The Spanish equalisation formula includes such criteria as population and per-capita incomes. In Italy, there is a major inconsistency between centralised taxing authority and decentralised spending authority. The share of total budgetary tax income raised directly by the regions fell from 4.3 per cent in 1980 to 1.8 per cent in 1989 (Putnam *et al.*, 1993, p.211, note 20). Only the five autonomous regions have the power to impose their own taxes in exceptional cases (Bull, 1994, p.72).

Institutional setting

Various political forms of federalism in Canada can be distinguished for different periods of time – a sign that intragovernmental relations were very much in flux. By the late 1960s, the division of powers approach in form of *interstate* federalism was changed into an *intrastate* one, by which the central government tried both to represent and to incorporate provincial perspectives within national institutions (Simeon and Robinson, 1990, p.265). However, intragovernmental relations shifted dramatically from a *cooperative* model to a *competitive* one by 1980, the latter of which was not only characterised by rising levels of conflicts and intragovernmental disentanglement (*ibid.*, p.283), but also a shifting of effective decision-making capacity upwards to central institutions, which Cairns (1991, p.15) called a '*political* federalism'.

In 1984–7, Canada witnessed a renewal of *collaborative* federalism including the constitutional recognition of Quebec's five conditions, discussed above.[54] Since then, federal and provincial governments have had to decide jointly on constitutional amendments, the use of the federal spending power and the appointment of judges and senators (Simeon and Robinson, 1990, p.332). This unleashed a growth of large and powerful complexes of institutions and personnel with their own professional and personal interests and it multiplied the rate at which partially self-contained entities like commissions and departments were set up. These resulted in frequent competition and duplication of activity between governments (Cairns, 1991, p.5–6).[55]

Similar experiences of shifting effective decision-making capacity upwards to the centre, as well as of a growing administrative apparatus with central elites pursuing their own institutional self-interests, were also the case in federal Germany. Municipalities and towns have tended to be dependent more and more on the *Länder* and the federal state, particularly in financial terms (Stammen, 1994, p.53). Moreover, there was a growing tendency towards standardisation in the German federal system, in which the exclusive responsibilities of the *Länder* have been reduced in number, and have become more restricted in scope (police and education).

However, in contrast to Canada, the responsibilities of the German *Bundesrat* (the upper house of parliament), which consists of representatives of the *Länder* governments, have increased over the last years. In the Canadian Senate, members are appointed by the federal government, as a result of which there is a lack of provincial legislative representation at the national level of government. This lack of regional representation in the centre is reinforced by a highly decentralised party system, in which some provinces are governed by regional parties which are not represented at the federal level at all, while the three nationally dominant parties have an asymmetrical regional power base and are internally divided along regional lines (Hueglin, 1988, p.22).

Tendency towards devolution

The irony of modern intragovernmental relations is that while federal states tend to concentrate more executive power in the centre, unitary states have often embarked on policies of decentralisation and devolution, with different degrees of success in terms of effective subnational government.

In Belgium, constitutional revisions were undertaken in recent years which started a movement in the direction of a federal state. Subnational units were divided in two different functional ways:

1) *régions* (Wallonia, Flanders and Brussels-Capital) with such responsibilities of regional development as transport and public works, housing, economic and employment policy and environmental matters;
2) *communautés* (French, Flemish and German-speaking) with functions in cultural heritage, radio and television, education and language (Wagstaff, 1994, p.47). While the former are dealt with by a directly-elected regional council, the latter issues are subject to a complex tripartite regime composed of commissions for French, Flemish and joint responsibilities. After the 1993 revision of the electoral system, 31 out of a total of 71 senators derive their status from the *communautés* (*ibid.*, p.48).

The regional reform under Mitterand in France in 1981 put *communes*, *départements* and *régions* on an equal footing as *collectivités territoriales* with their specific attributes and functions. Moreover, the *préfet* was no longer to be the all-powerful representative of central government, but an adviser and observer (*ibid.*, p.31), who checks, in the same way as the President's representatives in Russian regions, on the legality of decisions taken by provincial officials.

In the UK, regional policy, the traditional objective of which was to maintain or to create employment, was overtaken by urban policy, specifically inner city concerns, after Mrs Thatcher's government embarked on devolution in the 1980s, dismissing the provincial tier of government, which resulted effectively in a further centralisation of public finances. However, Conservative politicians accepted limited public sector intervention in special areas to be linked, where possible, with private sector finance (Philip, 1994, p.104) like tax-exempt enterprise zones or the appointment of bodies directly funded by central government (London Docklands Development Corporation, the Black Country and Merseyside inner city areas).

After the regional reform in Italy in the early 1970s, in which regions moved from a prefectoral system to one of elected regional government, provincial governments acquired comprehensive legislative authority in such fields as social services and territorial planning, while fiscal provisions of the 616 decrees gave the regions responsibility for spending approximately one-quarter of the entire national budget and virtually full responsibility for the national hospital and health care system (Putnam *et al.*, 1993, p.22). Italian regions became, in contrast to many other countries, increasingly autonomous from outside forces, while exercising their newfound powers of supervision over local governments (*ibid.*, p.46).

Lessons for Russia

Elitist policy and vertical patron-client networks dominate Russian regions where, if one can generalise from Young's case study of Omsk *oblast'* (1994, p.156), resources remain hierarchically distributed and provincial leaders seem to be actively guided by economic elites. The social context of the political changes in 1989–90 had a profound impact on who gained control over economic resources and what kind of economic policy regional politicians pursued.[56] Russian central authorities will have to show an extraordinary flexibility to accommodate provincial governments' demands motivated by economic hardships with hopefully more sensitivity than has been shown in the bloody war in Chechnya. One major issue is the commitment to macroeconomic stabilisation including the liberalisation of prices for energy and agricultural products. The discrepancy between domestic and world market prices for oil in Canada in the 1970s showed what amount of revenues the federal government can lose and to what extent one province can be forced to subsidise other provinces.

What concerns fiscal arrangements, the continuation of an improved tax-sharing-cum-grant system has been proposed (Bahl, 1994, p.162). Russia should clearly not overemphasise regional equalisation at the current stage of economic decline and incorporate special circumstances and cost differentials (transport, energy) into the grant equalisation formula. Income redistribution (unemployment benefits, social welfare programmes) and capital investment, the benefits of which go beyond regional boundaries, should be expenditure responsibilities of the federal state.

Finally, major change in the administrative-territorial division in Russia is, except for the abolition of *raiony* in cities, currently hardly politically viable. However, experiences in Belgium could be used to create cultural confederations based on close ethnic, linguistic and religious features which do not coincide with the existing administrative structure in Russia and which should be given national institutional representation. The current movement for strengthening subregional local self-government, however, could result in a new growth of the administrative apparatus and lead to institutional confusion and duplication.

Not functional separation of politics and economics at the provincial level, but institutional entanglement and local corporatism appear to drive the dynamics of Russian regional development. This could confine economic activity to particular clusters of regions and strengthen regional monopolies. Instead of powerful central branch ministries, Russia might end up with all-embracing financial-industrial groups growing along regional lines. They would not only enhance the scope for economic autonomy in particular regions, but could easily reinforce political pressure on the centre.

4 The Revitalisation of Nomenklatura Power in the Altai

The separation of political power from state property was on the agenda on the eve of radical economic reforms in 1991–2. From a remote, predominantly agrarian region like the AK one would expect, following the conclusions drawn in the previous chapter, that traditional patron-client relations and elitist policies would characterise the political scene, promoting an unequal distribution of economic resources, institutional entanglement and local corporatism between the political leadership, the agrarian lobby, the industrial management and the military. It will be argued that the early stage of political liberalisation in 1989–90, which is scrutinised in the first section, did not provide strong horizontal networks of civic activity, which would be effective enough to deprive the nomenklatura of their capacity to acquire wealth and control its distribution. The second section looks at the regional elite and key political players, while turning the attention in the third section to the institutions in place. Particular features of traditionalist economic policies in the region are the subject of the fourth section, leading to a special focus on the challenge of the national reform agenda in the last section.[1]

4.1 THE DEMOCRATIC WAVE OF 1989–90

The democratic movement in the Altai took its origin at the grassroots level mainly among members of the intelligentsia (doctors, teachers, university lecturers and lawyers) of big cities, establishing informal platforms within the structure of the Communist Party.[2] In 1988–9 they set up an 'Association for the Support of *Perestroika*', which consisted of reform Marxists, *solidaristy*,[3] Monarchists and members of trade unions, all being united by a common anti-CPSU and anti-nomenklatura stance. Its coordinating council of 10–15 people organised meetings, suggested the candidature of their members for the first free elections to the RSFSR Supreme Soviet and regional soviet and used newly emerging, democratic newspapers like *Svobodnyi kurs* and *Molodezh Altaya* as a public platform.[4]

However, effective organisational structures, which would bundle different interests and concentrate the political thrust towards thorough reform, were not set up. The only serious attempt was the creation of an informal 'Deputies Club' in the newly elected regional soviet in 1991, which tried to initiate new legislative acts on local government, land reform and the introduction of a new banking system (Sarychev, 1994, p.2). It also addressed questions of the need to restructure big industrial enterprises and to reform the executive power in the province (AP, 4 August 1994, p.2). Although its real influence on political decision making remained marginal, according to one leading member of 'Democratic Russia's Choice' in the Altai, K. Emeshin,[5] they managed to create a special atmosphere of competition for reform among the newly elected deputies in the regional soviet, effectively contributing to the political break-up of the old system and helping to change public opinion on land reform, particularly among city dwellers.

In addition to being in a numerical minority, democratic forces could not overcome ideological differences among themselves and a lot of them changed sides when they saw which way the political wind was blowing. As in most other Russian provinces, democratic leaders in the AK became incorporated into the 'bureaucratic market' after the August 1991 putsch, where an exchange of material wealth, political power and privileged access to resources took place (Gaidar, 1995, p.125). NTS defected from the democratic movement at an early stage, opposing the election of the first governor.[6] Anti-nomenklatura slogans emanating from different political camps appeared only on the façade, while the nomenklatura transformed itself quietly into private owners during the pre-1992 reform, effectively retaining a guarantee of local political power. Thus, the political context of 1989–90 did not put the Altai on track to establish horizontal networks of civic engagement and an effective democratic self-organisation of institutions which would change traditional elitist policies and hierarchically-structured patron–client relations.

4.2 THE REGIONAL ELITE AND KEY POLITICAL PLAYERS

The social base of the regional elite can be identified with nomenklatura members in leading positions of party and state organs, industrial and agrarian management, the military and secret service, together with leaders of new cooperatives, dealers in the shadow economy, 'Komsomol businessmen' (Gaidar, 1995, p.150) and, as a new commercial activity, rent seekers using *de facto* control of land (RG, 12 November 1994, p.15), all of whom exerted direct or indirect pressure on political decision making in the province. Old and new structures remained closely intertwined, limiting the access for outsiders and newcomers, while distributing economic wealth, political power and special rights among each other. Only after the August 1991 putsch was there an influx of democratic activists into decision-making positions, which changed the configuration of local political power for the period from late 1991 until early 1994.

This was mainly due to the appointment of a new reform-minded governor and his young, enthusiastic team in office, which produced, as in many other Russian regions, a classical stalemate between executive and legislative power, the latter of which was dominated by a conservative regional soviet with traditionalist nomenklatura members in leading positions opposing economic change. Three men were running for the new governorship in autumn 1991: Yu. Zhil'tsov (the former head of the regional executive committee),[7] A. Nazarchuk (the leader of the regionally influential agrarian lobby of *Agropromsoyuz*) and V. Raifikesht (a *sovkhoz* director from Novoaltaisk near Barnaul). The proposal by the regional soviet to appoint Raifikesht as governor meant the first victory for the 'democratic platform' in the Altai soviet. Whether the latter's German nationality played a decisive role in the outcome of the vote remains an open question.

The new governor took over the main staff of the former regional executive committee, but appointed six new heads for the eight committees, which were organised according to industrial sectors, and one gubernatorial apparatus. He brought with him from his home town of Novoaltaisk the new head of the economics committee, A. Sidorov, who had worked there before in the city council's committee for the construction industry.[8] Two doctoral candidates became the new heads of the committee for property administration (S. Potapov) and for the health service, culture and education (V. Kulikov). The most interesting figure in the new team, however, was the then 25-years-old chief-of-staff, V. Ryzhkov, who was Raifikesht's 'political brain' and driving force for market reforms.[9]

While additional executive power was given to the new governor to speed up reforms at the regional level, Raifikesht used it, in practical terms, mainly to cut shortages and to mitigate hardships (machinery for the harvest, fuel in winter). In July 1993, for example, he ordered *Altainefteprodukt* to supply *kolkhozy* and *sovkhozy* without prepayment with petrol from its reserve stocks. During these days he also pressed *Altaidizel'* to send an additional 600 diesel engines to Krasnoyarsk in exchange for 800 harvesting machines (AP, 21 July 1993, p.1).

The new regional administration got additional executive support from the new representative of the President in the AK, N. Shuba, who was sent there to watch closely the implementation of Yeltsin's decrees and to coordinate federal institutions of executive power (army, police, secret service).[10] As a former soldier in Afghanistan and head of the regional committee of Afghanistan veterans, he could rely on an informal network of colleagues within the armed forces. He has also actively supported the new Cossack movement in the Altai (AP, 19 May 1994, p.2). In order to implement central decrees, he works closely with the army and the prosecutor's office, while lobbying, in exchange, for better housing conditions for army officers (AP, 23 November 1994, p.2). His own label for himself, the 'prefect' of the region, might be a bit exaggerated, but could well be the case during martial law. After Yeltsin's edict 'On the Stage-by-stage Constitutional Reform in the Russian Federation' of 21 September 1993, Shuba became increasingly involved in public debates and used the local press to explain not only the content of this edict but also the main legislative innovations in the new Russian Constitution.[11]

However, the elections to the new federal and regional parliaments in late 1993 and early 1994 changed the configuration of political power dramatically in favour of traditionalists of the former nomenklatura, as a result of which leading democratic reformers left office and governor Raifikesht quit his job. This period also witnessed an incorporation of reform-minded officials of the administration into the 'bureaucratic market' (Potapov, Sidorov) and a marginalisation of democratic forces in the legislature power.

Three candidates were running for the two regional mandates on the Federation Council. The outcome of the vote was victory for A. Surikov, the chairman of the old regional soviet, and Ya. Shoikhet, the vice-chancellor of the Altai Medical Institute and head of the research team which analysed the consequences of the nuclear fall-out from the Semipalatinsk testing facility on the Altai territory (AP, 25 November 1993, p.2). The voters' preference for the latter against the third candidate, V. Safronov, the leader of the regional Communist Party, shows not only the minor role of party considerations but also the importance of voters' expectations that their deputies could get something concrete out of the centre; in this case, material compensation from the federal Semipalatinsk programme.

Four one-mandate voting districts for the elections to the State Duma were created in the region, in which a total of 13 candidates stood for office. The outcome showed a preference for lawyers and administrators. A. Sarychev, the deputy head of the regional judicial administration and leading member of the 'Deputies Club' of the former regional soviet, and V. Bessarabov, the deputy regional procurator, were elected in two of the leading cities, Barnaul and Rubtsovsk. Furthermore, the head of the agricultural committee of the AK administration, P. Efremov, won in the city of Biisk and the head of the Rodinsk *raion* soviet, S. Openyshev, took the first place in the agricultural centre of Slavgorod. Moreover, 13 'voting associations' registered in the party list for the two remaining seats in the State Duma (AP, 24 November 1993, p.2). The outcome of the vote was victory for V. Ryzhkov from 'Russia's Choice', the head of the governor's apparatus, and A. Nazarchuk, the leader of the regional *Agropromsoyuz*, and reflected the previous division between factions in the regional soviet.

Both Ryzhkov and Sarychev had a clear party affiliation with 'Russia's Choice' in the new State Duma, being subjected to severe public attacks in the local press by their counterparts, particularly Nazarchuk (AP, 9 June 1994, p.1). Ryzhkov became the head of the State Duma's Committee on Issues of the Federation and Regional Policy, where he was effectively responsible for the preparation of legislative acts on the formation of state power in the regions (AP, 16 August 1994, p.1), including local self-government (AP, 12 November 1994, p.4). Sarychev headed a subdivision of the Committee on Legal Affairs in the State Duma, where he expressed his clear commitment to privatisation, the free sale of land and the necessity of a law on bankruptcy (AP, 4 August 1994, p.2). However, both felt increasingly forced to play the populist card in the local media. While Ryzhkov started winking at the agrarian lobby (AP, 16 August 1994, p.1), Sarychev announced extensively his involvement in the preparation of new legislation on social benefits for 1996 (AP, 27 April 1995, p.2). These manoeuvres were probably due to forthcoming elections to the national parliament in late 1995.

Efremov, Openyshev and Bessarabov are a clear example of how Russian deputies can change their attitudes according to which way the wind is blowing. Efremov, who ran his election campaign as a member of 'Russia's Choice', worked later together with Openyshev in the central council of the Agrarian Party (AP, 27 December 1994, p.3).[12] Bessarabov worked in the faction 'New Regional Policy', where he was responsible for cooperation with the Agrarian Party (AP, 9 August 1994, p.2).[13] All of them seemed to feel it imperative to report in the local press the amount of soft credits and transfers they could get from the centre.[14] Finally, Nazarchuk was right from the beginning an active member of the faction of the Agrarian Party.

With hardening fiscal policies in early 1994, Moscow's budgetary cuts yielded less of a local political dividend, from which traditional politicians in the AK tried to gain political capital. This resulted in a revitalisation of nomenklatura power, leading effectively to a self-sustaining bureaucratic dynamic of regional politics in which Altai deputies in the national parliament and democratic movements were more and more marginalised. Since summer 1994 key political players can be divided into representatives of the conservative nomenklatura, which is split into a Communist/Soviet-type and an agrarian camp, and the pragmatic nomenklatura (Shvedov, 1994, p.2).

Communist and Soviet-type nomenklatura

This grouping is represented by Surikov, the chairman of the old regional soviet and now the new governor, and Safronov, the leader of the regional Communist Party and deputy chairman of the parliament. It is a fusion of the bureaucratic apparatus of the former soviet and party officials. They get support from old structures of trade unions, the Communist Party and veteran's unions, which consist mainly of pensioners, who were the most active part of the electorate in 1993–4. Their political aims include the control of the executive power, the stop of privatisation and the free sale of land and the control of prices for energy and foodstuff.

Surikov worked for many years as director of such construction associations as *Altaiavtodor* and *Altaistroi* (AP, 25 November 1993, p.2). In 1985 he was appointed the deputy head of the regional executive committee and in August 1991 he was elected as chairman of the regional soviet.[15] He has been described as a prototype of a narcissistic, charismatic leader, who does not want to be affiliated with any political structure, being only interested in himself and his power, while applying a distinctive administrative approach to maintain controlling and redistributory functions.[16] His populism in public speeches consists typically of addressing problems of the agro-industrial complex (APK), social issues like low wages and pensions (AP, 29 June 1994, p.1), 'excessive' privatisation (AP, 8 September 1994, p.1), calls for state regulation and price controls for energy and transport tariffs (AP, 11 October 1994, p.1) as well as for the control of federal structures in the region like the tax inspection, the treasury office, extrabudgetary funds (pension, employment) and the prosecution office (AP, 31 December 1994, p.3).[17]

Safronov, who worked up the party career ladder until he became the first secretary of the Altai CPSU committee in the old Soviet system, stands clearly in the shade of the strong personality of Surikov. He has a paternalistic approach aimed at protecting those who lose from the reform, while expressing anti-Western resentments and anti-liberal positions.[18]

Agrarian nomenklatura

This clan is represented by the former leader of *Agropromsoyuz*, Nazarchuk, who was appointed as the Russian Minister for Agriculture in October 1994. He can rely on remaining structures of *kolkhozy* and *sovkhozy*, trade unions of the APK, directors of processing industries and producers of agricultural machinery. His programme after becoming minister included a requirement of at least 10 per cent of the federal budget expenditures for the APK, the setting up of food funds and related semi-state corporate structures, the creation of an investment fund for agriculture and the halting of privatisation of processing industries (AP, 17 November 1994, pp.1–2). He then declared his intention to return to the Altai to continue his political career. It is widely believed that he weakened the positions of the Communist/Soviet-type nomenklatura by defecting with his agrarian clan, but his own influence decreased after he left for Moscow.[19] Not surprisingly, he is using his new portfolio to lobby in the Russian government for the APK (*Segodnya*, 24 February 1995, p.2 and 16 March 1995, p.2).[20]

Pragmatic nomenklatura

This grouping is represented by the old governor, L. Korshunov, who came to power after Raifikesht announced his intention to resign and to return to his former *sovkhoz* on 13 January 1994 (AP, 15 January 1994, p.2).[21] Korshunov worked before as head of *Altaipromstroi* and *Altaikoksokhimstroi* as well as head of the Rubtsovsk city executive committee (AP, 22 January 1994, p.1) and he considered himself 'radical in economics and a centrist in politics'.[22] He was originally clearly in favour of market reforms and, in his opinion, prices for energy and agricultural products should have been freed right at the beginning of the radical reform programme (AP, 12 February 1994, p.3). However, although he admitted that credits received from the centre were squandered, since they tried to give every enterprise an equal share, and that there was a net drain on budgetary resources by the existing social infrastructure, he favoured a further emission of money 'as long as it keeps enterprises going'.[23] He also announced a 'reorientation of his team' (AP, 12 February 1994, p.3), which could only mean a reconciliation with the regional soviet, since the most radical reformers (Raifikesht and Ryzhkov) had already left.

Korshunov could naturally rely on the heads of local administration, whom he appointed personally, but also the industrial management – mainly the 'Directors' Council' – and the military-industrial complex

(VPK) – new entrepreneurs from the old nomenklatura and traditionalist members of the intelligentsia (Shvedov, 1994, p.2). Main political aims included the completion of the nomenklatura privatisation and the attempt to stay in power, possibly for a new period, in close institutional entanglement and local corporatism with the industrial management.[24] In the second half of 1994 he took an increasingly populist stance (AP, 18 October 1994, p.2) and a protectionist approach for the region (AP, 31 December 1994, p.5).

However, the momentum of regional politics was more and more set by the conservative nomenklatura, while the pragmatic nomenklatura had to back down and compromise in their attempt to restructure the economy.

4.3 INSTITUTIONS

Apart from the executive and legislative power, there are a number of other institutional structures which are involved in economic policy making, including corporate, monopolistic structures (holding companies, regional FIG), federal institutions (treasury office, extrabudgetary funds) and, to a lesser extent, political parties, trade unions and other social movements.

Executive power

The regional administration is increasingly losing ground in terms of controlling the economy.[25] The functions of its committees were originally modelled on industrial sectors as they were taken over from the former executive committee. But there is a growing recognition that these functions have to be divided in future into two different blocs in correspondence with (a) attempts to influence national policies (for example on privatisation, banking regulation and so on) and (b) 'autonomous' intervention in the local economy.[26]

However, different committees were searching for new spheres of activity to legitimise their existence. The economics committee concentrated its efforts not only on preparing new programmes for grain and flax production and the extraction of polymetallic ores and coal (AP, 28 September 1994, p.1), but it also started geological surveys looking for gold, jasper and marble.[27] According to the head of this committee, Sidorov, the preparation of state programmes for the region, in which federal institutions got involved, was the most effective way to attract federal funding in 1995. This included, apart from the setting up of a grain fund for the supply of other regions, programmes for the production of low-nitrogen refrigerators, the recognition by federal authorities of the AK as a depressed region, and the setting up of a health centre and a sanatorium in Belokurikha.[28] The committee for agriculture was involved in the creation of a wholesale market for foodstuffs, in which it tried to retain old redistributory functions (AP, 29 June 1994, p.1).

The regional administration was also increasingly forced to compromise with the new parliament and other institutional structures. After voucher privatisation came to an end on 1 July 1994, the committee for property administration announced the conversion of unused vouchers for social programmes to build homes for orphans and disabled people and to set up a fund for social support (AP, 2 July 1994, p.1).[29] In August 1994 the administration proposed a document for 'social partnership' which would involve trade unions and employers (AP, 27 August 1994, p.2). These initiatives seem to have been launched by the new regional parliament.

Officials of the executive branch used the interregional association 'Siberian Agreement' to agree on energy and transport tariffs, grain supply and the handling of payment arrears. They got involved in barter exchange of grain and agricultural machinery for coal and electroenergy (AP, 28 June 1994, p.1). They strongly resisted separatist activities on the part of leaders of the association and the latter's claim for a special budget and executive functions including the collection of federal taxes (AP, 1 October 1994, p.6). Altai officials seem to have a fairly pragmatic approach to the 'Siberian Agreement', using its structure 'to exert more pressure on the government' (Sidorov), while coming to specific agreements between two or three regions independently of this association.[30]

Finally, while trying to search for new functions, authorities in the executive branch also became increasingly involved in informal commercial activities, which included cases of corruption. For example, two officials of the administration were held in custody in April 1995, accused of accepting bribes favouring companies applying for commercial credits (*Svobodnyi Kurs*, 20–27 April 1995, p.1). There is also less institutional coherence to local administrations who have to cope with growing problems of running the social infrastructure handed over from state enterprises and found their own solutions in setting up local grain funds (AP, 17 August 1994, p.2), and writing off debts for electricity supplies (AP, 27 August 1994, p.2). Local (subregional) self-government in the AK did not go further than the organisation of housing associations carrying out repair work at local schools, cleaning roads and checking sanitory conditions (AP, 13 September 1994, p.2).

Legislative power

The old regional soviet, elected in 1991 and consisting of 230 deputies, had two opposing factions, one of which was a core of orthodox communists and agrarian hardliners (about 35–50 people), resisting privatisation, land reform and new tax policies.[31] The other grouping (as previously discussed), was the reform-minded 'Deputies Club'. However, for day-to-day business, a 'small council' of 36 deputies, who worked on a full-time basis, was set up. It consisted of eight committees which were modelled on industrial sectors and copied the structure of the administration. Headed by its new chairman, Surikov, its distinctive administrative approach was to maintain controlling and redistributory functions. Permanently interfering in the sphere of executive power, the 'small council' tried to have the final word in privatisation and the distribution of state credits and other budgetary resources (Sarychev, 1994, p.2).[32]

At its special session after the announcement of Yeltsin's edict on constitutional reform on 21 September 1993, the regional soviet declared this document 'anti-constitutional' and announced that it would comply, from then onwards, only with Rutskoi's rule (AP, 25 September 1993, p.1). There was an attempt to force the representative of the President, Shuba, out of office, according to the latter. After Yeltsin forcibly disbanded the Supreme Soviet in October 1993, Surikov diplomatically changed his position, claiming now that both sides were responsible for these tragic events and, most importantly, resisted all calls by democratic deputies for the regional soviet to disband itself (AP, 12 October 1993, p.1).

While there was still a division of voting preferences in favour of either the agrarian-communist faction or the democratic platform during the elections to the federal parliament, the former enjoyed a clear victory at the elections to the regional parliament on 13 March 1994. This was mainly due to mass political apathy in urban centres (most of the nine voting districts in which the turnout was less than 25 per cent were in Barnaul and Rubtsovsk),[33] where the majority of support for democratic parties is expected to be. But there is also increasing disillusionment among the population. According to an earlier sociological survey, only 15 per cent of the AK population supported radical economic reforms at the beginning of March 1994 (Grigor'ev and Rastov, 1994, p.4), compared with 24.8 per cent in August 1992 (Rastov, 1993, p.22). Moreover, the more efficient structures of the Communist Party and the Agrarian Party in rural areas strengthened this urban-rural cleavage in voting patterns.

The importance of workplace background and the marginal role of party affiliation, which were mutually exclusive alternatives in the candidate list, becomes clear from Table 4.1.

For the 50 seats in the new parliament, one-mandate voting districts were created with an average of 38 400 eligible voters, but with a difference between the smallest and the largest one of nearly 1:2 (AP, 12 January 1994, p.1).[34] Candidates had mostly been proposed by working collectives or voting groups which had, according to the election regulations, to be 30–50 people; each candidate needed the support of at least three per cent of all eligible voters in one of the voting districts (AP, 1 February 1994, p.2). Table 4.1. shows that members of the executive branch were the most effective of all (from a 20.2 per cent share of candidates to a 34.0 per cent share of elected deputies or, in absolute figures, every third candidate was elected), while the intelligentsia suffered a considerable defeat. The only party worth mentioning in absolute figures is the Communist Party, which won two seats.

At its first session on 29 March 1994, the 41 elected deputies (re-elections for the remaining seats took place on 24 April) voted for Surikov as their new (and old) chairman, while the leader of the regional

Table 4.1 Candidates and elected deputies of the Altaiskii *Krai* regional parliament by workplace background and party affiliation, 1 3 March and 24 April 1994

	Candidates	% of total	Elected deputies	% of total
Total	233	100.0	50	100.0
Executive power	47	20.2	17	34.0
Regional soviet	10	4.3	2	4.0
Khozyaistvenniki	76	32.6	17	34.0
Intelligentsia	51	21.9	7	14.0
Communist Party	11	4.7	2	4.0
Other	38	16.3	5	10.0

Note: 'Executive power' refers to heads and deputy heads of *raion* administrations. *Khozyaistvenniki* includes directors and deputy directors of joint stock companies, *kolkhozy*, *sovkhozy* and poultry farms. Intelligentsia refers to teachers, doctors and staff of research institutes.

Source: Compiled from AP, 22 February 1994, p.2; 23 February 1994, p.2; 17 March 1994, p.1 and 27 April 1994, p.1

Communist Party, Safronov, became his deputy (AP, 31 March 1994, p.1). A few days later, Surikov announced publicly the regional parliament's intention to stop privatisation[35] and to control prices for energy (AP, 5 April 1994, p.1). Only six of the elected deputies were willing to work on a full-time basis (AP, 12 April 1994, p.2), four of whom were heading one of the new committees (economics, budget and finance, legislation and social policy). In the run-up to the second session at the end of April 1994, a faction of 25 traditionalists, supporting the communist-agrarian lobby, was formed, which gave them virtual control of parliament.[36] Democratic forces could rely on only five deputies,[37] but they did not set up a democratic faction, since this would require a minimum of 10 deputies according to the regulations of the AK parliament.

At their second session, the conservative nomenklatura started its open political struggle against the pragmatic nomenklatura in the regional administration, rejecting the latter's programme on privatisation for 1994 and pressing for local self-government, which meant, in clear terms, the election of local heads of administration in order to undermine the vertical control of executive power from Moscow (AP, 30 April 1994, p.2). In a paternalistic manner, they set up a commission for cooperation with political parties and social movements in order to condemn all kinds of factionism and, in effect, restrict competition between parties.

The new regional parliament started to press local administrations systematically to increase their share of social spending (which was now easily possible since a large number of deputies were, at the same time, heads or deputy heads of local executive power) and they started to oppose privatisation in the localities (AP, 1 June 1994, p.2). Both budgetary spending and privatisation shaped the main thrust of their political struggle against the regional administration. Its budget and finance committee set up a special accountancy chamber to control the expenditure of budgetary resources and federal programmes (AP, 15 June 1994, p.2). This led to amendments for the 1994 regional budget adopted at their third session in mid-June 1994, including populist measures leading to a higher expenditure of R19.7bn (AP, 18 June 1994, p.1), which amounted to 1.2 per cent of total income.

The head of the economics committee of the new parliament, V. Boldyrev, made clear right from the beginning that he wanted to have a say on privatisation which, according to him, should be stopped in key sectors of the economy (AP, 16 June 1994, p.2).[38] His committee had a strong influence on amendmends made in the programme on privatisation in 1994, raising questions of renationalisation and trying to oppose the free sale of land (AP, 30 July 1994, p.1). However, 'nomenklatura privatisation' continued to be a widespread phenomenon, which included the setting up of limited companies and production associations by managers, the sale of industrial assets and social infrastructure and leasing of workshops for private commercial interests.[39] However, it is hard to estimate to what extent local politicians benefited materially from privatisation. At least in one case, the Russian central press reported accusations made against the former head of the AK committee for property administration, Potapov, who allegedly embezzled 20 000 vouchers through the commercial bank *Sibirskii Al'yans*, where he was, at the same time, the head of the bank's council (KD, 17 June 1995, p.20).

The next three sessions in summer and autumn 1994 witnessed the regional parliament's attack on the political structures of provincial and federal executive power. This included debates on the structure of the provincial administration at the fourth session (27 August 1994, p.1), the committee on health services of the latter at the fifth (AP, 1 October 1994, p.2) and the regional fund for social support (AP, 15 November 1994, p.2) and the control of the federal pension fund at the sixth session (AP, 22 November 1994, p.1). This struggle for the control of the executive power had its political climax at the eleventh session in April 1995, when the new statute of the AK was overwhelmingly adopted, including a clause on the election of the governor by the deputies of the regional parliament (AP, 22 April 1994, p.1).

Federal structures of executive power

These include law enforcement organs (police, army, secret service, tax inspection, prosecution office), extrabudgetary funds and the treasury office. The latter two came under particular public scrutiny in terms of their impact on economic policy making.

The federal treasury office was set up to bundle the flow of federal finances in the region and to check on budgetary and extrabudgetary income and expenditures. In theory this should make the withholding of federal taxes technically impossible. However, the treasury office found itself in competition with the Central Bank branch in the Altai, which refused access to documents, trying to hide certain infringements and wanting to retain its monopolistic control function over commercial banks. The former was subjected, in the course of this conflict, to severe attacks in 1994.[40] As a result of its financial investigations, 2400 cases were disclosed in 1994 when the transfer of federal finances was withheld, totalling R6bn in that year (AP, 27 September 1994, p.2).

The medical insurance fund came under particular public criticism in 1994. The estimated total revenue of R30bn in 1994 compares with more than R3.2bn which were reportedly embezzled by officials of local health committees to buy cars and pay higher salaries, an amount they originally received as soft credits and federal transfers to acquire medicine and technical equipment and to use for medical treatment (AP, 30 June 1994, p.1). The crisis of the health system has its roots partly in the fact that six different administrative and commercial structures are running the health service in the AK, which led to overlapping competences, a growth of bureaucracy and presumably an unnecessarily heavy budgetary drain, given the services provided. This was aggravated by relatively low insurance contributions and price control of medicine and medical treatment (AP, 25 April 1994, p.2).

The region's pension fund disposed of an even larger amount of money from its 28 per cent levies on salaries in industry and 20.6 per cent in agriculture which are to be paid by employers. Its revenue totalled R675 581mn in 1994,[41] while employees in local post-office counters made a fortune by capitalising on extra amounts of transferred pensions received in their office. However, although the regional parliament started an investigation, it had to admit that it could not change the situation (AP, 22 November 1994, p.2).

Monopolistic and corporate structures

These tended to arise from the institutional entanglement of former state enterprises and production associations with the regional administration, which allows them to control a large share of the regional market and to impose prices. The growing importance of holding companies and FIGs on economic policy making in the AK is particularly evident in agriculture, energy production and the VPK. The 'Director's Council', a structure inherited from the old Soviet system to implement party commands in industry, is now exerting strong pressure for price control of energy and transport tariffs. According to the head of the 'Director's Council', V. Kargapolov, the director of the military enterprise *Barnaultransmash*, 'the administration has to take the opinion of the industrial management into account'.[42] They can rely on a number of deputies in the AK parliament to lobby for their interests. The provincial administration for its part pursues, according to Sidorov,[43] a policy of 'sticks and carrots', giving money at critical periods (harvest, preparation for winter), while applying severe budget constraints for the rest of the time.

The agrarian lobby of *Agropromsoyuz* – which has its roots in former state structures of agricultural production, processing and material supply as the regional administration of the Soviet Union's *Gosagroprom*, created under Gorbachev – set up its own commodity exchange, trade and commercial companies; this structure is currently being duplicated by the agricultural committee of the AK administration with its own channels of wholesale trade, marketing and foreign trade (AP, 21 April 1994, pp.1–2). Successor state organisations and the provincial administration in general, nonetheless, remain closely linked. *Altaiagropromsnab* dominates the supply of agricultural machinery, spare parts for tractors, tyres and batteries in the region (AP, 17 November 1993, pp.1–2). *Altaimolprom* managed to use its position to force the price for 1 kg of milk down to R80 (at a time when farmers were seeking R100–10), while, at the same time, a stock of 5000 t of butter and cheese was accumulating in their warehouse in late September 1993 (AP, 11 September 1993, p.2).

Officials from *Altaiagropromsnab* showed a particular eagerness to get federal funds for the supply of fuel and petrol to the region, suggesting the organisational fusion with the agricultural committee of the administration (AP, 27 April 1994, p.2). This provided them with a direct access to soft credits and subsidies from the centre. In fact, they received R3bn for spare parts and another R30bn for agricultural machinery from the federal budget in 1994, which compares with their own debt of R2bn in mid-1994 (AP, 26 July 1994, p.1). However, these were desperate attempts to hold on to former monopolistic positions. The head of *Altaiskotoprom*, A. Ernst, admitted the loss of their material base including the reduction of their livestock from 54 000 in 1992 to 31 000 in 1994 (AP, 13 September 1994, p.2). *Altaizernoprodukt* had a total debt of R102bn in mid-1994, while the regional administration bypassed their structures after the latter received R14.7bn from the centre for grain delivery, passing on the money directly to local administrations (AP, 2 August 1994, p.1). Finally, the setting up of a regional food corporation headed by the former first party secretary of the AK, A. Kuleshov, was announced in spring 1995, which is operating as a semi-state intermediary for interregional food delivery in exchange for spare parts and fuel (AP, 16 May 1995, pp.1–2).

Officials in the administration showed a strong commitment toward the setting up of holding companies and FIGs. This was often an open encouragement to keep former monopolistic structures together like *Altaisel'mash*, the leading producer of agricultural machinery in the region, which separated its workshops, set up new cooperatives and associations, but kept all structures under the control of the former directorate in the form of a holding company (AP, 29 October 1994, p.4). The creation of the first FIG in the AK, based on an agreement between the regional 'Union of Entrepreneurs' and the Moscow-based *Kreditprombank*, was first reported in September 1994. It was intended to bring together 13 joint stock companies and private enterprises operating in agriculture, construction and machine-building (AP, 6 September 1994, p.2). The head of the 'Union of Entrepreneurs' in the AK, V. Tverdokhlebov, who is also the leader of the regional organisation of PRES,[44] tried to use his old contacts in the administration to get tax relief and soft credits for this FIG.

However, it is not clear whether this structure ever came into existence. This kind of local press release reports only the intention to set up new structures, while local newspapers have not continued to report further developments. Similarly, the creation of the FIG 'Golden Grain', unifying grain producers, elevators, mills and *Zernobank*, was reported in spring 1995 (*Svobodnyi kurs*, 27 April–4 May 1995, p.2). It certainly indicates a tendency towards growing corporate structures.

In this context, more serious efforts were made by *Altaienergo*, the monopoly producer of electricity in the region. In order to solve the payments crisis, various bills-of-exchange-schemes were elaborated, mainly between the spheres of power production, mining, metallurgical industries and transport.[45] For that purpose, a special company, *Altaienergouglesnab*, was set up, which, under Zubkov, initiated closer ties between companies of 11 other Siberian and European regions and *Sibenergosnab* (AP, 1 March 1994, p.2). From such structures, huge intersectoral monopolies and new industrial groups could arise, completely controlling mining and energy production in particular clusters of regions.

Political parties and trade unions

The creation of national party structures is only in its infancy. Only two national leaders came to visit the region in the run-up to the elections on 12 December 1993. The leader of PRES, S. Shakhrai, arrived in Barnaul on 29 November 1993 and announced his intention to unite all Russian regions (AP, 30 November 1993, p.1). However, his party had no clear social base in the AK and his candidate in the region, Tverdokhlebov, did not do very well at these elections.

A few days later, the leader of the Agrarian Party, M. Lapshin, visited the Altai and declared in an interview (AP, 9 December 1993, p.1) that he intended to create, together with the then Vice-Prime Minister, A. Zaveryukha, regional structures for his party, relying mainly on employees of state and collective farms. In the meantime, his representative in the AK, Nazarchuk, was trying to combine commerce and politics. While he was using his direct access to the then head of the Russian Central Bank, V. Gerashchenko, to get central credits and to set up *Altaisel'khozbank* (AP, 2 December 1993, p.1), he started, at the same time, to restructure the regional *Agropromsoyuz* into the Altai organisation of the Agrarian Party (AP, 16 March 1994, p.1), the founding congress of which took place in April 1994 (AP, 19 April 1994, p.1).

In an earlier interview, Nazarchuk declared openly his intention to get control over both legislative and executive power in the province (AP, 16 March 1994, p.1). For these high ambitions, Zaveryukha provided him with political capital, bringing during his visit to the Altai an additional credit of R17bn to buy petrol for spring tilling (AP, 30 March 1994, p.1). After Nazarchuk took on his new job of Minister for Agriculture, his successor, V. Fominykh, announced his intention to strengthen the representation of members of the Agrarian Party in local executive power and indicated his willingness to cooperate with the Communist Party (AP, 27 December 1994, p.2).[46]

This could have been a recognition of the stronger support for the latter in rural areas. The Communist Party of the Russian Federation (KPRF) claimed in April 1994 to have 12 000 active members in the AK, of whom 30 per cent were pensioners, according to Safronov. He also had 11 old trade union structures under his control, which he reportedly mobilised for industrial action, giving the blessing of the regional parliament (AP, 2 July 1994, p.1). In his paternalistic manner, he set up a pro-communist voters' movement, incorporating parties (including the Agrarian Party), trade unions and social movements.[47] This provided them with an overwhelming victory in the election to the new regional parliament.

Similarily, in early October 1993, 'Altai's Choice', a voters' movement on the basis of the regional organisation of 'Russia's Choice', was set up, the founding members of which were, apart from democratic groupings, the 'Union of Afghanistan Veterans', Cossack groupings, a number of entrepreneurs, heads of *raiony* administrations and directors of state enterprises as well as members of the intelligentsia (AP, 7 October 1993, p.1). This provided the basis from which its leader, Ryzhkov, was elected to the State Duma, receiving about 100 000 votes (AP, 12 January 1994, p.1). However, it could not rely on a clear social base and did not manage to create a workable party structure. As a result, the movement was almost marginalised during the elections to the new regional parliament.[48] 'Democratic Russia's Choice' claimed a membership of about 100 people in the province in April 1995.[49] In their campaign for democratic changes they can rely on support from two deputies in the regional parliament and from former governor Korshunov and three of his deputies (Potapov, Mishin and Kandaurov), according to Emeshin.

However, most of the former democratic activists were incorporated into the 'bureaucratic market', becoming effectively hostages of the administrative system.[50] Despite the appeal for Russian patriotic and traditional family values in the statute of 'Democratic Russia's Choice',[51] most of the people active in 'democratic' politics in the province became disillusioned. Potapov's recent attempt at setting up the democratic movement 'Our *Krai*' in the region (KD, 17 June 1995, p.20) – which is not linked to Chernomyrdin's bloc – probably failed after he was arrested following accusations against him of embezzling privatisation vouchers.

Apart from the growing importance of Cossack groupings in the Altai (*Svobodnyi Kurs*, 27 April–4 May 1995, p.3), other social movements are operating merely at the grassroots level with no real political influence on economic decision making. For example, the NTS has, according to its regional leader Shvedov,[52] an active membership of about 10–15 people in the province and cooperates with other structures at the cross-regional level like the miners union in the Kuzbass or a private publishing house in Khakassiya. Their activities of civic engagement include the opening of a library in Barnaul and the reconstruction of churches and cemeteries, but they are too weak to break traditional patron-client relations and the hierarchical distribution of economic resources in the region.

4.4 ECONOMIC POLICY

Important issues of economic policy making in the AK included institutional restructuring, price control and, due to the region's established sectoral specialisation, agricultural policy. Budgetary and social policy played a significant regulatory role in this depressed region, while the federal programme of compensations for the nuclear fall-out from the Semipalatinsk testing facility provided additional resources from outside.

Institutional restructuring

Due to the reform-devoted, enthusiastic team in the committee for property administration, privatisation had proceeded fairly successfully in most of those enterprises which were on independent balance and released for privatisation by federal branch ministries. By the end of 1994, it was reported that about 70 per cent of them had some percentage share of private ownership, including 92 per cent in industry, 53 per cent in construction and 67 per cent in agricultural production.[53] However, it was also recognised that a proper restructuring at the enterprise level in terms of ownership, material supply and sales networks has still to take place. As shown in the previous section, former monopolistic structures were resistant to any change in their economic behaviour.

A classic example of the need for proper restructuring in the region is the military enterprise *Barnaultransmash*, which was mainly producing diesel engines for tanks. It suffered a drop in output of 60 per cent and made one-quarter of its workforce redundant in 1993 (from an original total of 16 000).[54] It switched over from an original three-fourths output share of military orders to the production of engines for Hungarian 'Ikarus' buses – which the Soviet Union imported on a mass scale a decade ago and which are now in need of new engines – as well as to the production of diesels for *Kamaz* lorries and other energy equipment. While six production lines were initially split up, they were later reunited as subsidiaries in a new holding company (*Svobodnyi Kurs*, 27 April–4 May 1995, p.4). However, it still had 16 kindergartens, one hospital, one sanatorium, one sports centre and a huge housing stock on its balance sheet in 1994.[55] Resources were still wasted on lighting and heating empty workshops over the winter, while paying, at the same time, high property taxes.

The creation of an alternative financial and banking sector is only in its infancy. Eight voucher investment funds were set up in the AK in 1994 to convert vouchers into shares which could be traded for money after 1 July 1994. Having converted 190 000 vouchers, their operation was practically paralysed by a presidential decree in the second half of 1994, establishing high taxes on the issue of shares.[56]

The regional branch of the Central Bank is broadly responsible for monitoring the regional credit and securities market. It checks accounting procedures and the financial liquidity of commercial banks, issuing licences for hard currency operations and regulating the issue of shares.[57] Financial settlements between commercial banks are carried out through one of the 50 clearing centres of the Central Bank branch. One-fourth of all investment finances in the region still went through this branch in 1993 (AP, 16 August 1994, p.2). As a new method of distributing central credits to commercial banks, auctions were started in early 1994, in which only nine of the total of 23 commercial banks could participate, since the others did not meet the requirements for liquidity and quality of accounting. A logical reaction to these measures was a relative increase of cash operations in 1994.

Finally, a first step towards the mobilisation of internal resources was the issue of bonds to finance housing construction at an original amount of R5bn by *Altaistroizakazchik* in 1994, using property in regional ownership as collateral (AP, 28 July 1994). In 1995, new bonds were issued by the regional administration to buy coal to a value of R20bn, which were sold within four days, according to Sidorov.[58] They afterwards planned to issue an even higher bond for R60bn to acquire gas and grain, but provision of collateral to cover this larger amount of money became a serious problem.

Price control

Tables A.19 and A.20 in the appendix show not only considerable retail price differentials between various cities in the AK, but also in comparison with other West Siberian provinces in August 1994. Low food prices are certainly due to the Altai's large agricultural production, but those for petrol, coal and electric power, for which the province is heavily dependent on outside supply, can only be explained by populist price controls (the 'consumption bias' as discussed in the previous chapter) by the political leadership.

According to the director of *Altaienergo*, Zubkov, large stocks of coal were accumulated in the region to provide reserves in case of supply interruptions, which created the illusion of high demand and an artificial price increase within the price targets set by AK officials (AP, 22 June 1994, p.2). But this could only happen, because domestic prices for fuel and energy resources were still much lower than world market prices as is shown in Table A.21 for May 1994. Grain procurement prices in the Altai were about R170 000 per t in summer 1994 (AP, 31 August 1994, p.1) compared with a Russian average of R210 000 at the same time (FT, 30 August 1994, p.18).

However, after the Russian government started to pursue a tougher policy to control federal budget expenditures, provincial authorities could not carry on indefinitely with their low price commitments. Price increases for household consumption were particularly high for water supply and municipal housing rents in the first quarter of 1994 (AP, 28 July 1994, p.2). This was followed by a further upsurge in the third quarter of 1994 for water supply, housing and central heating, which amounted to a total price increase by 47.8, 44 and 25 times respectively for the first nine months in 1994 (AP, 9 November 1994, p.3).

Agricultural policy

Institutional entanglement between government and corporate structures was particularly evident between the AK administration and agricultural producers and processing industries due to a strong agrarian lobby, price controls and half-hearted institutional restructuring. General problems in Russian agriculture include the price disparity between agricultural and industrial products, a growing local monopolism of processing industries and increases in real transport costs. This led, in Russia as a whole, to a fall of the agricultural share in national income from 20.7 per cent in 1990 to 7.3 per cent in 1993, which could be due partly to the price disparity, but probably most of all to the drop of gross agricultural output by 30 per cent in 1991–3 (NG, 29 November 1994, p.4). This was aggravated by lower crop yields due to the decreasing use of pesticides, soil erosion and problems with the supply of fertilizers, machinery and fuel (AP, 27 April 1995, p.2).

Although the Russian government's programme on agrarian reform for 1994–5 called for 'socially acceptable prices', it had a clear commitment to the free sale of farm land (except for foreign investors who can only lease) and the privatisation of processing industries (Ekizh, no.32, August 1994, p.20–2). It contained a long list of forms of state financial support including soft credits, federal programmes and preferential tax treatment. State investment policy was not primarily concentrated on grain production, but the reconstruction of processing industries for milk, sugar and meat products.

In the first nine months of 1994, grain production in the Altai APK fell by 39 per cent, hay by 53 per cent and cattle by 16 per cent in comparison with the same period in 1993, which could be only partly compensated by production increases of farmers and at private plots (AP, 3 November 1994, p.3). This was despite huge financial commitments by the federal and regional budgets. The latter spend R35bn for capital investment and social infrastructure in rural areas and another R25bn to maintain the existing livestock in 1993.[59] In the same year, the federal budget provided subsidies and compensation payments of R11bn. Preferential tariffs for fuel and energy and tax holidays were also granted, according to governor Korshunov (AP, 21 June 1994, p.1).

In July 1994, the regional administration provided a credit of R1bn to buy fertilizers (AP, 30 July 1994, p.1). The harvest in summer 1994 was, however, largely secured by a soft credit of R200bn from the Ministry of Agriculture and another loan from the federal budget of R48bn (AP, 21 September 1994, pp.1–2).[60] This was despite the regional authorities' unilateral decision to reduce the amount of grain supply to the federal fund by 50 per cent in 1994 (*ibid.*, p.1). These federal transfers compare with a guaranteed budgetary income of R872.7bn in the AK in 1994.[61] The regional administration, on its part, set up a fund for the support of agriculture, from which it granted R79bn for fodder production to compensate for price differentials and another R6.2bn for livestock (AP, 19 November 1994, p.2).

The regional agricultural programme for 1995 included further restructuring of procurement and processing industries, the creation of a credit reserve in the Central Bank branch for the milk industry, the setting up of a regional fodder fund and tax holidays for poultry farms (AP, 15 December 1994, p.1). In spring 1995, a special 1.5 per cent tax levy for the financial support of the regional APK was announced (AP, 26 April 1995, p.2). However, this was apparently not sufficient to provide tangible results, since new administrative measures had to be taken by the former Vice-Prime Minister, Zaveryukha, at a meeting of regional officials in the Ministry of Agriculture in April 1995 to supply agricultural producers in the AK with fertilizers (AP, 27 April 1995, p.1).

Budgetary and social policy

There were traditionally substantial differences in terms of existing social infrastructure and services not only between urban and rural areas, but also between various villages in the Altai (Sergienko, 1992, pp.51–2). Moreover, excessive industrial specialisation, concentrated in particular cities like Rubtsovsk, led to severe hardships after enterprises had to close down as a result of falling demand for their products. Schools and hospitals had to be closed, while teachers and doctors, who continued to work in their jobs, had to wait sometimes for several months to get their salaries.

The regional budget could not bear the increasing social costs after the responsibility for social infrastructure was shifted down from central branch ministries in 1992. Expenditure could only be covered to the extent of about 50 per cent from income in 1993–4.[62] The provincial budget deficit increased from R220bn in the first quarter of 1994 (AP, 30 March 1994, p.1) to R400bn in the third quarter of the same year (AP, 14 September 1994, p.1). The federal budget could compensate only by a transfer of R30bn and R72bn respectively. This federal transfer increased reportedly to a total of R180bn by the end of 1994 compared with an amount of R565bn demanded (AP, 30 November 1994, p.2).

However, as will be discussed in Chapter 6, there were numerous other budgetary channels and funds to cover social commitments and to support certain sectors in the regional economy through the AK budget. For example, the region received help from the 'Fund for Financial Support of the Subjects of the Russian Federation', allotting 6.3 per cent of the total to the AK compared with 7.9 per cent for neighbouring Novosibirsk *oblast'* in 1994 (AP, 27 April 1994, p.2). There were also specific grants from the federal budget like R3bn for four higher educational institutes in the province and another R5.1bn for the radio and television station *Altai* in 1995 (AP, 18 April 1995, p.1).

Different budgetary and extrabudgetary funds covered costs for social benefits. The federal employment fund in the AK spent R459.3mn on job creation for disabled people, R94.1mn for the opening of small-scale businesses by unemployed people, R5.7bn on unemployment benefits in 1994, while the pension fund granted 1231 people an earlier retirement for a total of R840.2mn in the same year. The regional reserve fund provided R635mn for unemployment benefits and further R1.1bn for job creation.[63]

Finally, in-migration fell to 27 200 in 1993 from 34 760 the year before, but remains a serious problem, mainly due to refugees from Central Asia, while out-migration is continuously increasing: 4421 people in 1991, 9600 in 1992 and 10 100 in 1993.[64] In 1994, another 8046 refugees came to the AK, which increased the number of officially registered refugees in the province to 14 075 people,[65] resulting in additional expenditures from the AK budget. In recognition of the 50th anniversary of VE-day in Russia, the government decreed higher pensions and more social benefits for veterans, but it was not clear who would pay for it (AP, 26 April 1995, p.3).

The Semipalatinsk programme

The most prominent federal programme in this region is state compensation for the nuclear fall-out from the neighbouring Semipalatinsk testing facility in Kazakhstan. It is officially recognised by the Russian government that 48.5 per cent of the AK territory was subject to nuclear radiation as a result of 470 nuclear tests between 1949 and 1990, an area in which 59.6 per cent of the total population lived in 1991 (Loginov and Trotskovskii, 1992, p.15). The economic loss for this period was estimated at R65bn (in 1992 prices) as a result of loss of labour (Rodionova, 1993, p.77) and another R123bn due to loss of cattle (Sazonov, 1993, p.24). This compares with a total budgetary income of R33.4bn in the province in 1992 (Aleinikov and Mikhailyuk, 1994, p.42). Caesium-137 can be mainly found in the surface soil used for tilling, adding to problems of flooding and soil erosion (Mishchenko and Mishchenko, 1993, p.45).

A new decree by President Yeltsin on 20 December 1993 announced special state compensation for people who suffered the highest radiation, which included, among other things, the reduction of pension age by 10 years, free health care, one free treatment at a sanatorium per year and a 50 per cent cut in rents for housing and other communal services (AP, 26 January 1994, p.3). For social compensation and other investment for housing and health services, the authorities of the AK spent R6.3bn from federal funds for this programme in 1992 and about R40bn in 1993 (Melkov and Gotfrid, 1994, p.51).

In 1994, the Russian government confirmed a list of settlements in the AK, which were subject to the largest amount of radiation after nuclear tests in 1949 and 1962.[66] As a result, the region received nearly R18bn in the first quarter of 1994 for the improvement of the health service, food industry, housing and communal services (AP, 21 June 1994, p.1). By mid-1994, the province got another R24bn from the official state programme and R1.3bn after a special presidential decree (AP, 20 July 1994, p.2). This added to one-tenth of total Russian compensation for nuclear radiation in that year. However, complaints were made that this amounted to only 14 per cent of the originally planned sum of money by summer 1994 (AP, 23 August 1994, p.2).[67]

In this context, a speech made by the deputy head of the AK administration, V. Germanenko, at a joint session of the Russian government and the Presidium of the Council of Ministers on 21 October 1993 gives an excellent example of special lobbying techniques by regional authorities (AP, 4 November 1993, pp.1–2). As at old party congresses, he started with the importance of the region for the whole country in terms of agricultural products, natural resources and machinery. Then he went on to argue that a stable situation in his region depended, first, on the fulfillment of the state programme of compensation for the nuclear fall-out from the Semipalatinsk testing facility, enumerating accurately all the negative consequences (in reduced life expectancy, increased infant mortality and numerous diseases) and, of course, exaggerating, claiming high radiation throughout the AK territory. Then he turned back again to the general problems in his region, outlining the traditional backwardness in the social sphere. This prepared the ground for his arguments for necessary investment, while repeatedly coming back to existing shortages. Finally, he informed the audience about projects already started as a part of the Semipalatinsk programme since 1992 and emphasised, in a typical Soviet manner ('first start with building the site, then find necessary funding'), that they could only be finished with additional financial help from Moscow.

One problem with nuclear radiation is that the consequences for life expectancy and infant mortality cannot be detected immediately. As shown in Table A.22, both birth and death rates per thousand inhabitants in the area officially recognised as subject to Semipalatinsk radiation were always just about one percentage point higher than those for the rest of the AK in the period 1950–92. Moreover, a sociological survey carried out by specialists from the Altai State University revealed that 80 per cent of the respondents in that area indicated inconsistencies in social compensation provided and 63 per cent complained about injustice (Rastov, 1993, p.27). By the end of 1994, only 9752 people officially received social benefits from the Semipalatinsk programme compared with a total of 1.5mn people living in the area of high radiation (AP, 19 November 1994, p.2).

Although there is no doubt about the serious damage to people's health and the natural environment, general social indicators are not as dramatic as they are presented as being by regional leaders. While birth rates per thousand inhabitants were falling from 12.9 in 1992 to 9.1 in 1993, death rates were increasing from 11.1 in 1992 to 14.0 in 1993 (Mel'nik and Rodionova, 1994, p.27). These figures were close to the corresponding Russian average for birth rates, which dropped from 10.7 in 1992 to 9.2 in 1993, and death rates, which rose from 12.2 in 1992 to 14.6 in 1993 (Ekizh, no.6, February 1994, p.9). Claims by a few leading regional officials that the AK suffered dramatic demographic changes appear to be mere populism (Surikov, 1993, p.2).

4.5 THE CHALLENGE OF THE NATIONAL REFORM AGENDA

Regional authorities in the AK never threatened seriously to secede in the way ethnically-based republics and some other standard provinces did in order to press for preferential tax treatment and higher subsidies and soft credits. But they challenged the reform approach of the Russian government by adopting their own law on privatisation and in the statute of the region in 1994–5, both of which strengthened the position of the traditionalist nomenklatura in the regional parliament.

The new law on privatisation in the AK was adopted in summer 1994. It coincided with the end of voucher privatisation, and entailed a switch from mass-privatisation forced by the centre to a specific individual approach in the region, in which regional authorities wanted to have a greater say on property evaluation, forms of privatisation and the change of business profile in communal enterprises (AP, 30 June 1994, p.1). The committee for property administration, which had, in fact, prepared this law, resisted the administrative approach towards privatisation by federal authorities, the latter's neglect, as they argued, of specific regional and sectoral features, the fact that the division between federal and regional property remained blurred, excessive preferences for working collectives which could not provide the necessary investments and no clear specification of what to do with the social infrastructure of enterprises (Potapov and Bobrovskaya, 1994, p.8–13).

However, the adoption of this law at the third session of the regional parliament in mid-June 1994 (AP, 18 June 1994, p.1) meant effectively a complete U-turn by a formerly reform-minded team in the committee for property administration, which became now incorporated into the 'bureaucratic market', using their access to information and industrial assets to their own advantage. From now onwards, privatisation of enterprises in the province had to be agreed between the working collective and both executive and legislative power, which all together would set up a special commission (AP, 26 July 1994, p.2), meaning effectively a further bureaucratisation of the whole process.

After the regional parliament had rejected the original programme on privatisation for 1994, the committee for property administration had now clearly backed down. According to this law, the housing stock of the enterprise was excluded from privatisation and a long list of preferences for the working collective was provided. Although the federal committee for property administration (GKI) put up fierce resistance against the Altai law on privatisation (AP, 10 August 1994, p.1), the fourth session of the regional parliament triumphantly announced a change of policy towards privatisation (AP, 30 August 1994, p.1).

In September 1994, Surikov publicly called for corrections of the regional programme on privatisation, which could now take place only with the special agreement of the provincial parliament, and he also declared the renationalisation of processing industries (AP, 20 September 1994, p.1). The amended programme included the halting of privatisation of educational and health institutions; the provision that the sale of land could only be carried out by permission of the regional parliament; extensive preferences for the working collective were provided, including a guarantee that the workforce had to be kept for at least one year after privatisation; and foreign investors were largely excluded (*ibid.*, p.2–4). This could not provide the necessary legal framework for thorough institutional restructuring and private investment. As discussed above, the regional committee for property administration set up new quangos to justify its further existence.

The second challenge to the national reform agenda, the adoption of the new provincial statute in April 1995, has to be seen in the context of the configuration of political power in the region. It officially declared the principles of power sharing between executive and legislative institutions, local self-government and the separation of functions and the control over resources between the centre and the region.[68] Its main political thrust was, however, that the governor of the region would be elected not by general elections, but by the regional parliament (*Svobodnyi Kurs*, 27 April–4 May 1995, p.3).[69] Leading officials of the provincial parliament argued that they wanted to cut costs and save time by this way of electing the governor (Safronov), but it clearly opens the door for them to get the executive power under complete control in future.

According to the President's representative in the region, Shuba, Moscow was seriously concerned about these developments and governor Korshunov appealed to the Constitutional Court.[70] This appeal was approved in early 1996, which marked not only an unprecedented defeat for the conservative nomenklatura in the Altai, but was also a sign of the institutional independence of the Constitutional Court despite the overwhelming victory of the Communist Party in the December 1995 parliamentary elections (*Segodnya*, 19 January 1996, p.2).

Four candidates competed for the governorship in March 1996: the mayor of the city of Barnaul, V. Bavarin, Korshunov, Nazarchuk and Surikov. According to the Constitutional Court's decision, free general elections of the governor were held in the Altai. However, those with the best chance of winning were undoubtedly members of the conservative nomenklatura. In a fierce neck-on-neck contest, Surikov won the second round of the governor's elections in 1996 against Korshunov. This would mean the complete revitalisation of nomenklatura power in the province with gloomy prospects for democratic changes and market reform.

5 The Rise of Authoritarian Power in Russia's Gateway to Pacific Asia

The examination of reform attempts in the PK in 1992–5 provided evidence that regional leaders sought an advantage in combining public office with private business, but this link already started to fall apart with a growing particularisation of interests and individualisation of society.[1] What made the PK differ from other regions, though only in its extreme appearance, was the assertive style and intransigence exhibited by regional leaders in demanding preferential treatment from Moscow (subsidies, soft credits), their continuous search for a special economic regime, the ruthless suppression of all oppositional forces, who were perceived as a threat to the current administration, and the emergence of an absolutist leader as governor. It will be argued that the centre was not only too weak to resist these developments, but that certain national leaders had a particular interest in keeping, on the periphery, such an authoritarian governor in power.

First, both key political players and institutions in place are investigated. This discussion culminates in an analysis of the open showdown with the centre, while forces of resistance and possible constraints on authoritarian power in the region will be examined afterwards.

5.1 THE REGIONAL ELITE AND KEY POLITICAL PLAYERS

This section examines the configuration of political power in the province by focusing on key political players. Two opposing political camps can be found represented in the present governor, Evgenii Nazdratenko, who is backed by the industrial management, the military and other federal structures, on the one side, and the newly reinstated mayor of Vladivostok city, Viktor Cherepkov, who receives support from various democratic groupings and some of the local media, on the other. The former camp is influential on regional policy making today and they are responsible for market reform and institutional restructuring, while the role of trade unions and parties in this process remains marginal.[2] However, this constellation became more complex after members of the new private business class and the criminal underworld entered the political scene, while the alliance that had formed Nazdratenko's camp was splitting up following a growing diversification of interests.

The ruling establishment in the PK consists of members of the second echelon of the former party and management nomenklatura, who came to power at the wave of public disillusionment with rapid systemic reforms, while being able to rely on considerable private capital (Savvateeva, 1994, p.5). The first governor of the region, Vladimir Kuznetsov, was for this alliance a newcomer and intellectual troublemaker. He was devotedly reform-minded and embarked on different economic experiments in 1991–2, the most prominent of which was the 'Greater Vladivostok' FEZ project. His liberal market approach and his liking for extended travel abroad caused strong resentments among traditionalists in the old regional soviet and industrial management.[3]

After Kuznetsov suspended the regional communist newspaper *Krasnoe znamya* in the aftermath of the August 1991 coup, its editor-in-chief, V. Shkrabov, started a campaign against him with the aim of promoting a new governor, who would be closer to the regional elite's thinking.[4] He joined traditionalists in the regional soviet to launch a coup against Kuznetsov in April 1993, after the Russian parliament had withdrawn its support of Yeltsin's power to appoint regional governors, as discussed in Chapter 3. The regional soviet suggested to the President the new candidature of Evgenii Nazdratenko, assuring him in advance of the support of the majority of the soviet (UR, 19 May 1993, p.1). Shkrabov revealed later (BBC interview on 28 September 1994) that they had chosen Nazdratenko because of his 'practical experience' and his allegedly close connections with Yeltsin.

The new governor was originally described as having a 'progressive conservatism' (Gainutdinov, 1993, p.2). In 1983, he finished a degree at the Far Eastern Technological Institute and became, in 1990, the director of the mining company *Vostok* in Dal'negorsk, as well as a deputy of the Russian parliament (UR, 20 May 1993, p.1). Nazdratenko provides an excellent example of how industrial management was pouring into power in Russian regions, seeking advantage in the combination of public office with private business. In a special interview, he referred explicitly to his friends, who are directors of enterprises of the defence industry and local entrepreneurs, which he called a 'legal union of industrialists' (UR, 2 June 1993, p.2).

Over a period of four months, Nazdratenko managed to appoint a new team in his administration[5] in which a number of deputies (A. Pavlov, I. Lebedinets, V. Shkrabov) were, at the same time, leading executive members of the joint-stock company PAKT.[6] This was devised as a 'model to rule the Primorskii *krai* independently of Moscow' (Shkrabov in the BBC interview on 28 September 1994) and the responsibility for large-scale privatisation gave the additional opportunity to control the regional economy (Vacroux, 1994, p.43). It allowed the combination of tax-evasion, embezzlement of public money and control of political power (including the issue of export licences and distribution of regional quota), which became famous as 'Primorskii Watergate' (Ostrovskaya, 1993, p.5).

The 213 founders (people, not enterprises) of PAKT represented 36 leading industrial enterprises, including six defence plants (among others, *Varyag* and *Radiopribor*), four fishing and fish-processing companies, producers of chemicals and electronic circuits (RFEU, March 1994, p.11). The member enterprises of PAKT employed 90 000 people or nine per cent of the total regional workforce in August 1993 (Vacroux, 1994, p.41). PAKT became a vehicle for its founders' interests. It acquired 236 600 shares of privatised enterprises for half the market price through manipulated, non-public auctions (Kucherenko, 1994, p.7). This was justified under the pretext that the local economy had to be protected against the capital pouring into the region from outside (Vacroux, 1994, p.41).

Credits were taken at *Promstroibank* and afterwards PAKT executives distributed loans among themselves to buy a majority of shares of privatised enterprises. Lebedinets, for example, acquired more than 28 000 shares through this kind of procedure (RG, 20 October 1994, p.3). PAKT founders received also interest-free loans from the regional budget, which totalled R500mn in 1993 (Kucherenko, 1994, p.7). The former representative of the President in the PK, V. Butov, claimed that PAKT embezzled money from the regional budget to the extent of R25bn in 1993 (UR, 12 January 1994, p.1), compared with a total budgetary income of R753.7bn in that year.[7]

Pavlov, the former head of the regional trade administration during the late Soviet period, who is today the director of the company *Kommersant*, originally held the reins as the general director of PAKT (UR, 4 November 1993, p.1). In 1992, the year when PAKT was set up, he seemed to be the real key player of the whole business, while Nazdratenko may have been at first only a political puppet.[8] Pavlov alone was accused of tax-evasion at *Kommersant* of R2.5bn in 1992 (UR, 19 October 1993, p.2). While Pavlov was trying to control the newly emerging commercial sector, Nazdratenko attempted to control the military-industrial complex. He takes a strong nationalist stance and wants Russia to restore and maintain its leading position in global arms sales alongside the United States: 'I support, by nature, a strong military-industrial complex … . Without the help of this complex, I would never be able to run the economy of the region.' (BBC interview on 1 October 1994) This is an astonishingly revealing statement, showing the extent of Nazdratenko's ambitions and his understanding of his functions as governor of the region!

Another important member of PAKT was the former deputy head of the regional tax inspectorate and, at the same time, the deputy director of the Vladivostok-based trawling and refrigerator ship fleet, Igor Lebedinets, who later became not only Nazdratenko's chief of staff, but also the first chairman of the new regional Duma. Finally, the fourth decisive player of PAKT was originally Shkrabov, a former member of the Primorskii CPSU committee and, as mentioned above, the editor-in-chief of the regional newspaper *Krasnoe znamya* (the former party organ), who was appointed as the head of the committee for mass-media in the regional administration, becoming, in fact, his own boss (Ostrovskaya, 1993, p.5). He described himself as the 'ideologist' of PAKT (BBC interview on 28 September 1994). The administration acted as the co-founder of this newspaper in an attempt to get its own media mouthpiece.

This fusion of politics and business in the activities of the highest ranking regional leaders marked a decisive step towards absolutist power in the second half of 1993. But this would not have been possible without the involvement of criminal gangs in local politics, privatisation and foreign economic activities. They were reported to have frequently offered their 'services' to the regional administration (*Novoe vremya*, no.40, 1994, p.14). This is not surprising for a region, which used to be a closed military district for many decades, subjecting people under military rule and patron-client relations, and where now many military servicemen are made redundant. Criminal activities are not only pervading all capillaries of social life, but they produce a special public atmosphere of compliance and patronage.

One clear example of their methods and political influence was provided by the criminal gang *Sistema*, which hired the highest ranking security officers from the Pacific Fleet and copied, with their help, the structure of the fleet's espionage system to carry out racketeering and blackmail of new commercial structures (UR, 12 May 1995, p.2–3). A sophisticated scheme was set up to acquire the control package of shares in the privatisation of *Vostokrybkholodflot* (UR, 13 May 1995, p.2). Each district in the city of Vladivostok has its own criminal hierarchy with a *Polozhenets* on top, who sorts out troubles between the groupings and presides over money. This structure not only parallels that of official state power, but former procurators and police officers are now working for the criminal underworld.

At least in one reported case, in the FEZ Nakhodka, the local elite seems to be ruled by the criminal underworld and local politics appears to be driven by feuds among criminal gangs (Korol'kov, 1995, p.3). The story of the city of Nakhodka is a particularly striking example of how authorities in Russian regions became, by their own hand, hostages of the criminal underworld, since gangs were originally hired by local officials to fight the perceived threat of the expansion of businesses owned by Caucasian people.

5.2 INSTITUTIONS

The strong stress on personalities in the analysis of the configuration of political power in the PK is due not only to blurred regional institutional structures, but also to the weak coherence of national parties and their low representation in the province. Institutional restructuring in the PK did not proceed toward a division of power as envisaged by national leaders and established in the new Russian Constitution, but toward a subordination of regional legislature and judiciary under the executive branch and, in particular, the concentration of authoritarian power in the hands of governor Nazdratenko.

Executive branch

Nazdratenko's predecessor, Kuznetsov, had already taken over a huge bureaucratic apparatus. He did not change the structure of the former executive committee and retained almost all of the old personnel. In September 1993, the PK administration employed 718 people and consisted of 16 committees and 28 departments.[9] In late 1994, Nazdratenko announced a reduction of members of staff down to 300 people altogether, including his deputies from 13 to only five, and also structural changes between committees and departments (UR, 5 November 1994, p.1). This was hardly an attempt to save public expenditures, but to get a close entourage of state employees, which would be more easily controllable, particularly with respect to the kind of information leaking out from the administration.

The distinctive approach of Nazdratenko's team was to take over the role of former central branch ministries and to converge, within the structures of PAKT, to an all-encompassing conglomerate aiming to control the main spheres of the regional economy. Administrative measures were taken to stop large-scale privatisation in 'crucial and socially significant' enterprises in August 1993. This category encompassed 64 regional and 108 federal enterprises (Vacroux, 1994, p.41).

In its organisational goals, PAKT claimed the leading role in structural reorganisation of the regional economy, the setting up of a financial system and a 'socially stable and economically protected structure for voucher investment' (*ibid.*, p.40). This would not only mean a replacement of old sectoral monopolies that dominated the regional economy until then, but also a new institutional entanglement of politics and economics at the regional level and a fierce resistance towards outside competition. In a letter to the President, signed by Egor Gaidar and other members of the democratic factions in the State Duma, it was claimed that PAKT controlled more than 200 of the total of 360 large enterprises in the province in September 1994 (*Segodnya*, 29 September 1994, p.2).

The redistribution of fishing quotas, for example, remained an important form of administrative leverage in a region so heavily dependent on this sector. The total regional quota for fishing within the 200-mile zone was 1.68mn t in 1994, which was 48 per cent of the Russian Far East total and a 70 000 t increase over the 1993 quotas (RFEU, February 1994, p.4). Seventy per cent of the total quotas in 1994 (as handed down by *Roskomrybolovstvo*, the national controlling body) were distributed by the committee for the fishing industry, while the remaining 30 per cent (destined for export) were administered by the committee for foreign economic and regional relations of the regional administration, which evidenced an overlapping of administrative competences.

There was no clear formula or criterion for this redistribution, but it was carried out by former planning methods (given capacity, achieved level from the previous year) and subjective factors.[10] It is clear that outsiders or newly established private companies had no chance under this system. Moreover, it opened the door for corruption. For example, the private company *Dal'vent* was not only denied fishing quotas for a number of years, but its boats were requisitioned by decree of the regional administration in July 1994 because these boats were allegedly 'not supervised' (*Izvestiya*, 2 September 1994, p.4).

The system of regional quotas and export licences left a strong lever of control over foreign trade for the authorities. The administrative distribution of fishing quotas for export in the region implied price agreements and financial help for the former regional monopoly (in terms of sale of fish on foreign markets) *Dal'moreprodukt*, which led naturally to new cartels and conglomerates (UR, 28 January 1994, p.2). *Dal'moreprodukt* created an investment holding company in May 1994 which included 11 subsidiaries, seven foreign co-founders (mainly Japanese banks) and a huge armada of fishing boats, issuing 30 000 shares.[11] Its market power became even stronger after its regional competitor *Primorrybprom* was run-down by corrupt management (UR, 19 May 1994, p.2).

Moreover, in order to pursue its populist price policy for fuel and energy, the regional administration initiated in May 1994 the creation of a new conglomerate, *Energiya Vostoka*, in which the regional energy company *Dal'energo* and the mining company *Primorskugol'* were incorporated (UR, 6 May 1994, p.2). The executive branch reportedly backed Central Bank credits to the conglomerate by passing on subsidies from the federal budget (*Segodnya*, 20 October 1994, p.11), which is a clear example of how regional authorities contribute to the federal budget deficit.

Finally, the PK administration not only tried to control former sectoral monopolies of the regional economy, but it also interfered in newly emerging market structures. In late August 1994, Nazdratenko set up a new commission for securities under his administration which was supposed to control the issue and turnover of securities in the region (KD, 27 August 1994, p.7). The commission's remit gave its members the right to check on participants of Vladivostok's stock exchange and to give them binding instructions.

The head of the regional property fund, V. Lutsenko, issued a decree in September 1994 to stop the free sale of shares of privatised enterprises at the city's stock exchange (KD, 3 September 1994, p.6). This was part of a new attempt at manipulating large-scale privatisation by the use of closed, non-public auctions to which leading executives of PAKT had access. Kucherenko (1994, p.7) reported that officials in Lutsenko's property fund allowed applications by serious competitors and independent entrepreneurs to 'disappear', making sure that PAKT members could cheaply acquire the best enterprises in the region. At a press conference in October 1994, Nazdratenko made the following statement after being accused of mixing public office with private business: 'One cannot separate me from industry ... I am not against privatisation, but I am against the methods being used. For that reason, I tried to keep a large package of shares in the hands of the administration to talk with the commercial structures in a civilised way.' (*Segodnya*, 26 October 1994, p.2)

Legislative branch

The traditionalist majority in the regional soviet rejected Yeltsin's edict 'On the Stage-by-stage Constitutional Reform in the Russian Federation' of 21 September 1993 (UR, 28 September 1993, p.1) and Nazdratenko declared on 22 September: 'There is only one solution to this mess: the whole Far East has to split up' (RG, 1 October 1994, p.2). However, after Yeltsin forcibly disbanded the Russian parliament in early October 1993, Nazdratenko made a complete u-turn, pledging allegiance to the President and ordering strong subordination of the local executive power under his command (UR, 6 October 1993, p.1). Moreover, he decided to disband the regional soviet on 28 October 1993 (UR, 29 October 1993, p.1) – a move which affected most of those deputies who originally proposed his appointment.

This gave Nazdratenko the opportunity to rule without being faced with a legislative counterbalance for more than a year, since he postponed in March 1994 the elections to the regional parliament, which were originally scheduled for that month by presidential decree, until 23 October. Whether he did not feel safe enough, remains an open question, but he claimed that there was not enough money to pay for them (*RFE/RL Daily Report*, 22 March 1994). Moreover, there was a rising apathy among voters disillusioned with local politics. A public survey conducted in the run-up to the elections of the new regional Duma in October 1994 still indicated that one third of the eligible voters were willing to participate at the elections (UR, 11 October 1994, p.2). But the results of the elections had to be declared invalid because of low turnout. In only 19 of the 39 voting districts the necessary quorum of 25 per cent was achieved (UR, 3 November 1994, p.1). Nevertheless, the analysis of candidates and elected deputies by workplace background[12] gives a clear indication of the revitalisation of the power of former nomenklatura members, as is shown in Table 5.1.

Even if the regional parliament had convened at that time, it is clear that it would have been dominated by representatives of the executive power and industrial management. Both members of the intelligentsia and social organisations lost considerably in this tentative estimate of the configuration of power.

As in other Russian provinces discussed above there was a particularly low turnout in urban areas such as Vladivostok, Artem and Nakhodka (UR, 25 October 1994, p.1). Unpleasant candidates like Pavlov, who departed from the PAKT alliance only a few weeks before, were reportedly denied their proper number of votes (UR, 3 November 1994, p.1). The same applies to Nazdratenko's main political opponent, Cherepkov, who won with a large margin in his voting district, but so-called 'dead souls' (non-existing or not eligible voters) were added on the list, as a result of which the necessary quorum of a 25 per cent turnout was not achieved and the elections were simply declared invalid (UR, 16 June 1995, p.2).

Moreover, new procedures for the re-elections scheduled for 15 January 1995 were adopted which clearly violated the President's decree on voting regulations:

Table 5.1 Candidates and elected deputies to the Primorskii *Krai* parliament by workplace background, 23 October 1994

	Candidates	% of total	Elected Deputies	% of total
Total	149	100.0	19	100.0
Executive power	41	27.5	8	42.1
Khozyaistvenniki	55	36.9	8	42.1
Military	9	6.0	1	5.3
Intelligentsia	22	14.8	1	5.3
Social organisations	8	5.4	–	–
Other	14	9.4	1	5.3

Note: Percentage figures in the last column do not add to 100.0 per cent because of rounding. 'Executive power' includes heads and deputy heads of regional and local administrations. *Khozyaistvenniki* refers to directors, managing directors and chief engineers of joint-stock companies, state enterprises, banks, *kolkhozy* and *sovkhozy*. Intelligentsia includes academics, teachers, doctors and engineers. 'Social organisations' apply to members of independent trade unions, consumer associations and so on. 37 of the candidates (24.8 %) were former deputies of the regional soviet (UR, 15 March 1994, p.1).

Source: Compiled from UR, 12 March 1994, p.2 and 3 November 1994, p.1

1) the candidate had now to collect signatures from only one per cent of all eligible voters instead of three per cent as required before;
2) the candidate could be proposed by only one supporter instead of a group of at least 30 supporters;
3) better conditions were provided for members of the executive branch including the possibility to be relieved from public duty for the time of the pre-election campaign (UR, 17 December 1994, p.1).

It is intriguing that no further information on the new deputies elected in January 1995 was released in the local press.

The first information came in the national press, reporting on the attempt of some of the new deputies to declare the primacy of the legislative over the executive branch in the draft of the new provincial statute, but its new chairman and close ally of Nazdratenko, Lebedinets, quickly distanced himself from this clause (*Segodnya*, 22 February 1995, p.2). Two committees out of a total of five are headed by former deputies of the regional soviet, while the former head of the federal treasury office in the

PK, N. Sadomskii, was, at the same time, the head of the budget committee of the regional Duma (UR, 24 February 1995, p.1), resulting in overlapping administrative competences of officials in federal and provincial institutions.

Moreover, the leadership of the new regional parliament pursued a provocative policy against the centre right from the beginning, trying to mobilise various trade unions during the miners' strike in the province in spring 1995 by declaring, allegedly in their name, that they would block ports and the Transsiberian Railtrack if the centre would not provide further subsidies and soft credits for defence-related enterprises (NG, 30 March 1995, p.2) and the coal industry (NG, 7 April 1995, p.1). This was widely considered as a deliberate attempt by the highest provincial officials at using industrial action to destabilise the political situation in the region (*Segodnya*, 11 April 95, p.2).

However, conflicts arose between the executive and legislative branches, particularly between Lebedinets and Nazdratenko, who started an uncompromising battle over absolutist power in the region. The regional administration fiercely resisted the attempt by leading officials of the regional Duma to set up a huge apparatus by simply not providing office space (UR, 7 June 1995, p.2). Nazdratenko changed a clause in the new law on the status of deputies in the PK Duma, which gives only him the right to appoint the deputies' aides (UR, 14 June 1995, p.2). This conflict culminated in Lebedinets' forced resignation, following his attempts to disclose the findings of a special governmental commission on abuse of power and corruption in the PK administration (KD, 15 June 1995, p.15) and his open appeal for the sacking of Nazdratenko and a number of his deputies (*Segodnya*, 22 June 1995, p.3). As a result, Nazdratenko was by summer 1995 the only survivor from the original alliance of top officials in public office and executive members of PAKT.

Federal structures of executive power

Nazdratenko tried also to get the structures of federal power in the region under his control. He was at loggerheads with the first representative of the President in the PK, Butov. Butov was a former soldier in Afghanistan and later the deputy military procurator of the Pacific Fleet (UR, 26 November 1993, p.2), who started, in the second half of 1993, to report more frequently on abuse of power by the administration and to reveal publicly cases of corruption by leading executives of PAKT. Nazdratenko started a campaign against Butov and pressed the centre to replace him. On 4 January 1994, Yeltsin acceded to the demands of the regional administration and sacked his representative. In a later interview, Butov referred to the personal friendship between Nazdratenko and the former head of the President's bureau, V. Ilyushin, who not only suggested to the President the candidature of Nazdratenko as the new governor in May 1993, but also the sacking of Butov (UR, 12 January 1994, p.1). Whether Yeltsin knew what was going on in the region while signing this document remains an open question.

The new representative, Vladimir Ignatenko, was clearly Nazdratenko's man, a former head of a local administration in the province. He condemned democratic groupings and the mass-media supporting Cherepkov as being 'scandalous and provocative' (UR, 13 August 1994, p.2) and openly resisted the reinstatement of the sacked mayor in his former office (*Izvestiya*, 27 December 1994, p.4). In mid-1995, he started increasingly to go beyond his official mandate, openly interfering in matters within the competence of the PK administration (UR, 20 June 1995, p.1).

Two attempts were made by the governor to suggest in Moscow the former head of the Dal'negorsk police office (where Nazdratenko's company *Vostok* is based), Lieutenant-Colonel Shul'g, as the new head of the regional tax police (UR, 26 November 1993, p.1). The appointment of the new head of the regional police department, V. Ipatov, was largely promoted by Nazdratenko's team (UR, 16 November 1993, p.1), who, in return, then showed his gratitude by delaying the legal investigation into the case of PAKT's tax-evasions and embezzlement of public money by special commissions from Moscow (UR, 26 November 1993, p.1). One year later, Nazdratenko promoted Ipatov to the rank of general (UR, 6 January 1995, p.2).[13] Moreover, the commanders of the regional office of the secret service, the border guards and the Pacific Fleet have, reportedly, 'close relations' with governor Nazdratenko (*Segodnya*, 29 September 1994, p.2).

This applies also to newly set up federal committees. The former head of the tax police in the province, A. Bondarenko, was one of Nazdratenko's close allies (*Novoe vremya*, no.40, 1994, p.14), before he was arrested in July 1995 for being involved in the campaign against Cherepkov (*Izvestiya*, 22 June 1995, p.1). The head of the pension fund, P. Nazarov, gave Nazdratenko's administration R25bn in July 1994, because the latter decided to increase pensions by 50 per cent – a populist action in Nazdratenko's campaign to be elected as governor in October 1994.[14] Whether the newly created treasury office – which is supposed to control the flow of federal finances[15] – will stay independent from the regional administration's intrusion, remains doubtful. All the more so as its former head, N. Sadomskii, had already become a member of the commission for securities of the administration as well as the head of the budget committee of the new regional Duma, discussed above. Finally, the regional parliament now also claims the right to confirm the appointment of heads of various federal institutions in the region (UR, 23 February 1995, p.2), which could be merely another way to legitimise the governor's authoritarian power.

Monopolistic and corporate structures

The strongest impact on economic decision making in the region is made by the above mentioned industrial conglomerate PAKT, whose members are closely linked with the provincial administration. Nazdratenko tried to justify the establishment of such a FIG by drawing parallels with Japanese conglomerates, arguing that they would be better suited to absorb economic shocks (UR, 27 August 1994, p.2). PAKT executives reportedly have a particular interest in the fuel and energy complex, ports, oil pipelines and sites of natural resource extraction, while all programmes of geological investigation in the region are under personal control of Nazdratenko (*Novoe vremya*, no.40, 1994, p.14).

According to Savvateeva (1994, p.5), PAKT never did engage in any production activity; it only redistributed money and industrial assets. In late 1994, the Moscow-based *ONEKSIM bank* was chosen by the regional administration to operate as its financial agent in foreign economic activities, to settle payment arrears between provincial enterprises for which bank officials hoped to get treasury bills from the Ministry of Finance, and to engage in new investment projects in the PK (KD, 16 December 1994, p.5).[16]

The regional administration's attempt at halting privatisation and setting up new conglomerates impeded proper institutional restructuring, resulting in a growing commitment from both the federal and the regional budgets. In return, industrial managers' response was to lobby for new subsidies and soft credits, while not undertaking thorough-going structural changes at the enterprise level. The mining company *Primorskugol'*, for example, which had to be subsidised almost completely by the state as a result of regional authorities' price policy for fuel and electricity, started with privatisation only in autumn 1994, employing reportedly, at that time, more people for management and subsidiary jobs than miners (UR, 29 September 1994, p.1). The only solution is to close a number of unprofitable mines, but no programmes for retraining were started until the miners' strike of spring 1995 (*Izvestiya*, 26 April 1995, p.1).

Moreover, the PK administration still claims the right to dispose of federal subsidies handed down for this company, from which R17bn were reportedly embezzled and passed on to commercial structures (*Izvestiya*, 7 April 1995, p.1). The provincial administration also acted as the intermediary in negotiations between the national energy company, *Rosugol'*, and *Primorskugol'*, at which the former promised to provide R500bn in 1995 for technical re-equipment, new housing and additional pensions, while PK authorities wanted to lobby for tax and customs exemptions for *Primorskugol'* in the centre (KD, 20 July 1995, p.9).

The institutional entanglement of politics and economics in the PK resulted in growing cartels along the regional boundary, the institutionalisation of inflationary behaviour and rent seeking, which was politically supported by the executive branch. Monopolies in timber-processing industries were exempted from local taxes (UR, 19 April 1995, p.2), while the set up of a new transport conglomerate sponsored by regional and Moscow-based banks was also reported (UR, 1 April 1995, p.2). The management of the fishing company, *Primorrybprom*, acquired 55 per cent of all shares after having received money from the regional budget for 23 per cent of the shares alone (UR, 20 April 1995, p.2). The provincial bread cartel, *Primorkhleboprodukt*, got a $3mn credit from the regional hard currency fund to buy grain abroad, but less than one tenth of the agreed total was imported, which fuelled speculations about new corruption (UR, 19 May 1995, p.1).

Without these institutions and structures under his control, Nazdratenko not only could not have afforded to press the centre for preferential treatment (subsidies, soft credits) and to require a special economic regime, but also would not have been able to suppress ruthlessly all oppositional forces in the province, who were perceived to be a threat to the regional administration.

5.3 THE OPEN SHOWDOWN WITH MOSCOW

Nazdratenko's administration was certainly not the only regional executive in Russia to press the centre for a special economic status. But what made the PK differ from other regions, apart from its important strategic location, was the combination of close private connections to top officials in Moscow, the subjection of the majority of regional branches of federal institutions to the command of an authoritarian executive branch and the reliance on the military and criminal gangs for political ends.

Kuznetsov had already lobbied for a special economic status as part of his 'Greater Vladivostok' FEZ project, asking for more regional power and control than the RF was inclined to grant at that time, including the setting up of an economic development fund based on the transfer of assets from the federation to a regional authority (RFEU, April 1992, pp.6–7). However, he attracted the interest of central authorities and managed to keep a part of the 40 per cent mandatory transfer of hard currency revenues (that would normally have gone to the centre) in the PK in 1992 to buy foodstuffs from abroad and to set up a regional hard currency fund. Thanks to his lobbying efforts in Moscow, the region could also keep 10 per cent of customs duties, collected in the province in 1993, for the setting up of infrastructure to promote foreign trade. Furthermore, the authorities also managed to get additional export quotas for mineral fertilizers in 1992.[17]

Most of the deputies in the former regional soviet resented ambiguities in the Federation Treaty of March 1992; in particular, as they perceived it, lesser rights in terms of taxation and control over territorial resources compared with Russian republics. As a result, the 'small council' (consisting of full-time deputies) prepared its own draft of a law 'On the Status of the Primorskii *Krai*', emphasising its special geopolitical location for 'long-term Russian interests in the Asian-Pacific region' (UR, 24 March 1993, p.1). As 'state priorities' in the province it defined, among other things, transport facilities to Asian-Pacific countries, the modernisation of processing industries for increased value added to local raw materials and the maintenance of military capacity in this region. This definition of 'state priorities' reflects traditional thinking, in which the state (central or local) is assumed to be responsible for the development of various industries. The soviet, for its part, sought special authority in the following main spheres:

1) the right of use and disposal of land, raw materials and other natural resources in the province;
2) the retention of five per cent of the amount of VAT going to the federal budget;
3) the licencing of export of regional products;
4) the right to reduce customs duties for regional export producers;
5) the registration of foreign enterprises and joint ventures;
6) the right to establish a 'special economic regime'.

In summer 1993, the regional soviet embarked on a bolder political course. At its session on 8 July 1993, it declared its 'intention to establish, on the territory of the Primorskii *krai*, a state-territorial entity that has the constitutional-legal status of a republic in the Russian Federation' (UR, 16 July 1993, p.1). The vice chairman of the regional soviet, V. Butakov, called this a 'political step' and justified it by the desire to obtain equal rights with autonomous republics in the budgetary sphere and in the use of natural resources.[18] However, at the same time, the soviet required even more preferential treatment in foreign trade (tax holidays for joint ventures, customs preferences with the right to keep a portion of those duties within the province for infrastructural development).

Butov reported to the Russian President on 14 September 1993 that Nazdratenko seriously considered separating the region from the RF and that preliminary agreements on this with other Far Eastern provinces were reached (RG, 1 October 1994, p.2). Referring to information obtained from the chairman of the regional soviet, D. Grigorovich, Pavlov and Lebedinets were described in Butov's report as the ideologists of the proposed new state, who offered Grigorovich the post of President in exchange for his support.

The obvious political intention to press for more soft credits and further state subsidies becomes clear if one returns to the distinctive industrial structure. As was shown in Chapter 1, the regional economy was dominated by resource extraction and there was evidence of subsidised consumption implied by the official statistics showing that the region's national income utilised was 1.6 per cent of the Russian total in comparison with 1.3 per cent for produced national income in 1991 (Osipov, 1992, p.14). Moreover, transport from European Russia and Siberia had been subsidised. This suggests that a self-sufficient, independent economy could only have been attained at considerable cost. That in turn gives an idea of the high ambitions of the political leadership and its attempts at getting not only greater fiscal and budgetary autonomy, but also absolutist power in the region and, at the same time, perhaps, to seek continued subsidy from Moscow.

However, these actions attracted the attention of the central authorities, leading to a visit by the Russian Prime Minister, Viktor Chernomyrdin, in late August 1993. The Prime Minister's Far Eastern trip, which included stops in Kamchatka, Sakhalin and the Kurile islands, ended with a visit to the PK. The visit focused on 'key questions' of the fuel and energy complex, transportation and agriculture. The main regional demands included lower import duties and export tariffs, the consignment of all federal taxes to the province for three years, independence in determining annual export quotas and issuance of export licences (in fish and wood products) and the introduction of special local taxes on transit cargoes (RFEU, September 1993, p.6). As a result, the Prime Minister announced, once again, the preparation of a new decree on the socio-economic development of the PK and promised, in the form of an 'experiment', to leave all tax payments in the region (UR, 21 August 1993, p.1). These promises eventually materialised in the form of decree no.1001 of the Russian government on 8 October 1993 'On Urgent Measures of State Support for the Primorskii *Krai* Economy in 1993–5', which included a subsidy of R17bn for *Dal' energo* to keep prices for electricity at a level of R40 per kWh for industrial enterprises (UR, 12 November 1993, p.1).

Apart from Nazdratenko's unilateral decision to stop privatisation in vital spheres of the economy, this meant a further blow for substantial institutional restructuring, since prices for coal were also controlled at an even lower real level than during the Soviet period (taking inflation into account) of R1500 per t of coal until June 1994. The price which has now to be paid is much higher, since 90 per cent of the expenditures of local mining companies are subsidised by the federal budget,[19] payment arrears are rocketing and former interregional trade has been interrupted. This implied an open-ended commitment from the central authorities, who provided a further subsidy of R138bn in the first quarter of 1994 (Savalei, 1994, p.10),[20] but it is questionable whether they can afford to continue acceding to regional demands. After all, the fate of Russian economic reforms is at stake in this kind of bargaining and ensuing conflicts between the national agenda and different regional interests. Meanwhile, it gives a clear sign of what kind of influence regional leaders currently have on national policy making.

The exchange of political declarations only fuelled resentments at the regional level and helped to legitimise authoritarian power in the province. In late summer 1993, Nazdratenko's team continued to initiate 'democratically adopted resolutions' by the regional soviet, including the refusal to transfer federal taxes amounting to R71.8bn, which they claimed the Ministry of Finance owed them (UR, 17 September 1993, p.3), as well as the above discussed rejection of Yeltsin's edict on constitutional reform in September 1993 (UR, 28 September 1993, p.1). Only Yeltsin's reassertion of power after the October 1993 events could give the central authorities a short breathing space from regional demands and pressures for soft credits.

However, the election campaigns for regional parliaments in March 1994 very soon revived the old habits of regional leaders. At a press conference on 20 March 1994, Nazdratenko announced not only the delay of elections to the new regional parliament until October 1994, but also his renewed demand for a special economic status for the province as well as the administrative subordination of the Kurile islands to the jurisdiction of the PK (*Izvestiya*, 22 March 1994, p.1). These two demands remained among the most important regional policy issues challenging the centre for most of 1994.[21]

In summer 1994, Nazdratenko announced still more assertively his proposal to the President to subordinate the Kurile islands to his (Nazdratenko's) control, claiming to have a stronger position than Sakhalin *oblast'* to help the islands' economic problems. This came at the time when his own campaign to become the elected governor started. It was then considered as an additional attempt to get votes from fishermen as a potentially supportive electorate (KD, 3 August 1994, p.3). Using the fact of a difficult demographic situation with a high rate of out-migration in 1993 (261 from a total population of about 5000 in the Northern Kurile islands),[22] Nazdratenko accused the Sakhalin authorities of not supporting these territories and promised large investments by PK fishing and mining companies, if these islands were put under his rule (*Segodnya*, 6 September 1994, p.3). As with 'fighting' the mass influx of Chinese people into Russian territory, he tried to present himself again as the defender of Russian national interests, since all four islands are still under territorial dispute with Japan.

Yeltsin passed Nazdratenko's proposal on to governmental authorities for 'further investigation' (KD, 18 August 1994, p.3), but more importantly Nazdratenko could rely on strong encouragement by top officials in Moscow, notably the former head of the Russian secret service, S. Stepashin, who mentioned the possibility of an administrative fusion of Sakhalin *oblast'* and the Kurile islands with the PK at a meeting with businessmen in Nakhodka in June 1994 (RG, 1 October 1994, p.2). This rather supports the assumption made by Venevtsev and Demkin (1994, p.4) that the idea of bringing the Kurile islands under the jurisdiction of the PK comes from people in the President's entourage who are aiming not only to strengthen Russia's political assets against the Japanese, but also to make cuts in subsidies previously promised to these territories.[23] Furthermore, typhoons in the region in September 1994 and a devastating earthquake affecting the Kurile islands in October 1994 showed to what extent both regions are still dependent on the help of central authorities in emergency situations (*Segodnya*, 18 October 1994, p.2).[24]

Nazdratenko reiterated in summer 1994 his intention to get a special economic status granted to the region. He announced that a development programme for his region had been elaborated which included a 'preferential tax and investment policy regime for two to three years' (RV, 19 July 1994, p.2). However, this press release could be a big understatement of the scale of the special regime plans. In March 1994, he had already given a hint of a long term 'Hong Kong solution' during an interview for the American business journal *GQ*.

The internal version of his economic programme, which was made available to this author in September 1994, contained demands adding up to a total of R175.3trn (in August 1994 prices) to be paid by federal institutions in the period up to 2010.[25] These demands included among others:

1) higher revenues for regional authorities from state-controlled transit cargoes and freight transport which are crossing provincial territory;
2) federal subsidies for fuel and energy;
3) additional payments for regional enterprises in form of a special federal programme;
4) the consignment of all federal taxes to the region for a period of ten years;
5) the consignment of all state customs duties to the region for a period of four years;
6) restricted entry to the province for non-residents for a period of 10 years.

Nazdratenko justified these requirements later on the grounds that the region faced high transport charges for shipments from the rest of Russia, and that customs duties, export quotas and most taxes were controlled by central authorities (BBC interview on 1 October 1994). Most of the regional authorities agreed that these demands were unrealistic, but they also emphasised that they stood a better chance of getting more by putting higher requirements forward. For example, regionally collected state customs duties were expected to be left in the province at a rate of 35 per cent in 1994 compared with 10 per cent the year before.[26]

The third and politically most serious challenge to the centre was Nazdratenko's announcement of the election of the governor of the PK, which was to take place on 7 October 1994 in the form of an 'experiment' (KD, 30 July 1994, p.3). It was peculiar that this election was scheduled before the elections of the new regional Duma on 23 October 1994, which alone would have the legislative power to call for elections of the head of the executive branch (KD, 12 August 1994, p.3). Nazdratenko had the backing not only of main institutions in the region (FT, 27 October 1994, p.3), as was discussed above, but also of influential national leaders. The former head of the President's administration, Sergei Filatov, tried to delay Yeltsin's new decree, which would reassert the postponement of elections of provincial governors until the next Presidential elections in 1996, until the last minute (*Segodnya*, 29 September 1994, p.2). The then chairman of the Federation Council, Vladimir Shumeiko, supported publicly the election of the governor in the PK (*Segodnya*, 5 October 1994, p.2).

Five local democratic parties united to fight Nazdratenko in this election and announced Igor Ustinov, the former head of the Nakhodka FEZ administration and current deputy of the State Duma, as their candidate (KD, 19 August 1994, p.3).[27] However, Nazdratenko unilaterally took the decision that 32 000 signatures would be necessary for registration as a candidate (the Russian legislature requires merely 10 000) in an attempt to make sure that he would not face any serious competition (*Segodnya*, 29 September 1994, p.2). Ustinov could collect only 25 000 signatures,[28] which left merely two 'puppet opponents', who were promoted by Nazdratenko to give the whole campaign a democratic appearance. Nazdratenko also enforced public pressure on Ustinov by making a joint statement with Stepashin on Russian television about alleged fraud and embezzlement of public money by Ustinov when the latter was the head of the Nakhodka FEZ administration (KD, 31 August 1994, p.14).

This scheduled election had strong political implications. It was widely believed that this was a new attempt at separating the region from the RF. A new constitution of the province was already in preparation (*Vladivostok*, 20 September 1994, p.4), as the President requested from all provinces, and the day after the election a referendum could have been called for setting up an independent republic (RG, 1 October 1994, p.2). Only when the leaders of the democratic factions in the State Duma, Egor Gaidar, Boris Fedorov and Grigorii Yavlinskii, published a report in late September following their independent investigation of human rights' abuses, corruption and authoritarian power in the region (*Segodnya*, 29 September 1994, p.2), was the attention of the Russian public attracted. At this point President Yeltsin issued a new decree to strengthen his power in appointing governors until 1996 (RG, 7 October 1994, p.1). Nazdratenko backed down from his election two days before it was scheduled (*Segodnya*, 6 October 1994, p.3).

The two main challenges of the centre by Nazdratenko's administration until mid-1995 included a demand for the unilateral denunciation of the 1991 Russian-Chinese treaty on border demarcation in early 1995 and the new showdown with the government over subsidies as a result of the miners' strike in spring 1995, briefly discussed above.[29] In the second half of 1994, the regional leadership reinforced its nationalistic policy, expressing xenophobic paranoia against all non-Russian nationalities. This applied particularly to people from neighbouring China. In the border town of Ussuriisk, local officials declared Chinese traders as criminal elements, intimidating them with armed police, and stopped all foreigners from trading at the local market (UR, 25 October 1994, p.2). According to witnesses, Chinese people were regularly robbed and beaten up by the police, while a special repatriation camp for Chinese citizens was set up in one of the suburbs of Vladivostok during the police operation 'Foreigner', from which arrested people could get free only after paying $300 to the police (*Segodnya*, 3 March 1995, p.6).

This was encouraged by the Russian central press, which reported mass in-migration of Chinese people, the alleged robbery of Russian resources and the setting up of Chinatowns on Russian territory, which could lead, according to Russian commentators, to renewed territorial claims (DM, 6–12 March 1995, p.42).[30] One of the few realistic reports in the Russian central press was published in *Izvestiya* (16 March 1995, p.3), in which the author dismissed the Russian hysteria about a 'silent colonisation' by the Chinese, after he carried out close investigations in the Russian bordering regions and conducted interviews with their governors. A new police operation *Rubezh* was launched in the PK in April 1995, but only 200 illegal residents of Chinese nationality were identified (UR, 27 May 1995, p.1).

However, this xenophobic atmosphere was used by Nazdratenko to present himself to the public as the defender of Russian national interests in the periphery and to denounce the 1991 Russian-Chinese treaty on border demarcation in early 1995, declaring the 1500 ha of territory under question to be 'strategically important' (*Segodnya*, 14 February 1995, p.2).[31] This was reiterated by the new regional Duma (*Segodnya*, 23 February 1995, p.2), effectively embarrassing the Foreign Minister, Kozyrev, before he left for his official visit to China (*Izvestiya*, 3 March 1995, p.3). The regional leadership's position on this issue was enacted in the new provincial statute, which required a referendum in the PK before state borders could be redrawn (UR, 15 June 1995, p.2).

5.4 FORCES OF RESISTANCE

Nazdratenko did not for a long time face any serious institutional opposition, either from regional or from federal structures. As discussed in the previous chapter, politics in the RF is chiefly the politics of individual personalities due to a weak coherence of national parties and the turmoil in institutions. Hence, only a few people in the PK dared to resist authoritarian power and they could not rely on political or judicial structures. Among them were journalists working in the opposition press and media, the mayor of Vladivostok, Cherepkov, who became the spokesman for democratic groupings, defecting members of PAKT with their own economic and criminal structures as well as the democratic factions in the State Duma.

Nazdratenko's most blatant exercise of absolutist power was, apart from the attacks on the President's representative, Butov, the suspension of the critical mass-media in the province and the open showdown with the first democratically elected mayor of Vladivostok, Cherepkov. The commercial television channel PKTV was prevented from running its programmes, after compromising Nazdratenko's reputation by showing him publicly embracing putsch leader Alexander Rutskoi, and an assassination attempt was made on the author of this programme, M. Voznesenskii, on 15 November 1993 (Ostrovskaya, 1993, p.5).

Under the command of Lebedinets, fierce attacks were launched against the oppositional newspapers *Bolshoi Vladivostok* and *Utro Rossii*. Both were suspended on 21 March 1994, when it was claimed that there was a shortage of paper, while electricity and heating in their offices were switched off (*Izvestiya*, 6 April 1994, p.2). Critical journalists were regularly beaten up by hired criminal gangs (KD, 22 July 1994, p.14). When the former deputy governor and member of PAKT, Shkrabov, started to express a different opinion to that of Nazdratenko's team, there was an attempt to sack him as editor-in-chief and to suspend his newspaper *Krasnoe znamya* (UR, 17 September 1994, p.2). The regional publisher's monopoly, *Dal'press*, was under Nazdratenko's control and could deny newspapers paper, office space and other technical facilities (KD, 14 December 1994, p.3). For example, the printing and sale of those central newspapers, which maintained critical reporting on the events in the PK, was restricted in the region under the pretext that there was not sufficient paper (*Izvestiya*, 17 November 1994, p.1).

Systematic measures were undertaken to undermine the authority of Vladivostok's mayor, Cherepkov, including the switching-off of water and electric power, a cut in the city's share of the consolidated regional budget from 16.8 per cent to 8.4 per cent, the sudden off-loading of one-third of the total housing stock of Vladivostok from former sectoral ministries onto the municipal authorities and acts of sabotage on heating systems (Smirnova, 1993, p.2). In order to undermine the city's tax base, local enterprises had to pay their taxes directly into the regional budget and the city administration was denied export quotas for fish, wood and mineral fertilizers in 1993 (KD, 7 June 1995, p.14).

Cherepkov was elected in summer 1993 and embarked on a number of measures that were unpopular with the huge administrative apparatus in the city. His main suggestion for administrative reform was to dissolve city districts, which would reduce the number of state employees from 6500 to 1000 (UR, 8 October 1993, p.2). In reply, the regional administration issued a statement that city district councils should not comply with Cherepkov's commands (UR, 11 March 1994, p.1). The mayor, for his part, sought popular support by providing free public transport and trying to break the bread and fish monopolies through opening new bakeries and fish markets (Smirnova, 1993, p.2).

The campaign against Cherepkov was reinforced at the end of 1993. On 30 December 1993, Lebedinets sent an emergency call to Moscow, reporting the alleged breakdown of the heating system, paralysed public transport and medical aid not working in Vladivostok, for which he blamed Cherepkov (UR, 6 January 1994, p.1). On 11 February 1994, an apparent plot was started against the mayor, when the city procurator and a number of armed policemen investigated his office for alleged acceptence of bribes. During the inspection, R1.2mn were reported to have been placed in his safe and another R1mn to have been left in one of his coats, during an investigation of his flat (UR, 15 February 1994, p.1). Cherepkov was kept in custody for a day or so and his son was also arrested, being accused of theft of a computer from his school a year earlier, for which he was later sentenced to prison for seven years (FT, 27 October 1994, p.3). At this time, Vladivostok's mayor had to be released after public protest; he was later evicted from his office on 17 March 1994 by armed police under orders from Nazdratenko (UR, 18 March 1994, p.1). He was also beaten up by criminal gangs on 2 August 1994 (KD, 4 August 1994, p.14).

In late 1994, Cherepkov was cleared of all charges of accepting bribes by the Russian attorney general A. Il'yushenko (*Segodnya*, 6 December 1994, p.2). However, only a few days later Yeltsin sacked Cherepkov for 'violating the legislation of the Russian Federation and for not fulfilling his public duties for a long period of time' (*Izvestiya*, 27 December 1994, p.4). For Cherepkov, who was kept in custody and not allowed to get into his office for more than four months, this could not have been a more ridiculous statement, and it is questionable whether Yeltsin really knew what he was signing. In spring 1995, three former police officers, who took part in Cherepkov's eviction from his office, were made scapegoats and arrested, while no charges have been made against Nazdratenko at the time of writing (KD, 25 May 1995, p.14).

One of the 'famous representatives of the local criminal underworld',[32] and a close ally of Nazdratenko, K. Tolstoshein, who received less than one per cent of the votes during the election of the new mayor of Vladivostok in June 1993 (UR, 16 June 1993, p.1), was appointed by the governor as Cherepkov's successor. He sought popular support among former military officers and soldiers who had served in Afghanistan and war veterans (RG, 11 May 1994, p.3). He also hired criminal gangs to beat up journalists, who produced a critical programme about him on radio (UR, 7 June 1995, p.2).

The strong stress on personalities in the analysis of the regional political situation is due not only to the blurred regional institutional structures, but also, as has been noted, to the weak coherence of national parties and their representation in the province. Voters' preferences and political sympathies are scattered, as is shown in the analysis of the results of the elections to the new Russian parliament in December 1993 in Table 5.2.

One of the striking features was that the Communist Party and the Agrarian Party received a considerably smaller share of the vote in the PK than they did in both Russia as a whole and Nizhnii Novgorod *oblast'*, which is widely perceived as a region with a strong reputation for reform. While 'Women of Russia' got substantially stronger support in the Far Eastern region due to the prominence of its regional leader and former Yeltsin aide, Svetlana Goryacheva, the same importance of personalities applied to Nizhnii Novgorod for the Yavlinskii-Boldyrev-Lukin bloc, since Yavlinskii had chosen this region for his market reform experiment.[33]

However, the support for Yeltsin's policy in the PK decreased from 730 000 votes in June 1990 and 572 000 at the April 1993 referendum to 244 000 (total vote for the four leading democratic parties) on 12 December 1993, while 130 000 citizens in the province voted for

Table 5.2 Results of the Federation-wide election to the State Duma in the Primorskii *Krai* by party consideration compared with Russia as a whole and Nizhnii Novgorod *oblast'*, 12 December 1993 (in per cent of the total vote)

Party	Russia	Primorskii *Krai*	Nizhnii Novgorod *Obl.*
Liberal Democratic Party	22.8	21.9	19.2
Russia's Choice	15.4	13.2	13.4
Communist Party of RF	12.3	8.1	11.8
Women of Russia	8.1	14.3	9.3
Agrarian Party	7.9	2.3	8.7
Yavlinskii-Boldyrev-Lukin	7.8	7.9	11.6
Party of Russian Unity and Accord	6.8	7.5	5.3
Democratic Party of Russia	5.5	6.8	6.8
Russian Movement for Dem. Reform	4.0	5.2	n.a.
Other	9.4	12.8	13.9

Source: Compiled from *Kuranty*, 28 December 1993, p.1; UR, 16 December 1993, p.1 and Cline (1994, p.51)

Zhirinovskii's Liberal Democratic Party (Brodyanskii, 1994, p.2). The last two figures do not only reflect the lower turnout in the 1993 elections, but also confusion about different policies pursued by national parties in the regions. While Zhirinovskii's party is widely perceived in the West as an ultra-nationalist party, the local office of this party joined the 'Club of Democrats' in Vladivostok and supported mayor Cherepkov.[34] Moreover, the regional administration tried also to combat mass apathy during the run-up to the elections. It was reported that 'Igor Lebedinets ... sent a circular to factory managers asking them to "take exhaustive measures to guarantee that the referendum succeeds", including handing out grants for clothes, food and heating' (*The Guardian*, 13 December 1993, p.8). This resulted, at least, in a 71.7 per cent 'yes' vote for the new constitution (UR, 16 December 1993, p.1).

The activity of national political parties in the PK is characterised by weak links with their national party headquarters, and by low membership and generally weak potential support as indicated in Table 5.3.

Although the estimates in Table 5.3 are only tentative, they appear to support the notion of a revival of Communist Party structures, as has already been found in the previous chapter. Members of the provincial communist parties tried to integrate the Social-Democratic Party and the Democratic Party of Russia in a patriotic movement 'Accord in the Name

Table 5.3 Estimated membership and potential voters for leading national parties in Primorskii *Krai*, September 1994 (in absolute figures)

Party	Members	Potential Voters
Communist Parties	150	20–30 000
Party of Russian Unity and Accord	100	n.a.
Social-Democratic Party	40	300–400
Russia's Choice	20–30	500
Democratic Party of Russia	15–20	200
Party of Economic Freedom	15	150–200
Liberal-Democratic Party	5	n.a.

Note: 'Communist Parties' refers to both the 'Russian Communist Workers Party' and the 'Communist Party of the Russian Federation'.

Source: Compiled from interviews with lecturers of the department of political science of the Far Eastern State University in Vladivostok, I. Sanachev and G. Kulikov, on 15 and 19 September 1994

of Russia' (UR, 10 September 1994, p.1), but it remains to be seen what real impact this could make on regional policy making. The representation of political parties in the new regional Duma was only marginal, as was shown in Table 5.1, and they could not organise strong opposition to the rise of authoritarian power in the province. In contrast, Nazdratenko became the Far Eastern coordinator of Chernomyrdin's centrist political bloc 'Our Home Russia' in spring 1995 (*Segodnya*, 13 May 1995, p.2), which gave him additional institutional backing for his power.

Other forces of resistance to Nazdratenko included defecting members of PAKT, notably its former general director, Pavlov, after executives of this conglomerate, representing three leading regional enterprises, split up in summer 1994 (KD, 2 August 1994, p.3). Pavlov then claimed the role of a 'shadow governor' and declared his aim of setting up a strong oppositional group to force Nazdratenko to step down. However, although he even sought a rapprochement with Ustinov and Cherepkov, his prediction that Nazdratenko would not survive the summer of 1994 was not borne out.[35] Strong resistance to an important element of Nazdratenko's policies came also from the energy lobby, which declared that they would increase, from 1 November 1994, prices for electric power for households from R4–6 to R25 per kWh and for industrial enterprises from R40 to R54 per kWh. This announcement was made immediately after the election of the governor was cancelled (KD, 14 October 1994, p.11).[36]

In Moscow, opposition to Nazdratenko's autocratic power is of a somewhat ambiguous nature. Although the State Duma had a hearing on human rights' abuses in the PK on 5 October 1994 (*Segodnya*, 4 October 1994, p.2) and several governmental commissions had already been sent to the region to investigate, Nazdratenko is still, at the time of writing, firmly in power. The only explanation for this seems to be that certain top officials in the centre have a particular interest in keeping such an authoritarian governor in power on Russia's periphery. Apart from Nazdratenko's allies Filatov, Stepashin, Ilyushin and Shumeiko, who were already mentioned above, he could also use his contacts with the former attorney general, Alexei Ilyushenko, to delay all investigations when he was accused of violating human rights (UR, 18 March 1994, p.1). Direct access to the office of the then Vice-Prime Minister Oleg Soskovets was used while lobbying for preferential treatment.[37] Soskovets was Nazdratenko's boss as the former Minister for Metallurgy in the USSR (*Izvestiya*, 19 January 1995, p.5), when the latter still worked as the director of the mining company *Vostok* in 1991. The former also headed several governmental meetings to solve financial problems in the PK (UR, 29 October 1994, p.1).

The positions of President Yeltsin and Prime Minister Chernomyrdin are ambivalent. Nazdratenko accompanied them frequently when they went on state visits to Asian countries. Yeltsin rewarded Nazdratenko with the medal 'For Personal Bravery' after the rather mysterious explosion at an ammunition store in Novonezhino in May 1994 (KD, 12 August 1994, p.3). Nazdratenko reportedly used to spend his weekends in the President's dacha. In late 1994, Nazdratenko was invited to join the 'President's Club', an informal group of advisers consisting of 30 members (UR, 19 November 1994, p.1).

Chernomyrdin was a strong supporter of subsidies for the region to keep prices for electricity at a level of R40 per kWh. For this purpose, R134bn was received in the first quarter of 1994 (KD, 30 July 1994, p.3). However, the centre seems to have used these subsidies as a strong political lever, since they were not given after the beginning of August 1994, when Nazdratenko announced the election of the governor, while payments were resumed after he backed down (KD, 14 October 1994, p.11). This suggests an ambiguous and dangerous policy on the part of national leaders. They were apparently not prepared to challenge authoritarian rule by politicians like Nazdratenko even at the price of human rights' abuses, corruption and crime; at the same time, they seem to have resisted an attempt on his part to acquire democratic legitimacy. Nazdratenko finally managed to get a popular mandate when earlier elections of the governor were staged in December 1995, winning more than 60 per cent of the votes.

5.5 ARE THERE ANY CONSTRAINTS ON AUTHORITARIAN POWER?

Although Nazdratenko's apparently omnipotent power had been reduced in 1994–5, at the time of writing he is still firmly in control of his public office and private business.[38] While his former closest allies and leading executives of PAKT defected (Pavlov, Shkrabov, Lebedinets), Nazdratenko's power base, which is represented by the regional management nomenklatura, is still largely intact. The regional Duma, which started its legislative work after the re-elections in mid-January 1995, is mainly composed of local heads of administration (who were appointed by Nazdratenko before), managers and the military. Thus, there is a complete subordination of the legislative branch to the executive administration; even more so after Lebedinets was ousted from his post as chairman of the provincial Duma in June 1995. Only a few days later, the provincial parliament approved a law on the election of the governor in the PK (KD, 23 June 1995, p.4), which would take place – according to the newly-adopted statute of the region (UR, 15 June 1995, p.4) – six months after the latter was enacted, which ensured Nazdratenko a confident victory.

Moreover, the judiciary provides no guarantee of due process and proper legal order in the region. Oppositional political forces can be brutally intimidated and suppressed with the help of criminal gangs. The local media can be muzzled. Finally, national leaders in Moscow seem not only to have only limited real leverage over Nazdratenko, but they also appear to have a strong interest in keeping such an autocratic politician in power in a peripheral province, which is perceived to be vital for Russian national interests. Thus, there seems to be a real danger of regional warlordism and little constraint on authoritarian power.

This applies particularly to institutional arrangements. Nazdratenko controls not only the appointment of officials of both the regional executive and legislative branches, but also of authorities of the federal structures in his province (army, police, tax inspection). He could simply capitalise on the fact that institutional arrangements in Russian centre-periphery relations remained blurred, administrative competences were not clearly defined and that Moscow did not draw a clear line between central and provincial/local property and taxes, which left the struggle for control over economic resources open-ended. Most importantly, there were a number of contentious constitutional issues in which shared functions between the centre and standard provinces (ownership of territorial resources, foreign trade) were not clearly defined. The sheer mountain of contradictory central decrees and regulations enabled regional authorities to interpret law to their own advantage.

This also strengthened existing elitist policies and vertical networks of patron-client relations in Russian regions, of which the PK provides a striking example. Not functional separation of politics and economics at the provincial level, but institutional entanglement and local corporatism appear to drive the dynamics of Russian regional development. This could confine economic activity to particular clusters of regions and strengthen regional monopolies. Instead of powerful central branch ministries, Russia might end up with all-embracing FIGs growing along regional lines. One might speculate whether an organisation like PAKT can succeed in monopolising the regional economy in the medium and long term, in particular if operating in geographic proximity to leading financial and trade centres like Japan and South Korea, but it can clearly slow down the development of an open and competitive regional economy in the short term.

During the last few years, Vladivostok has become one of the main centres of drug trafficking, arms deals and money laundering in Russia. Its autocratic leadership, pursuing a policy of insider control and administrative protectionism of the economy, strong nationalism and political suppression of all oppositional forces, could be on the way to marginalising the region and realising the city's potential to take on a role for Russia that Palermo has for Italy. Hopes for a successful transformation from a formerly closed military fortress to a gateway for active integration of the Russian economy into the world market, even in Nazdratenko's vision of an authoritarian Hong Kong solution, could then be buried quickly.

6 Gateway Versus Agrarian Region: Institutional Restructuring and Economic Adaptation

The process of economic transformation as it affects Russian regions includes two major elements that influence centre-periphery relations: the depoliticisation of the economy and the setting up of a new institutional structure, which would force both policy makers and economic agents to respond effectively to price and interest rate signals, and would introduce competition from outsiders and the hardening of soft budget constraints. While the first issue was extensively discussed in the previous two chapters, we now look at institutional restructuring in terms of its profound impact on new centre-periphery relations as a result of the change of ownership rights, fiscal arrangements and capital investment. Although traditional practices and attitudes of regional authorities such as rent seeking and risk aversion prevailed, they were also increasingly forced to search for new ways to mobilise internal resources, and this will be examined with respect to foreign trade and municipal bonds.

Whereas the first chapter introduced the industrial structure and economic performance of the PK and AK as of late 1993, this one investigates institutional changes under way in 1994 and early 1995, focusing on privatisation, regional price policy, fiscal arrangements, capital investment, and foreign trade in subsequent sections. This should give a better understanding of the kind of policy factors on which economic adaptation currently depends in Russian regions, given their substantial differences in geographical location, resource endowment, industrial structure and provincial politics.[1]

However, available quantitative data should be treated with considerable caution. Reported results on privatisation differed substantially between various provincial institutions, while budget figures were constantly being corrected, unregistered retail trade and unlicenced foreign trade remained unreported.[2] As outlined in the first chapter, information based on statistical data received from regional administrations and *Goskomstat* provincial offices (and in some cases published in the local press) will be preferred in this analysis,[3] while also, where possible, incorporating total figures for

Russia as a whole. Finally, budget figures for 1994 were hardly available due to an increasing secretiveness of provincial authorities towards outsiders (including central officials).[4] There were particular difficulties in obtaining end-1994 data for the PK, which makes it necessary in some cases to provide figures either for the third quarter of 1994 or the first quarter of 1995.

6.1 PRIVATISATION

In previous chapters it was argued that regional authorities' attitude towards market reform had a major impact on institutional changes, and also played an important role in determining how and at what speed privatisation would be carried out as well as who the potential beneficiaries would be. This makes it necessary to provide, beside numerical data, some background information on qualitative changes in major sectors of the economy in both regions. This combination of quantitative and qualitative analysis will be applied for medium- and large-scale privatisation, small-scale privatisation, private farming and housing privatisation.

Medium and large-scale privatisation

Table 6.1 indicates results of privatisation of medium- and large-sized enterprises by industrial sector relying on data provided from regional committees of property administration.

Despite the time difference of nine months for the available data in Table 6.1,[5] higher percentage results in the AK seem to indicate a much stronger privatisation policy in this region, which was mainly due to a reform-minded team in charge of privatisation in 1992–4. In contrast, as described in Chapter 5, governor Nazdratenko stopped privatisation in 'vital spheres of the economy' in the PK in August 1993, putting a large number of enterprises under the control of the regional conglomerate PAKT – which probably explains the difference in the number of enterprises which applied for privatisation and those actually privatised.

According to regional *Goskomstat* information, a total of 1195 privatised enterprises in the PK in the first quarter of 1995 (UR, 27 April 1995, p.2) compares with a total of 2182 in the AK at the beginning of 1995 (AP, 29 April 1995, p.6), but this gives no indication of the number of all enterprises (including those not released for privatisation) in both regions. Since the branch coverage in Table 6.1 is incomplete, there is no reason for columns 2 and 5 to sum to anything close to these total amounts. One

Table 6.1 Privatised medium- and large-sized enterprises in the Altaiskii and Primorskii *Kraya* compared with Russia as a whole by some sectors of industry, July 1994–April 1995 (in absolute figures and % of applications)

Sector of Industry	PK (1 Sept 1994) applied	priv.	%	AK (1 April 1995) applied	priv.	%	RF total (1 July '94) priv. %
Light industry	23	7	30.4	n.a.	n.a.	–	48.0
Food industry	107	18	16.8	120	113	94.1	47.0
Construction industry	172	46	26.7	315	250	79.4	35.0
Construction materials	73	15	20.5	n.a.	n.a.	–	46.0
Agricultural industry	100	32	32.0	262	214	81.7	n.a.
Transport industry	73	4	5.5	99	91	91.9	n.a.
Wholesale trade	62	23	37.1	39	35	89.7	47.0

Note: Going through the procedure of 'applying' for privatisation was mandatory for many enterprises, so the number that 'applied' should not, in principle, be dependent on local initiative.

Source: *Osnovnye pokazateli khoda privatizatsii na territorii Primorskogo kraya po sostoyaniyu na 1 sentyabrya 1994*, Komitet po upravleniyu gosudarstvennym imushchestvom Primorskogo kraya, Vladivostok: 1994 (mimeo); *Osnovnye pokazateli khoda privatizatsii na territorii Altaiskogo kraya po sostoyaniyu na 1 aprelya 1995*, Komitet po upravleniyu gosudarstvennym imushchestvom Altaiskogo kraya, Barnaul: 1995 (mimeo) and Radygin (1994, p.155)

intriguing fact is that in both statistical reports used in Table 6.1 none of the defence-related sectors (machine-building and metalworking) nor those structures under state control (fuel and energy production) were included, which may reflect a central monopoly on information about these sectors.[6]

Some specific features of the industrial structure in both provinces have to be taken into account. A large amount of industrial infrastructure in the PK was traditionally under direct control of defence-related ministries or was declared of significant state importance. This complicated, for example, the privatisation of shipping companies and ports. Although 15 per cent of the shares of the 'Far Eastern Shipping Company' were acquired by foreign investors by the end of 1994, the control package was still officially under control of the state at that time, which led to numerous regulations about management and employment (UR, 15 October 1994, p.1–2).[7] Foreign investment could not bail out the Vladivostok based trawling fleet, which was reported to be on the brink of bankruptcy in late 1994 (*Segodnya*, 15 November 1994, p.3).[8] As discussed in Chapter 5, both companies were not only under the control of PAKT, but also involved in corruption and money laundering.

Despite the involvement of foreign investors, they remained under strong insider control, which was criticised in the Western academic discussion not only in terms of equity and efficiency, but also for state intervention, paternalism and protectionism (Sutela, 1994, p.431). Such structures could use the PAKT conglomerate for rent-seeking and they managed to commit the government to what Frydman and Rapaczynski (1993, p.41) called a 'system of political enterprise governance'. Similarly, the management of the fishing fleet *Primorrybprom*, which was also incorporated into PAKT, got 55 per cent of the shares under their control in early 1995, for 23 per cent of which they reportedly received money from the regional budget (UR, 20 April 1995, p.2). Such examples provide hardly any evidence of thorough-going market reform, which requires companies to be open to competition and to the possibility of effective outside control.

The lack of structural changes in the PK may be illustrated by the mining company *Primorskugol'*, which employed 34 000 people in September 1994 and had to be almost completely subsidised due to Nazdratenko's populist policy of controlling prices for coal at R1500 per t until June 1994, which was far less than production costs.[9] This probably contributed to a decline of annual output from 22.4mn t in 1988 to only 11.4mn t in 1994 (UR, 12 April 1995, p.1). Forty per cent of the shares remained under the control of the management (UR, 18 April 1995, p.2), which was reportedly not interested in any restructuring, keeping their former social infrastructure and workforce (UR, 7 April 1995, p.2). Loss-making coal mines were not closed down, which led to further payment arrears, while workers did not receive any wages between December 1994 and April 1995.[10] This provoked industrial action, including a miners' hunger strike in Partizanskii *raion*, which attracted national attention, because regional authorities tried, as discussed in the previous chapter, to use the strike immediately for their own political ends, demanding more subsidies and central credits for the region (*Izvestiya*, 26 April 1995, p.1).

The considerably higher number of enterprises released for privatisation in construction and agricultural industries in the AK, as shown in Table 6.1, is probably due to the traditional industrial specialisation of the Altai. While a reform-minded team was in charge of privatisation in the AK in 1992–4, they were, as described in Chapter 4, increasingly assimilated to the power base of the traditional nomenklatura through the adoption of a new provincial law on privatisation in summer 1994. The law not only demanded the agreement of both executive and legislative branches as well as the working collective, but also included new preferences for the working collective to acquire shares (AP, 26 July 1994, p.2) and the setting-up of quangos for post-privatisation support of enterprises. A typical feature of local corporatism in the Altai was the creation of holding companies such as the monopolist-producer of agricultural machinery in the region *Altaisel'mash* (AP, 29 October 1994, p.4) and the defence-related enterprise *Barnaultransmash* (AP, 7 December 1994, p.1), which left industrial ministries strong legal control; and a special regime of tax holidays for holding companies was proposed (AP, 4 April 1995, p.2).

Small-scale privatisation

There was a somewhat greater availability of data for privatisation in the spheres of retail trade, public catering and services, as evidenced in Table 6.2, but a great deal of caution in interpretation is necessary here as well. For example, 250 outlets in Vladivostok city were reportedly privatised by the end of 1993, which amounted to 75.7 per cent of the total according to official statistics (UR, 11 December 1993, p.2). However, the comparison with 1990, when Vladivostok had more than 1000 shops, catering and service outlets, reveals that at least two-thirds of the original premises were restructured, closed or passed on to other commercial structures, without the city authorities getting control of them, which gives reason to doubt any favourable interpretation of the official statistics.

Despite the considerable time differences in available data, a certain pattern of privatisation policy becomes clear. While the PK was far slower

Table 6.2 Results of small-scale privatisation in the Altaiskii and Primorskii *Kraya* compared with Russia as a whole, September 1994–April 1995 (in absolute figures and % of applications)

Sphere	PK (1 Sept 1994)		%	AK (1 April 1995)		%	Russia (Nov 1994)		%
	appl.	priv.		appl.	priv.		appl.	priv.	
Retail trade	811	680	83.8	706	478	67.7	84 857	57 703	68.0
Public catering	133	114	85.7	207	143	69.1	21 056	14 739	70.0
Services	361	288	79.8	546	472	86.4	38 451	29 992	78.0

Source: see Table 6.1 and RET, 3(4) 1994, p.97

in medium- and large-scale privatisation than the AK (and presumably Russia as a whole), its regional authorities adopted a high-speed small-scale privatisation with reported results far exceeding those of the Russian total even two months earlier.[11] This resulted reportedly in the breakdown of retail trade and the provision of services in many rural areas in the PK (UR, 21 April 1995, p.2).

Whereas the AK had, in contrast, a much higher rate of privatised medium- and large-sized enterprises compared with the PK, its reported results in retail trade and public catering were just in the range of those for Russia as a whole (but only five months later), while those in services were generally high in most parts of the RF. The lower results in small-scale privatisation in the AK are mainly due to the strong resistance towards privatisation in rural areas. Moreover, the change in ownership rights did not necessarily lead to an improvement in the quality of provided services, with many new owners just closing down or trading their premises,[12] while the widely criticised decline in trade of basic food products is probably more a result of local price controls. This applies much more to the AK, while the PK was 'flooded' with cheap imports, particularly from neighbouring China.

Private farming

The regional authorities' attitude towards institutional restructuring is also reflected in results of private farming as shown in Table 6.3. The AK with

Table 6.3 Private farming in the Altaiskii and Primorskii *Kraya* compared with Russia as a whole, late 1994–early 1995

Indicators	Russia (1994)	AK (Q3'94)	% of Russia	PK (Q1'95)	% of Russia
Number of private farms	279 200	6917	2.5	4022	1.4
Used arable land ('000 ha)	12 005.6	729.9	6.1	73.3	0.6
Average size of land per private farm (ha and % of Russian average)	43.0	105.5	245.3	18.2	42.3
Average percentage of the total arable land in the examined territory	5.2	10.0	–	10.0	–

Source: Compiled from RET, 3(4) 1994, p.69–70; AP, 3 November 1994, p.3 and UR, 27 April 1995, p.3

1.0 per cent of Russia's territory and 1.8 per cent of its population has a relatively high number of private farms, which are cultivating 6.1 per cent of the total privately used arable land in Russia, having more than twice the national average size of land per private farm. Although 10 per cent of the total arable land in the PK is also privately owned (which is twice the RF average), the average size of land per private farm amounts merely to less than half of the national average, which indicates a lower proportional total of arable land in the PK.[13]

However, one should not read too much into these figures. In the PK, 20 000 ha of land were reportedly given to Cossacks for farming in 1994 (UR, 25 October 1994, p.3), but it is not clear whether they really engaged in private farming, since they were used by regional authorities as an additional force to protect the Russian border against Chinese illegal migration, and land guards are part of the traditional Russian state 'deal' with Cossacks.[14] Moreover, the committee for land reform of the PK administration had a distinct anti-reform stance, calling for 'regulation of the state agro-industrial complex' and 'new cooperation' (UR, 13 April 1995, p.2).

The same is true for regional authorities in the AK, where the head of the provincial *Agropromsoyuz*, Nazarchuk, rejected publicly the free sale of land only a few months before he was appointed Russian Minister of Agriculture (AP, 9 June 1994, p.2). The AK administration gave a soft credit of R350mn to the regional farmers' association in early 1995 (AP, 1 March 1995, p.1), which looks rather meagre if compared with subsidies for former state structures (see Section 6.3).[15] Although successful private farming was reported for several *raiony* in the AK,[16] this could be further evidence for the view that the regional differentiation of privatisation procedures led generally to a strengthening of the existing industrial and agrarian elites.

Housing privatisation

The pattern of housing privatisation did not differ substantially among the investigated regions as evidenced in Table 6.4.

Both regions have an above average percentage share of privatised housing relative to their population. In Russia as a whole, 32 per cent of all flats to be privatised were reported to be in private hands by the end of 1994 (RET, 3(4) 1994, p.98), which compares with almost 50 per cent in the AK (AP, 2 February 1995, p.3) and about one third in the PK if the total housing stock is taken as a basis (UR, 28 July 1994, p.2).[17] The almost identical figures for living space per privatised flat indicate the standardised type of former Soviet housing. The above national average

Table 6.4 Housing privatisation in the Altaiskii and Primorskii *Kraya* compared with Russia as a whole, 1994–early 1995

Indicator	Russia (1994)	AK (1994)	% of Russia	PK (Q1'95)	% of Russia
Population ('000)	148 400.0	2684.3	1.8	2287.0	1.5
Number of privatised flats ('000)	10 923.0	284.9	2.6	225.0	2.1
Total living space ('000 sqm)	n.a.	13 600.0	–	10 676.3	–
Living space per flat (sqm)	n.a.	47.7	–	47.4	–

Source: Compiled from Table 1.1; RET, 3(4) 1994, p.98; AP, 2 February 1995, p.3 and UR, 27 April 1995, p.2

results in both provinces are probably due to the reform-minded leadership in urban areas, particularly in Vladivostok city in 1992–3 and Barnaul city in 1992–4. Moreover, as Struyk and Daniel (1995, p.206) found from their study of 5000 households privatised in seven Russian cities which did not show significant inter-city differences, ordinary Russian citizens seem to favour housing privatisation in general, particularly elderly people with a prospect of bequeathing the property.

Unemployment

A last issue to examine within the area of institutional restructuring is that of open and hidden unemployment as shown in Table 6.5.

Statistical data on open and hidden unemployment should shed some light on enterprise managements' adaptation to an increasingly changing economic environment, including more competition and hardening budget constraints. By international standards, Russia has still a relatively low rate of official unemployment. However, figures for hidden unemployment in both regions suggest that the real problem of unemployment is much more serious, while managers still favour a paternalistic survival strategy, maintaining the existing working collective. This is partly a result of the excess wage tax, which discourages labour shedding by taxing some of the savings in labour costs (Fan and Schaffer, 1994, p.168). Moreover, this is also due to the predominantly adopted second option of voucher

Table 6.5 Open and hidden unemployment in the Altaiskii and Primorskii *Kraya* compared with Russia as a whole, 1994–early 1995 (in absolute figures and % of total labour)

Indicator	Russia (1 May 1995)	%	AK (1994)	%	PK (Q1'95)	%
Population ('000)	148 400.0	100.0	2684.3	1.8	2287.0	1.5
Total Workforce ('000 and % of population)	73 540.7	49.5	1515.8	56.5	1006.3	44.0
Number of registered unemployed ('000)	1985.6	2.7	28.8	1.9	21.9	2.2
Hidden unemployment ('000)	n.a.	–	230.0	15.1	159.0	15.8
Number of people applying for one vacancy	6.0	–	8.3	–	4.0	–

Note: 'Hidden unemployment' refers to people, who are on short-time shifts or forced work-leave, while still being officially employed and receiving wages, which are mostly lower than normally.

Source: Compiled from Table 1.1; DM, 29 May–4 June 1995, p.42; *Sostoyanie zanyatosti na rynke truda kraya v 1994 godu*, Komitet administratsii Altaiskogo kraya po zanyatosti naseleniya, Barnaul, 1995, p.3–8; AP, 12 January 1995, p.1 and UR, 27 April 1995, p.2

privatisation, which gives the working collective the control over 51 per cent of the shares, exerting additional pressure on the management to avoid mass redundancies.

The lower percentage figure of total workforce in the PK relative to the population is probably due to earlier retirement of military personnel. The fact that twice as many people in the AK are applying for one vacancy compared with the PK is perhaps explained by the fact that there are more informal employment opportunities in the latter region including 'shuttle trade'. However, both regions seem to be faced with much smaller problems of unemployment if compared with the average rate in their macroregion as shown in Table A.23 in the appendix.[18]

6.2 REGIONAL PRICE POLICY

As discussed in previous chapters, regional authorities in most of the Russian regions had a considerable leverage over price liberalisation, developing a populist 'consumption bias', through which they tried to increase their votes at the ballot box by lowering transformation costs.[19] This applied to both investigated regions, where price controls impeded structural reforms and provincial officials had to cover an increasing bill for industrial and consumer price subsidies. Both provinces were heavily dependent on outside supply of fuel and energy, while authorities committed themselves to price compensations in these sectors in particular.

Industrial prices

While subsidies and soft credits from the federal budget were mostly for agriculture and the defence and coal industries, provincial officials provided additional financial help in these spheres as well. As noted before in Chapter 4, the first session of the new regional parliament in the AK announced price regulation as one of its main political goals in March 1994 (AP, 31 March 1994, p.1). One year later, a special agreement was signed between the AK 'Association of Entrepreneurs', trade unions and the regional administration to control not only prices for food, but also major industrial goods, tariffs and services, which were, however, not explicit in the document (AP, 21 March 1995, p.2). In a special report, governor Korshunov outlined his policy approach of keeping charges for fuel and energy at preferential terms, but he also admitted the increase of budgetary expenditures which these commitments caused (AP, 21 June 1994, p.1). Special subsidies for livestock production were provided from the provincial budget in summer 1994 (AP, 27 August 1994, p.2), while R6.2bn were reportedly spent from the AK budget offsetting price rises of concentrated feed in late 1994 (AP, 19 November 1994, p.2).

As outlined in the previous section, industrial prices for coal and electricity in the PK were heavily controlled by the regional administration, resulting in a drop of output by 15 per cent in the first half of 1994 alone (UR, 28 July 1994, p.2). The cheap energy is still a general feature of Russian economic policy. While the IPI rose by 235 per cent in Russia as a whole in 1994, average energy prices (including raw fuels, petroleum products and electricity) increased by only 200 per cent (RET, 3(4) 1994, p.41–2); energy became 11 per cent cheaper in real terms in that year. However, industrial prices between the regions differed widely.[20] For example, industrial enterprises in the PK were charged for electricity R40 per kWh in mid-1994, while those in Sakhalin *oblast'* had to pay R218,[21] which amounted to a price difference of more than 1:5.

As a consequence, payment arrears accumulated between coal mines, energy producers and industrial enterprises. Debts of *Primorskugol'* customers were reported to total R70bn by the end of 1994 (UR, 24 December 1994, p.1). This became a vicious circle, since coal producers could not pay for the electricity they used either; the only solution that was considered was to press for new subsidies and soft credits from the centre. However, after Moscow cut the monthly subsidies for the TEK in the PK to R43bn in the first quarter of 1995, industrial prices for electricity were raised to R287 per kWh, which reportedly increased the debts of coal producers in the region to a total of R200bn by 1 March 1995 (KD, 3 March 1995, p.11). This in turn produced arrears of wage payments in the mines.

After miners went on strike in the Partizansk *raion* and a special commission was sent from Moscow to investigate the financial situation of *Primorskugol'*, it was revealed that federal subsidies had been misused by regional authorities. For example, a R17bn transfer from the federal budget had reportedly ended up in various private and semi-private businesses (*Izvestiya*, 7 April 1995, p.1). This is a clear example of the extent to which inflationary behaviour was institutionalised in policy making circles and in industrial management in Russia in ways that combined rent-seeking and corruption. The company's subsidiary *Primorskuglesbyt*, which sells the coal, could still report a profit of R2.9bn in 1994 (UR, 18 April 1995, p.2). Moreover, funds earmarked for wage payments to PK miners, totalling R617bn, were sent from Moscow in early 1995, from which the miners had actually received only R23bn by April 1995 (DM, 13 April 1995, p.4).

Expenditures of *Primorskugol'* were reportedly subsidised from the federal budget by 80 per cent and those of the Far Eastern energy company *Dal'energo*, which controls the electricity grid in the PK, by 65 per cent in early 1995 (FI, 18 April 1995, p.11). According to this analysis, *Dal'energo* paid only 50 per cent of its debts to regional coal producers in 1994 and 10 per cent in the first two months of 1995. Moreover, provincial authorities had a strong leverage over the disposal of federal subsidies for the TEK, reportedly passing on R25bn from a *Minfin* transfer of R100bn in 1994 as a soft credit to the firm *Dal'vemo* and contracting for the import of 250 000 t of coal from China worth $41mn, of which, at the time of the miners' strike, only 10 per cent had been delivered.

This is a clear example not only of the extent to which access to public money is currently intertwined with private business in Russian regions, but also of the real political power provincial officials have in shaping economic policy. Apart from the previously transferred R200bn in the form of federal subsidies for the PK coal industry, another R850bn were allotted after the miners' strike was settled in April 1995 (*Segodnya*,

14 April 1995, p.2). That payment suggests that Moscow considered industrial action to be a political threat in the forthcoming parliamentary elections in December 1995; whether the regional authorities would in fact implement the federal government's political objective by allowing most of this money to reach the miners themselves, is an open question.

Apart from their 'consumption bias', populist measures taken by regional authorities have also to be seen in the context of their political struggle for control over territorial resources, in which provincial officials wanted to maintain a strong leverage over industrial management through administrative price controls (UR, 29 October 1994, p.2). Table 6.6 compares the increase of IPI and CPI in both regions with that in Russia as a whole and relates this to the increase in (cash) money supply.[22]

Whereas increases of IPI and CPI in the AK came close to the national average in 1994 and early 1995, those in the PK exceeded the Russian average considerably at the same time, while the growth in MO in the PK was above the increase of both IPI and CPI. This is probably due to two main reasons. First, its gateway location is linked with a large amount of 'shuttle trade', which increases the inflow of hard currency from abroad and domestic currency from other parts of the RF. The latter applies particularly to the trade in Japanese second-hand cars in the province.

Table 6.6 Comparison of increased IPI and CPI in the Altaiskii and Primorskii *Kraya* with Russia as a whole and rise of money supply (MO), 1993–early 1995 (multiples of previously indicated time period)

Indicator	Russia			AK			PK		
	1993	1994	Q1 95	1993	1994	Q1 95	1993	Q3 94	Q1 95
IPI	10.0	3.4	1.1	11.3	n.a.	n.a.	11.6	3.3	4.3
CPI	9.4	3.0	1.4	11.5	2.7	1.5	11.6	3.6	2.9
MO	7.7	2.7	1.2	n.a.	n.a.	n.a.	13.8	5.7	1.2

Note: Figures for the PK for Q1 95 apply for period 31 December 1994 to 31 March 1995, not from Q3 94 to Q1 95.

Source: Compiled from RET, 3(4) 1994, p.38; FI, 18 May 1995, p.II; *Segodnya*, 25 May 1995, p.2; Goskomstat Rossii, *Rossiya v tsifrakh 1995*, Moscow: 1995, p.170; Goskomstat Rossii, *Sotsial 'no-ekonomicheskoe polozhenie Rossii, yan-iyun' 1995*, Moscow: 1995, p.108 and various issues of AP and UR

Second, there is also a large inflow of cash into the PK for trading in the shares of enterprises from Siberia and the Russian Far East at the Vladivostok stock exchange (UR, 30 August 1994, p.2). In September 1994 alone, the total of its financial transactions amounted reportedly to R7.37bn (UR, 4 October 1994, p.1) or $2.95mn at that time. It reportedly paid R3.5bn in taxes into the regional budget in the first half of 1994 (UR, 30 August 1994, p.2). The inflow of cash into the PK increased even further after the sale of 3.7 per cent of *Gazprom* shares at the Vladivostok stock exchange was announced in November 1994, which was apparently personally agreed between Nazdratenko and Prime Minister Chernomyrdin (*Segodnya*, 5 November 1994, p.2). One per cent of *Gazprom* shares was estimated to be worth $2bn (UR, 6 December 1994, p.2), which immediately unleashed financial speculation in which traders acquired options to buy shares in order to resell them afterwards (KD, 9 November 1994, p.5).

However, the considerably higher increase of IPI and CPI in the PK compared with the national average in the first quarter of 1995 is clearly a result of the lifting of previous price controls in the region, which were no longer tenable by the end of 1994. Despite first signs of stabilisation in Russia as a whole in the first quarter of 1995, the substantial increase in money supply is still cause for concern.[23]

Consumer prices

As shown in Table 6.6, both regions had an above national average CPI in 1993, while it was in the AK lower than in Russia as a whole in 1994, probably indicating prevailing price controls for consumer goods (Table A.24 shows the increase of CPI by Russian macroregions in 1992–4). However, both provinces were faced with a significant upsurge of consumer prices for municipal services in mid-1994 and early 1995 as indicated in Table 6.7.

While the CPI was in the same range in both provinces in 1993, the upsurge of consumer prices in the first half of 1994 was at a different speed for the municipal services shown in Table 6.7. This indicates a tougher price control for fuel and household electricity in the PK at that time. Consumer prices for electricity in this region reportedly covered only 6 per cent of producer costs in November 1994 (UR, 26 November 1994, p.2).[24] However, household prices for electricity in the AK were also among the lowest in mid-1994 if compared with their neighbouring regions, as shown in Table A.25.

Table 6.7 Increase of consumer prices for basic municipal services in the Altaiskii and Primorskii *Kraya*, 1994–5 (multiples)

Indicator	AK		PK	
	Jan–June '94	Jan–March '95	Jan–June '94	Jan–March '95
Housing rents	44.2	2.4	17.0	2.0–2.5
Central heating	n.a.	2.1	16.0	2.0–2.5
Hot water supply	37.0	n.a.	8.7	2.0–2.5

Note: Data provided in the last column were only a rough estimate of a 2.0–2.5 times increase.
Source: Compiled from AP, 28 July 1994, p.3; AP, 29 April 1995, p.6; UR, 28 July 1994, p.2 and UR, 27 April 1995, p.2

Real consumption

While both regions had a different pattern of price policy and money supply, real consumption has to be analysed by comparing data for average monthly income, the price of the consumer basket (consisting of 19 basic consumer items) and savings as indicated in Table 6.8.[25]

Table 6.8 Incomes, prices and savings in the Altaiskii and Primorskii *Kraya* compared with Russia as a whole, late 1994–early 1995

Indicator	Russia		AK		PK	
	Nov 94	April 95	Sept 94	March 95	Sept 94	March 95
Average monthly income ('000 R)	280.7	385.0	181.0	320.0	158.7	285.0
Cost of consumer basket ('000 R)	83.0	n.a.	49.2	121.0	n.a.	n.a.
'Real' average income ('000 R)	197.7	–	107.3	–	–	–
Subsistence income ('000)	121.5	n.a.	78.0	n.a.	n.a.	288.5
Savings (as % of income, July '94)	29.5	n.a.	31.6	n.a.	23.6	n.a.

Note: For the concept of 'real' average income, see: Hanson (1994a, p.26).
Source: Compiled from RET, 3(4) 1994, p.51; Rutland (1994a, p.12); *Segodnya*, 25 March 1995, p.3; AP, 28 July 1994, p.2; AP, 9 November 1994, p.1; AP, 29 April 1995, p.6; UR, 28 July 1994, p.2; UR, 29 October 1994, p.2 and UR, 27 April 1995, p.2

The AK had a considerably less than average national monthly income with only half of the 'real' average income in the RF in September 1994, but slightly higher savings rates than the Russian average in mid-1994. This could be another confirmation of our earlier findings in Chapter 1 that people in the AK are probably really poorer, in terms of their monetised income, but rely much more than the Russian average on subsistence farming and/or informal, unreported trade for their consumption, while retail prices in the AK are lower.

Both figures for the PK are clearly an understatement and probably a result of censorship by the regional administration, since, according to Table 1.4, average real income was already R244 400 in December 1993 as reported by the same *Goskomstat* office a few months earlier. The claim that average monthly income was lower than subsistence income in March 1995 seems then to be unrealistic. Moreover, savings rates in this province would seem to be too high if this income figure were correct. It is certainly difficult to come to a final conclusion on real consumption for a gateway region where people have many more opportunities for informal income through trade with hard currency and 'shuttle trade' than their counterparts in a remote region like the AK would have.[26]

6.3 FISCAL ARRANGEMENTS

While the theoretical implications of the current turmoil in fiscal arrangements in the RF were extensively discussed in Chapter 3, this section provides quantitative data for budgetary revenues and expenditures in both provinces for 1992–3 and partly 1994–5. However, qualitative background information will also be given in the detailed exploration of the issues, while the compilation of data for extrabudgetary funds, federal subsidies and state programmes – which partly appear in the budget equation of Russian regions and provide much larger financial resources than the official budget would indicate – confirm the earlier finding that the current federal system in Russia has no transparent, fair and consensus-based intragovernmental financial framework, but consists of a series of bilaterally bargained, *ad hoc* deals and has no clear equalisation formula, despite some modifications in 1994–5.

Revenues

With traditionally only a small percentage of enterprises of both provinces under local jurisdiction, as in the former Soviet Union generally, regional authorities possessed a quite meagre independent income base and depended almost entirely on union and republic subsidies and allocations handed down as a percentage of locally-collected but centrally-determined turnover taxes and personal income taxes. This high budgetary dependence on the centre did not change with the fiscal reform and introduction of new taxes (VAT, profit tax) in 1992, as discussed in Chapter 3.

Table 6.9 shows a clear decrease of guaranteed income in the AK in 1993, while subsidies and soft credits from the federal budget rose considerably. In the PK, in contrast, there was a tendency for guaranteed income to increase. In terms of guaranteed income, the AK was clearly at a disadvantage due to its high share of agricultural production, for which prices are still not freed and VAT amounts to merely 10 per cent. Moreover, the 10.7 per cent 'credits', which appeared under 'regulated income', were, in fact, loans from local enterprises and organisations,[27] which create additional liabilities and future expenditures. As in the PK, the former regional soviet of the AK took the decision, in the summer of 1993, to refuse the payment of R21.6bn in federal taxes, the equivalent of which was claimed to be overdue for transfer by the Ministry of Finance (AP, 28 August

Table 6.9 Main income sources of the consolidated budgets of the Altaiskii and Primorskii *Kraya*, 1992–3 (in Rmn and % of total)

Income Source	AK				PK			
	1992	%	1993	%	1992	%	1993	%
Total	33 422	100.0	445 114	100.0	35 829	100.0	751 905	100.0
Profit tax	8 078	24.2	89 531	20.1	9 894	27.6	212 041	28.2
VAT	4 893	14.6	55 896	12.6	3 235	9.0	93 701	12.5
Personal income tax	6 067	18.2	57 399	12.9	7 819	21.8	97 088	12.9
Excise duties	2 579	7.7	18 292	4.1	1 411	3.9	15 516	2.0
Other	2 594	7.8	28 356	6.4	4 654	13.0	181 698	24.2
Total guaranteed income	24 211	72.5	249 474	56.1	27 013	75.4	600 044	79.8
Subsidies	5 135	15.4	50 638	11.4	–	–	72 923	9.7
Federal budget	2 926	8.7	96 841	21.8	7 286	20.3	73 792	9.8
Federal loans	1 150	3.4	300	–	1 526	4.3	5 146	0.7
Credits	–	–	47 861	10.7	–	–	–	–

Note: Because of rounded absolute figures for the PK, percentage figures do not always add to 100.0%.

Source: Compiled from Aleinikov and Mikhailyuk (1994, p.42) and interviews with the deputy heads of the budget office of the PK administration, L. Popova, on 13 and 20 September 1993, and V. Rybakova on 7 September 1994

1993, p.1). One immediate effect of this challenge was that VAT was left at its full rate in the region in the second quarter of 1994.[28] Table A.26 confirms this pattern of budgetary development for both provinces in 1994. Finally, the inefficiency of the tax collection system was a serious problem. Payment arrears to the AK budget were estimated at 4.8 per cent of total income at the beginning of 1994, and reportedly increased to 20 per cent or a total of R63bn by 1 June 1994 (AP, 5 July 1994, p.2).

As discussed in Chapter 3, there were some minor modifications of the Russian fiscal system in 1994–5, including the setting up of a federal fund for the financial support of regions as a first attempt at equalising budgetary income between Russian provinces and the incorporation of the extrabudgetary road and ecological funds into the RF 1995 budget. The AK got a 7.9 per cent share allotted from the federal fund for financial support of the regions in 1994 (AP, 27 April 1994, p.2), amounting to R155.5bn by November 1994 (RET, 3(4) 1994, p.18). This share slightly decreased to 7.6 per cent in 1995, while the PK got a 2.8 per cent share allotted in 1995 (RG, 7 April 1995, p.4).[29]

However, there were numerous other funds providing financial help to the regions included in the RF 1995 budget, such as a R1.7trn federal programme for the development of regions; R4.4trn as financial support for the Russian Far North; almost R200bn for the city of Moscow and another R104bn for closed cities (RG, 7 April 1995, p.3). It is not clear which regions could be potential beneficiaries in 1995. The incorporation of some extrabudgetary funds into the official budget equation could also provide for significant additional revenues. The road fund in the PK, for example, provided reportedly R50.9bn for the regional budget in the first quarter of 1995 alone (UR, 27 April 1995, p.2).[30]

In contrast, income from local taxes was almost negligible in both regions due to a lack of an efficient tax rate- or base-setting authority for local governments. Revenue from the 15 local taxes in the PK provided less than 10 per cent of the provincial budget income in 1994, while some of the local taxes (auctions and lotteries, ownership of dogs) could be considered as nuisance taxes (UR, 20 April 1995, p.3). A tax squeeze was applied by city administrations with respect to their municipal boroughs. For example, the city of Barnaul retained 12 per cent of all the taxes it collected in 1994, while its boroughs could reportedly keep only three per cent in the same year (AP, 13 September 1994, p.2).

Finally, as in all Russian regions, privatisation was not a significant source of revenue for the various budgets due to numerous exemptions and preferences granted to the working collective. Shares of joint-stock companies could be purchased by employees in closed subscriptions at bargain prices based on low valuations of the founding capital, while in voucher auctions money was paid only for the five per cent of shares sold for cash to cover privatisation agencies' expenses (Bornstein, 1994, p.448). Local budgets in the AK received reportedly R783.3mn from privatisation in the first half of 1994, while the regional budget received proceeds of R415.9mn at that time (AP, 27 July 1994, p.2). This increased the consolidated regional budget to R5542mn or 0.3 per cent of total budgetary income by the end of 1994.

Expenditures

The two main spheres of expenditure in both provinces in 1992–3 were the regional economy and the social and cultural sphere, as indicated in Table 6.10. What becomes clear from a comparison of the data in Tables 6.9

Table 6.10 Main spheres of expenditure of the consolidated budgets of the Altaiskii and Primorskii *Kraya*, 1992–3 (in Rmn and as % of total)

Sphere of Expenditure	AK				PK			
	1992	%	1993	%	1992	%	1993	%
Total	30 596	100.0	432 379	100.0	31 893	100.0	513 541	100.0
Regional economy	10 388	33.9	193 577	44.8	13 242	41.5	245 659	47.8
of which:								
Agriculture	1232	4.0	34 835	8.1	573	1.8	33 076	6.4
Transport	787	2.6	13 291	3.1	1446	4.5	19 122	3.7
Housing	6068	19.8	92 471	21.4	1030	3.2	163 800	31.9
Other	2301	7.5	52 980	12.2	10 193	32.0	29 661	5.8
Social and cultural sphere	15 631	51.1	180 329	41.7	14 779	46.4	199 489	38.8
of which:								
Education	7235	23.6	98 362	22.7	6928	21.7	99 482	19.4
Culture	955	3.1	10 408	2.4	596	1.9	6984	1.3
Health and sports	6580	21.5	64 748	15.0	6499	20.4	85 912	16.7
Social services	861	2.8	6811	1.5	756	2.4	7111	1.4
Administration	1205	3.9	16 467	3.8	919	2.9	13 902	2.7
Other	3372	11.1	42 006	9.7	2953	9.2	54 491	10.6

Note: Because of rounded absolute figures for the PK, percentage figures do not always add to 100.0%. It also appears that the figure for 'housing' in the PK in 1992 is not reliable, bearing in mind the traditional high subsidies for housing and its high proportional share in 1993.

Source: see Table 6.9

and 6.10 is that neither province had a budget deficit in 1992–3. For a region to have a deficit was, of course, virtually impossible because Russian regional authorities cannot increase the money supply by printing new money and the issue of municipal bonds was only in its infancy.[31]

Moreover, rising expenditures during the financial year were covered by additional federal transfers at that time. For example, a budget deficit of R220bn was announced in the AK for the first quarter of 1994, but Moscow reportedly sent soft credits amounting to R30bn in April 1994 to cover the deficit (AP, 30 March 1994, p.1). This transfer increased to R72bn in late summer 1994, but regional authorities claimed already a need of R400bn at that time (AP, 14 September 1994, p.1). In November 1994, governor Korshunov reported that the provincial budget had received a federal transfer of R180bn, but he expected a total one of R565bn by the end of the year (UR, 30 November 1994, p.2). This shows the extent to which the half-hearted fiscal reform in 1992–4 had forced Moscow into open-ended commitments to provide soft credits and subsidies for the regions.

The issue of housing bonds worth R5bn was first announced at the third session of the AK regional parliament in June 1994 (AP, 18 June 1994, p.1), while municipal bonds totalling R20bn were issued by the AK regional administration to buy fuel in spring 1995 (AP, 18 March 1995, p.1). However, these sums were too low to alleviate fiscal pressures significantly and they clearly could not perceptibly enhance the autonomy of regional authorities. A heavy dependency on the federal budget remained evident for both provinces.

At the same time, expenditure assignments became an issue in the power struggle between the executive and legislative branches in Russian regions. This led to numerous amendments and extensive delays in adopting the annual budgets. Deputies of the newly elected regional parliament in the AK originally rejected the proposed total of expenditures of R945.2bn and set an unrealistic target of R2.5trn (AP, 15 June 1994, p.1).[32] However, the budget amendment adopted at the third session in June 1994 included additional expenditures of only R19.7bn (AP, 18 June 1994, p.1). Moreover, the new statute of the AK adopted in April 1995 declared a commitment to free medical treatment and education (AP, 8 February 1995, p.3), but it left open how this was to be achieved.

Table 6.10 indicated that in both provinces the regional economy received an increased share of total budget expenditure in 1993, while the social and cultural sphere had a corresponding decline of almost the same percentage most conspicuously in the health service. In 1993, R35bn were reportedly spent from the AK budget for capital investment and the maintenance of the social infrastructure, while another R25bn were allotted to animal husbandry (AP, 21 June 1994, p.1). Agro-industrial producers of former state structures were among the main recipients of subsidies and soft credits from the AK budget. The regional monopoly for tractor production *Alttrak*, for example, was granted a soft credit of R7bn from the regional budget in 1994 and Rubtsovsk city, where this enterprise is located, R1bn to buy fuel (AP, 13 August 1994, p.1).

These subsidies were normally justified as a way of preventing mass-unemployment in factory cities like Rubtsovsk, but the money would probably have been better spent on new training schemes. In March 1995, a special 1.5 per cent provincial tax for the support of the Altai agricultural system was announced by the AK regional parliament (AP, 4 March 1995, p.1), which shows that at least some local fiscal effort was undertaken to fill the big budgetary hole, but it is still too early to judge its effectiveness.

In general, officially published data on spending for social needs look rather meagre if compared with expenditures on the regional economy, though it should be borne in mind. For example, the regional parliament in the AK announced at its fifth session in September 1994 to allocate R1.8bn for low income families (AP, 1 October 1994, p.2). Moreover, additional expenditures had to be provided by the AK authorities as a result of large in-migration of refugees from Central Asia, who were mainly of Russian nationality, amounting to 8046 people in 1994[33] and another 5300 people in the first quarter of 1995 alone (AP, 29 April 1995, p.6), but detailed spending data for this category were not available.

Extrabudgetary funds, federal subsidies and programmes

However, official budgetary figures do not reflect the whole picture, since various other flows of public money are not included in them. These are federal extrabudgetary resources, or 'off-budget funds', which are channelled through federal institutions at the regional and local level (pension fund, social insurance fund, employment fund and so on), regional extrabudgetary funds, state programmes, and certain subsidies and soft credits. These resources provide much more scope for autonomous regional development than official statistics would reveal, and help to account for the bargaining power different regions have in reality. Table 6.11 gives a rough estimate of actual regional public-sector income and expenditure in both provinces in 1993–4, incorporating extrabudgetary resources.

Table 6.11 shows that both regions had not only a budgetary surplus in 1993 (and presumably 1994 as well),[34] but that there was also considerably more public money available through extrabudgetary funds, federal

Table 6.11 Comparison of aggregated budgetary and extrabudgetary income and expenditure in the Altaiskii and Primorskii *Kraya*, 1993–4 (in Rbn)

Source	AK				PK			
	Income		Expenditure		Income		Expenditure	
	1993	1994	1993	1994	1993	first half 94	1993	first half 94
Total regional budget	445.1	1690.3	432.4	1213.3	751.9	820.1	513.5	803.7
Central Bank soft credit	207.0	64.6	207.0	64.6	45.4	n.a.	45.4	n.a.
Memorandum items	70.0	1088.6	70.0	1088.6	58.0	377.4	58.0	377.4
Total	722.1	2843.5	709.4	2366.5	855.3	1197.5	616.9	1181.1

Note: 'Memorandum items' contain 'off-budget funds', finances from state programmes and subsidies.

Source: Compiled from Tables 6.9 and 6.10; Melkov and Gotfrid (1994, p.51–2), several issues of AP and UR and interviews with officials in both provinces in 1994–5

subsidies, soft credits and state programmes, which were frequently used to meet increasing budgetary expenditures.[35] The substantially higher total for aggregated data for the AK if compared with official budgetary figures is striking and reveals the extent to which this region is really dependent on financial help from Moscow. Major federal transfers in 1994 contained R14.7bn for the regional grain fund (AP, 2 August 1994, p.1), R200bn for the 1994 harvest and a R48bn loan from the Ministry for Agriculture (AP, 21 September 1994, p.1–2). Revenues from extrabudgetary funds in the AK in 1994 included, among others, R675.6bn from the pension fund,[36] R41bn from the medical insurance fund (AP, 5 January 1995, p.2) and R84bn from the social insurance fund (AP, 29 March 1995).[37] The most prominent state programme in the AK was that of compensation for the nuclear fall-out from the Semipalatinsk testing facility, for which the authorities received R40bn in 1993 (Melkov and Gotfrid, 1994, p.51) and another R25.3bn by mid-1994 (AP, 20 July 1994, p.2).

There was a much less generous provision of information about extra-budgetary funds, federal subsidies and state programmes in the PK local press. 'Memorandum items' for the first half of 1994 contain R52.4bn from the road fund,[38] R83bn from the social insurance fund (for the third quarter of 1994),[39] R187bn from the pension fund,[40] while R55bn were reportedly provided as federal compensations for the devastating floods in the region in September–October 1994 (UR, 30 March 1995, p.1).

6.4 CAPITAL INVESTMENT

One important issue of economic transformation is how to find new forms of resource allocation by which the traditional state dominance in investment policy can be reduced, while private entrepreneurs and foreign investors are expected to play a much more important role. Whereas private savings were generally too low for substantial capital investments at the start of economic reform, later on, both foreign investors and the Russian *nouveaux riches* were discouraged by economic turmoil and political uncertainty. However, enterprises' own funds became the major source of capital investment in recent years, while state investment went mainly on the fuel and energy sector, agriculture and the defence industry. Table 6.12 indicates capital investment by sources of financing in both provinces compared with Russia as a whole in 1994.

Table 6.12 Capital investment by sources of financing in the Altaiskii and Primorskii *Kraya* compared with Russia as a whole, 1994 (in % of total)

Indicator	Russia (1994)	AK (1994)	PK (first half '94)
Total	100.0	100.0	100.0
State investment	24.1	32.0	27.0
from federal budget	(13.6)	(23.0)	(14.1)
from subnational budgets	(10.5)	(9.0)	(12.9)
Preferential state credits	1.4	2.0	1.4
Centralised off-budget investment fund	5.9	7.0	7.8
Enterprises' funds (own and borrowed)	64.5	58.0	63.0
Joint ventures and foreign firms	4.1	1.0	0.8

Source: Compiled from RET, 3(4) 1994, p.68; AP, 2 February 1995, p.1 and UR, 28 July 1994, p.3

Data in Table 6.12 confirm earlier findings showing heavy dependency of both regions on financial support from Moscow. This applies particularly to the AK, where central sources still provided one third of total capital investment in 1994. The 0.8 per cent share of foreign investment in the PK is somewhat surprising for such a gateway region, but probably reflects (through either real deterrent effects or deterrence to reporting) the frightening criminal situation in the region, as discussed in Chapter 5. The cities of Vladivostok and Nakhodka certainly have a higher share of foreign investment, which amounted for the latter, for example, to 18.4 per cent in the first quarter of 1995 (UR, 27 April 1995, p.3). Moreover, the use of mid-1994 figures for the PK could also distort the results.

The AK probably received more foreign investment than the figure in Table 6.12 would suggest. For example, the German government provided DM53mn in 1994 for social infrastructure and small-scale business for the German national district in the Altai (AP, 11 March 1995, p.2), which would amount to R159bn (DM1 = R3000) at the end of 1994. The official statistics probably did not incorporate this figure in the reported total amount of R865.5bn (AP, 2 February 1995, p.1), but if it were amended, the percentage share of the German financial help would still be much higher at 15.5 per cent of total capital investments. This is a clear example of one kind of methodological problems with Russian statistics.[41]

Both provinces suffered severe declines in capital investment during the period investigated, which amounted to 23 per cent in the AK in 1994 (AP, 2 February 1995, p.1) compared with a national average of 26 per cent in that year (RET, 3(4) 1994, p.67), while the PK reportedly had a decrease of 48.5 per cent in the first half of 1994 (UR, 28 July 1994, p.2). For Russia as a whole, another fall in capital investment of 24 per cent was reported for the first quarter of 1995 alone (FI, 18 May 1995, p.II).

The combined fall in output and decrease in capital investment led to significant structural changes by sector of industry at the national scale, as a result of which primary industries such as the energy and fuel sectors, ferrous and nonferrous metallurgy increased their relative share in total industrial output, while secondary sectors (machine-building and metalworking, chemical and construction materials industries) lost their former importance (DM, 16–22 January 1995, p.14).[42] At the same time, the percentage share of 'non-productive' investment increased to 44 per cent in 1994 compared with 31 per cent in 1991 (*Segodnya*, 25 March 1995, p.3), particularly in housing construction.

Both provinces received state investment finance, mainly for agriculture, food industries (fishing in the case of the PK), defence-related and coal industries. In 1995, it was announced by the Minister for Agriculture,

Nazarchuk, that a federal investment fund for the APK would be set up on the basis of shares from privatised enterprises and bills of exchange worth R200bn issued by the Ministry of Finance, while R4trn were planned for leasing of agricultural machinery and another R2trn for the improvement of soil fertility (AP, 11 January 1995, p.8).

State investments from the federal budget totalling R1.9trn were allotted to the fishing industry in 1995, while foreign investments in this sector are expected to amount to $550mn in that year (*Segodnya*, 17 May 1995, p.4). Finally, the state mining company *Rosugol'* was expected to provide 36 per cent of the total capital investment in the PK coal industry in 1995 (UR, 18 April 1995, p.1). These high commitments of central investment in the regions are a result of half-hearted institutional restructuring in the sectors discussed.

6.5 FOREIGN ECONOMIC ACTIVITY

Liberalisation of regional economies is one of the main cornerstones of economic change in the Russian provinces. By opening the economy to the outside world, reformers in the centre hoped not only to tackle the problem of shortages of consumer goods, but also to speed up technological modernisation of domestic production and to enhance its competitiveness on the world market. However, regional authorities had a considerable administrative leverage through the registration of export producers, the issue of licences for foreign trade, export quotas and import tariffs, which was overseen and enforced by representatives of the Ministry for Foreign Economic Relations in each province.

Foreign trade

In terms of revenues generated from foreign trade, the PK was naturally in a more advantageous position than the AK due to its close geographical location to Asian-Pacific markets and its disposition of resources that are tradable on the world market – mainly fish and precious metals. Table 6.13 shows that the foreign trade turnover of the PK was 2.5 times higher than that in the AK in 1993 even if trade with CIS countries for this region is excluded. This could still be an understatement, since non-registered 'shuttle trade' is not included in the regional data, which would increase their percentage shares relative to the RF total. However, the AK with a 1.8 per cent share of the RF population had clearly a lower than national average foreign economic activity, which is mainly due to its remote

Table 6.13 Foreign trade activities of the Altaiskii and Primorskii *Kraya* compared with Russia as a whole, 1993–4 (in $mn and % of Russia)

Indicator	Russia		AK				PK			
	1993	1994	1993	%	1994	%	1993	%	Q3 '94	%
Exports	112 000	83 000	143.7	0.1	228.1	0.3	442.3	0.4	279.9	–
Imports	75 100	66 600	140.2	0.2	154.3	0.2	253.0	0.3	118.4	–
Freight transport (in mn t)	3 600	n.a.	27.9	0.8	17.5	–	45.0	1.2	26.7	–

Note: RF exports include gold, but exclude gold swaps. RF imports include non-registered 'shuttle trade'. PK data include only trade with non-CIS countries. Freight transport includes export and import cargoes.

Source: Compiled from RET, 3(4) 1994, p.73–81; EkiZh, no.6, February 1994, p.7; Departament vneshne ekonomicheskoi deyatel'nosti administratsii Altaiskogo kraya, *Obshchie itogi po eksportu i importu*, Barnaul, 1995, p.4–5 (mimeo); AP, 9 February 1994, p.2; AP, 2 February 1995, p.3; UR, 3 February 1994, p.2 and UR, 29 October 1994, p.2

geographical location, undeveloped infrastructure and relatively poor endowment with resources tradable on the world market. In contrast, unreported 'shuttle trade' in the PK would probably increase its share of national foreign economic activity significantly, although it is hard to estimate what real difference it makes.

Table 6.13 also indicates what is probably a strong tendency across Russian provinces for each region's imports to be dependent on its export earnings, as the centre's control of export earnings declines, and, with that decline, centralised purchasing and central allocation of funds to purchase imports also falls. Moreover, the incorporation of figures for trade with CIS countries for the PK in this statistical analysis would probably not make a significant difference. CIS trade is probably of much less importance for this region than for the AK due to the latter's location close to Kazakhstan and Central Asia.[43] Finally, figures for freight transport indicate that capacity was underutilised. The volume of freight loadings had decreased to 61 per cent of the 1993 level in the AK (AP, 2 February 1995, p.3) and to 78 per cent in the PK in the third quarter of 1994 (UR, 29 October 1994, p.2). This is particularly striking for the PK with its high amount of foreign economic activities, associated with relatively high domestic tariffs for transport over long distances from and to European Russia.

Structure of exports and imports

As in most other Russian regions, the export structure was dominated in both provinces by natural resources, as shown in Table 6.14, while consumer goods and equipment were mostly imported. Whereas the RF had a clear domination of fuel, minerals and metals in its export structure,

Table 6.14 Export and import structure of the Altaiskii and Primorskii *Kraya* compared with Russia as a whole, 1993–4 (in % of total in US-$ prices)

Export products	Russia (non-CIS) 1993	1994	AK (incl. CIS) 1993	1994	PK (non-CIS) 1993
Total	100.0	100.0	100.0	100.0	100.0
Machinery and equipment	6.5	5.3	32.0	31.0	n.a.
Fuel, minerals and metals	63.7	66.7	38.0	45.0	n.a.
Food products (fish)	2.7	2.8	n.a.	n.a.	75.8
Lumber and wood products	3.7	3.8	n.a.	n.a.	15.1
Chemicals (fertilizers)	3.0	4.2	18.0	10.0	1.9
Other	20.4	17.2	–	–	–
Import products					
Total	100.0	100.0	100.0	100.0	100.0
Machinery, equipment and transportation	33.9	34.0	32.0	21.0	27.3
Fuel, minerals, metals and building materials	4.6	4.7	n.a.	n.a.	0.3
Chemicals and pharmaceut.	2.4	5.2	n.a.	n.a.	2.1
Foodstuffs	12.4	11.7	21.0	23.0	22.2
Consumer goods	12.8	5.7	13.0	12.0	24.0
Other	33.9	38.7	34.0	44.0	24.1

Source: Compiled from RET, 3(4) 1994, p.76–8; Departament vneshneekonomicheskoi deyatel'nosti administratsii Altaiskogo kraya, *Obshchie itogi po eksportu i importu*, Barnaul: 1995, p.4–5 (mimeo); Komitet po vneshneekonomicheskim i regional'nym svyazyam administratsii Primorskogo kraya, *Vneshne ekonomicheskie svyazi Primorskogo kraya: sostoyanie, problemy, perspektivy*, Vladivostok: 1994, p.9 (mimeo)

exporters from the PK were mainly selling fish products, and lumber and wood products on the foreign market. In 1994, 70 per cent of the total catch of the PK fishing fleet was reportedly exported to Asian-Pacific countries (UR, 22 April 1995, p.1).

The more diversified export structure in the AK is due to the fact that trade with CIS-countries was included in the available statistics according to which the AK is selling machinery and equipment mainly to Kazakhstan and Central Asian countries, but they would hardly be competitive at the non-CIS market. Moreover, the state security office in the AK took a particularly strong xenophobic position and objected to the extraction of natural resources by foreigners (AP, 14 February 1995, p.1).

The above national average import of food products in both provinces is a striking feature, particularly in the AK which traditionally specialised in agriculture. The AK reportedly imported food products totalling $12.1mn in 1994 (AP, 18 October 1994, p.1). The increase of cotton imports from Uzbekistan was announced in early 1995, for which barter agreements were found, trading 16 t of cotton for one tractor from the Altai (AP, 18 January 1995, p.1). The above national average import of consumer goods in the PK is certainly due to the region's geographical proximity to the Asian-Pacific market, while the proportionally lower figure for machinery, equipment and transportation could be an understatement bearing in mind the large amount of Japanese second-hand cars traded in the region. Finally, one has also to take into account the change of relative prices on the world market in 1992–3 (Illarionov, 1994, p.87–8), which affected main export and import products of both the provinces investigated.

State regulation

An important source for generating income at the regional level is the sale of rights for export quotas of 'strategically important' products (fish, wood, wheat, nonferrous metals). From this the PK administration earned $3mn in 1992 alone, which it spent on imports of sugar, frozen and canned meat, and other food products (RFEU, July 1993, p.7). Export licences were sometimes given only on the condition that food products (butter, meat) are imported by export producers with their hard currency revenues.[44] This system of regional quotas and export licences leaves a strong lever of control over foreign trade for regional authorities. The administrative distribution of regional quotas for fishing in the PK, for example, implied price agreements and financial help for *Dal'moreprodukt*, which led naturally to new cartels and monopolies (UR, 28 January 1994, p.2). Table A.28 indicates different export quotas for the PK in 1991–4, which varied considerably from one year to another and became a vehicle for rent-seeking in the centre.

Although it was originally announced that regional quotas were scheduled to be liquidated in summer 1994 (RFEU, May 1994, p.5), they still covered 20 per cent of oil exports and 35 per cent of other exports at the end of the year (Rutland, 1994a, p.18). However, some of the main export products of both provinces such as fish, timber, raw diamonds and nonferrous metals were freed of export quotas by a decree of the Russian government on 31 December 1994 (RET, 3(4) 1994, p.72). They are now mainly regulated by the demand on foreign markets and international agreements. Finally, state customs duties were partly a source for mobilising internal resources, since some of the provincial authorities managed to keep a share of it in their territory.[45]

Free economic zones

A very popular element in the regional authorities' attempt at gaining more scope for autonomous development and control over territorial resources was the idea, pursued in both regions, of setting up FEZs. The Russian governmental decision to give the AK the status of a FEZ was taken in 1990 on highly political grounds, as part of the struggle of the RSFSR authorities against the union government and the re-establishment of the German autonomous district in the AK, with the hope of attracting predominantly German capital to that region. The main conceptual inconsistency was, apart from its huge territorial size, the approach of opting to solve internal economic and social problems by introducing a preferential regime of tax holidays and freedom from customs duties, which, in fact, could never be provided in reality, since the regional budget's need for revenue was too pressing.

The concept of setting up a FEZ in Nakhodka originally appeared much more promising. It had relatively well equipped port, transport and infrastructural facilities. It received, alone among the 12 FEZs officially approved by the Russian parliament, governmental credits of R2.2bn in 1992 and R20.1bn in 1993 (FI, 10–16 December 1993, p.II). However, of this money, only R600mn were invested in port modernisation, while 70 per cent of the total reportedly ended-up back in Moscow in the accounts of various businesses (RFEU, April 1994, p.7). Other preferential treatment included the right to transfer all revenues from privatisation into a special account of the FEZ administration and the reduction of tax payments to the centre by 50 per cent.

The main problems for the setting up of a properly functioning FEZ were, apart from high inflation and the lack of legal regulations, the size of the territory and the multiple power structure in the region, including overlapping and duplication of administrative competences, which provided openings for the kind of corruption and embezzlement of public money mentioned earlier (UR, 7 October 1993, p.2). As a result, Nakhodka authorities found no common formula to articulate their interests and the preferential treatment originally provided was increasingly frozen, including tariff privileges that it had enjoyed (RFEU, April 1994, p.6).

The legal status of a FEZ on the whole territory of Nakhodka was changed by governmental decree in September 1994, reducing preferential treatment to five customs zones in the territory (KD, 14 September 1994, p.2). For their development, the administration in Nakhodka received a *Minfin* loan of R302.8bn in March 1995 (KD, 24 March 1995, p.2). However, one of the most promising projects in Nakhodka – the setting up of a South Korean technopark with the potential to create 20 000 new jobs – is currently in jeopardy, because the authorities reportedly need another five years to build a power station to provide the production units with electricity (UR, 29 March 1995, p.2).

7 Conclusion

The diversity of the RF in terms of natural resource endowment, population, climate, physical accessibility of its territories, industrial structure and local politics had a profound impact on the policy of implementing systemic transformation and the path its constituent administrative-territorial units would take. Moreover, the spatially intertwined co-existence of ethnically non-homogeneous nations as a result of Stalin's policy of 'divide and rule' complicated reform attempts, since it unleashed – after the collapse of the communist regime – a dynamic development of provincial elites wanting to define ethno-spatial identity in a new context and to control territorial resources. Under conditions of emergency, statehood came before nationhood in the creation of the new RF, but the centre did not dare to change existing administrative-territorial boundaries at the beginning of intended transformation in 1991–2. This mixed policy of speed and compromise included the granting of preferential treatment for various provinces in exchange for commitments by regional leaderships to preserve the territorial integrity of the RF.

The scale of different implementation policies

Under these conditions, the centre had to adopt different policies to implement intended transformation, which was not only adjusted to different local situations and personalities in power, but also entailed the devising of various institutional arrangements. This applies, first and foremost, to the distinction between autonomous republics and standard provinces, as enacted by the Federation Treaty of March 1992, which granted republics, for example, the right to have their own constitution and to elect their own President, while standard provinces could prepare only a statute and heads of administration were appointed by the Russian President in these regions. A second scale of different implementation policies applies to resource-rich regions in contrast to poorer provinces. The former were naturally more assertive in their effort to get granted tax exemptions and the right of retention of export revenues and customs payments.

Finally, a third distinction in different implementation policies, which was the subject of this thesis, can be discerned in terms of geographical location, particularly for peripheral regions. The most conspicuous examples are Chechnya, at the one end of the scale, where military force was used to try to stop the republic leadership's assertion of sovereignity, and Kaliningrad *oblast*', on the other, which enjoyed a regime of tax holidays in 1991–4. Although the above made distinctions are certainly not exhaustive, they confirm our earlier hypothesis that economic change and institutional restructuring in Russia's provinces imply a scale of different implementation policies, which range from an imposed form of transformation 'from above' to one of devolved regional autonomy.

The case of the regions investigated

Different implementation policies were also applied to both provinces examined in this thesis. Moscow reacted much more sensitively to the assertiveness of the political leadership in the PK than to that in the AK. As described above, the PK received exceptional subsidies to keep low prices for coal and electricity, while preferential treatment was given with respect to export quotas and the retention of customs payments. In contrast, the AK leadership lobbied mainly for special state programmes, while the fact that this province is one of the main agricultural producers in the RF gave its politicians a strong bargaining power against the centre. Hence, both provinces provide an example of what impact Russian regional elites currently have on the national policy agenda.

However, the second part of the hypothesis, namely, that the two provinces could be located at opposite ends of the scale of implementation policies has to be rejected. Among standard provinces, the PK enjoys undoubtedly some of the most preferential treatments, but Moscow stopped short of granting full autonomy by denying the region a special economic regime and objecting to the election of the governor in 1994. Revelations in the national media about embezzlement of public money, corruption and human rights' abuses brought the PK leadership into disrepute, but, at the time of writing, the team of the autocratic governor Nazdratenko is still firmly in power. This strengthened existing patron-client relations, while the criminal underworld has an increasing influence on regional policy making, as a result of which the PK became a Russian centre for drug trafficking, arms deals and money laundering. This combined with the lack of thorough-going institutional restructuring, while, at the same time, new cartels and conglomerates such as PAKT grew along the regional boundary, cast doubt on the PK's potential to become a pilot project for market reform due to its favourable gateway location.

In contrast, the leadership of the AK can hardly be described as anti-reformist for the period from late 1991 until early 1994. It adopted a fast-speed privatisation policy for large- and medium-sized enterprises, while some sectors of the regional economy (chemical industry, machine-building, nonferrous metallurgy) showed first signs of economic recovery in early 1995 through increasing interregional trade at the meso-level (Western Siberia, Kazakhstan) and the regional leadership tried to mobilise internal resources by issuing municipal bonds. However, as described in Chapter 4, there was a revival of nomenklatura power and the agrarian clan in the AK by mid-1994, and the region's leaders increasingly challenged the national reform agenda by adopting their own law on privatisation and approving a new statute of the province, according to which the new governor was to be elected by the regional parliament, which would implicitly mean a subordination of the executive power under the traditionalist legislative branch.

As a result, neither region represents a prototype to be located at one end of the scale of implementation policies, either that of transformation 'from above' or regional autonomy. Although both provinces did not lack autonomy in general, they did not move towards an open economy and a democratic political system either. What came out of this study is the profound impact regional leaders have on provincial (and partly national) policy making, which strengthened existing industrial and agrarian elites and not only made possible, as shown in the case of the AK, a revival of nomenklatura power and the reactivation of former social networks, but also allowed the fusion of nomenklatura power with private property. However, in contrast, with a growing pluralisation of society and particularisation of interests in the PK the all-encompassing power of PAKT was reduced after new private businesses and the criminal underworld entered the political scene.

This leads to the conclusion that the two-dimensional model of transformation 'from above' versus regional autonomy, which was certainly a serious academic issue at the beginning of intended transformation, has to be reconsidered with a view to further regional differentiation and general pluralisation of Russian society. Russian provinces move in rather different directions, which are not necessarily determined by the centre any more. This development became more complex since outside forces (migrants, foreign investors) and new players from inside (local private business, criminal gangs) have a growing impact on regional policy making.

Prospects of economic change in Russian provinces

The economic recovery and change in Russia's provinces have to be seen in the context of national economic policy. A drastic reduction of soft credits and subsidies would enforce, apart from stabilisation at the national level, structural adjustment at the regional level. The growth of cartels and conglomerates within regional boundaries is worrisome, since they are some of the main beneficiaries of state subsidies. Further liberalisation of prices for energy and agricultural products would not only undermine local price controls, but also introduce outside competition and price adjustment reflecting the relative scarcity of resources.

Thorough-going liberalisation of foreign economic activities would have to stop with the malpractice of granting preferential treatment to export producers (export quotas, retention of customs payments), excessive protectionism of domestic producers (import tariffs), while enforcing outside competition and promoting potential foreign investment. Finally, privatisation and proper institutional restructuring should act as an alternative to the current development of local corporatism and institutional entanglement of politics and economics at the regional level, evidenced in semi-state structures and conglomerates enjoying tax holidays and cheap credits.

This would enhance the chance of regional economic activity to reflect opportunity costs, which can already be seen in a relative shift towards primary industries and goods tradable on the world market (such as ferrous and nonferrous metals). It would also lead to a new pattern of economic activity at the meso-level, taking energy and transport costs fully into account and developing supplementary industries.

The viability of the Russian Federation

To make centre-periphery relations in the RF work, clearly defined and transparent institutional arrangements have to be found, handing down political responsibility to the appropriate level and enhancing accountability. There is also a need for strengthening law enforcement authorities, particularly the judiciary, while the currently used practice of setting up new commissions and quangos can only lead to new overlaps and confusions of administrative and legal competences. Russian central authorities have also to stop practices of dual subordination and *ad hoc* deals in fiscal arrangements. There is an urgent need for a proper tax reform, including the decentralisation of tax-base and rate-setting authority and the finding of a consensus-based and transparent equalisation formula.

Finally, Prime Minister Chernomyrdin's political movement 'Our Home Russia' appears to be a new instrument of Moscow-controlled elitist policy (though it performed badly at the December 1995 elections to the State Duma), while most of the regional elites were quick in joining this new 'party of power'. This was clearly a response to the weak institutional coherence between national parties' headquarters and their political representation in the provinces, as was the case in the 1993 Russian parliamentary elections. However, the development of new parties, social movements and trade unions, which might even have a particular regional thrust, should only be encouraged, since it could lead, as shown in Putnam's study (1993) of Italy's regional governments, to new networks of civic engagement, which would not only challenge the official establishment, but also contribute to more efficiently working institutions in Russia's provinces.

There seems to be currently no real threat of separation of regions from the RF for purely economic reasons (Petrov and Treivish, 1994, p.17). This provides a further argument for the granting of more economic autonomy to Russia's provinces in conjunction with more requirements for higher accountability and fiscal responsibility, which would enhance the efficiency of providing public services in the regions. Further decentralisation and liberalisation would also break the established configuration of political power in the provinces based on industrial management and former nomenklatura networks, which act, in most of Russia's regions, as an impediment to thorough-going market reform.

Appendix

Table A.1 Regional differentiation of levels of prices and real wages in Western Siberia and the Russian Far East, 1993–4 (R, in current prices)

Western Siberia	Cost of Consumer Basket (June 1994)	Average Monthly Wages (June 1994)
Altaiskii *krai*	74 973	150 400
Kemerovskaya *oblast'*	92 569	321 000
Novosibirskaya *oblast'*	65 685	185 700
Omskaya *oblast'*	75 280	174 300
Tomskaya *oblast'*	84 488	248 400
Tyumenskaya *oblast'*	n.a.	514 600

Note: No statistical data for the Republic of Altai were given in the used source.

Far East	Cost of Consumer Basket		Average Monthly Wages	
	August 1993	June 1994	August 1993	June 1994
Primorskii *krai*	34 954	114 228	83 878	329 400
Khabarovskii *krai*	36 250	107 497	92 608	335 100
Amurskaya *oblast'*	21 497	144 700	76 550	297 200
Kamchatskaya *oblast'*	49 784	143 715	135 541	562 000
Magadanskaya *oblast'*	92 216	260 617	161 871	712 200
Sakhalinskaya *oblast'*	36 390	200 810	103 534	412 100
Republic Sakha/Yakutiya	51 228	234 380	103 426	479 100
Evreiskaya avt. *oblast'*	n.a.	128 834	66 549	238 400

Source: Compiled from Goskomstat Rossii (Primorskii *krai* office), *Pokazateli otslezhivaniya khoda ekonomicheskikh reform v sravnenii s drugimi regionami*, Vladivostok: 1993; Goskomstat Rossii (Primorskii *krai* office), *Nekotorye pokazateli, kharakterizuyushchie khod ekonomicheskikh reform, po Primorskomu krayu v sravnenii s drugimi regionami Sibiri i Dal'nego Vostoka na 1 iyuliya 1994 goda*, Vladivostok: 1994

Table A.2 Average per capita income and minimum living standard by macro-region, second and third quarters of 1994 (in R '000)

Macro region	Average per capita income		Minimum living standard		Difference column 1–2 (multiples)	
	Q2 94	Q3 94	Q2 94	Q3 94	Q2 94	Q3 94
Russia	168.7	224.7	81.8	92.9	2.06	2.42
North	241.0	308.1	92.4	114.8	2.61	2.68
North-West	149.8	198.3	78.6	90.4	1.91	2.19
Central	204.1	288.4	79.3	91.3	2.57	3.16
Volgo-Vyatskii	131.8	165.4	68.7	77.9	1.92	2.12
Central Black Earth	117.1	156.7	59.2	67.9	1.98	2.31
Povolzhskii	130.0	166.6	68.0	77.3	1.91	2.16
North Caucasus	119.4	149.7	67.5	72.0	1.77	2.08
Ural	144.4	197.2	81.9	90.4	1.76	2.18
Western Siberia	221.7	281.6	81.5	93.4	2.72	3.01
Eastern Siberia	180.0	222.7	96.1	118.4	1.87	1.88
Far East	233.8	335.9	133.5	167.3	1.75	2.01

Source: NG, 1 November 1994, p. 4

Table A.3 Demographic features of Western Siberia and the Russian Far East, 1993

Region	Population ('000, 1989)	Natural Increase (per '000 people)	Migration (per '000 people)
Russia	148 400	–0.2	n.a.
Western Siberia	13 165	–4.0	1.9
Altaiskii *krai*	2 624	2.3	1.7
Republic of Altai	191	0.8	4.0
Kemerovskaya *oblast'*	3 154	n.a.	n.a.
Novosibirskaya *oblast'*	2 764	n.a.	n.a.
Omskaya *oblast'*	2 129	n.a.	n.a.
Tomskaya *oblast'*	995	n.a.	n.a.
Tyumenskaya *oblast'*	1 308	n.a.	n.a.
Far East	7 674	–2.2	–11.0
Primorskii *krai*	2 236	–4.3	–2.2
Khabarovskii *krai*	1 579	n.a.	n.a.
Amurskaya *oblast'*	1 039	n.a.	n.a.
Kamchatskaya *oblast'*	429	n.a.	n.a.
Magadanskaya *oblast'*	389	n.a.	n.a.
Sakhalinskaya *oblast'*	700	n.a.	n.a.
Republic Sakha/Yakutiya	1 090	6.1	–13.1
Evreiskaya auton *oblast'*	212	n.a.	n.a.

Note: Figures for natural increase and migration are for December 1993 in comparison with December 1992. However, a local source in the PK indicated a negative increase of –7.8 for the same time period (UR, 3 February 1994, p.2).

Source: Compiled from EkiZh, no.6, February 1994, p.9; AP, 10 February 1994, p.2; E. Skatershchikova and L. Smirnyagin: 'Zhiznennye migratsii rossiyan kak faktor territorial'noi splochennosti Rossii´, *Rossiya regionov*, Napravlenie regionalistika analiticheskogo tsentra pri Presidente RF, Moscow, no.1, October 1994; Goskomstat Rossii, *Sotsial'no-ekonomicheskoe polozhenie Rossii 1993g.*, Moscow: 1993, p.347

Table A.4 Economic and social indicators of Western Siberia and the Russian Far East, first half of 1994 (in current prices)

Region	Retail Trade (in Rbn)	Services (in Rbn)	Average Wages (R '000)	Official Unemployment ('000 people)
Russia	47 353.1	7 126.3	183.5	1 219.3
Western Siberia	4 353.8	823.7	226.7	90.8
Altaiskii *krai*	519.1	95.4	132.7	23.7
Republic of Altai	47.1	6.6	135.8	0.9
Kemerovskaya *oblast'*	1 026.5	149.5	300.3	13.2
Novosibirskaya *oblast'*	699.0	183.3	163.0	19.2
Omskaya *oblast'*	568.5	77.5	158.7	8.8
Tomskaya *oblast'*	289.7	53.6	215.1	7.6
Tyumenskaya *oblast'*	1 203.9	257.8	481.5	17.4
Far East	3 094.2	599.2	410.9	56.1
Primorskii *krai*	875.2	161.5	292.3	11.3
Khabarovskii *krai*	638.1	136.3	301.6	12.0
Amurskaya *oblast'*	379.3	59.5	266.7	9.4
Kamchatskaya *oblast'*	197.2	32.0	476.0	4.4
Magadanskaya *oblast'*	214.4	87.3	657.9	5.9
Sakhalinskaya *oblast'*	301.4	37.4	382.9	10.0
Republic Sakha/Yakutiya	422.5	77.7	436.1	1.9
Evreiskaya auton *oblast'*	66.1	7.5	226.5	1.2

Note: Figures for average wages and official unemployment are for May 1994.
Source: Compiled from Goskomstat Rossii, *Sotsial'no- ekonomicheskoe polozhenie Rossii*, Moscow, January–June 1994

Table A.5 *Territorial budgetary redistribution in the RSFSR, 1989–91 (in per cent)*

Region	Regional budgetary income as a share of their produced national income, 1989	Deduction norm from turnover tax into regional budgets 1989	1990	1991
Vologodskaya *oblast'*	11.0	6.3	6.7	47.6
Murmanskaya *oblast'*	26.2	64.1	87.3	100.0
Leningradskaya *oblast'*	14.8	38.2	14.0	12.7
Moskovskaya *oblast'*	11.4	8.8	3.4	5.4
Smolenskaya *oblast'*	15.6	6.2	9.3	39.1
Astrakhanskaya *oblast'*	19.8	16.8	34.9	100.0
Kurganskaya *oblast'*	24.3	33.4	23.1	54.5
Sverdlovskaya *oblast'*	12.3	6.5	30.0	57.6
Chelyabinskaya *oblast'*	12.9	4.4	51.2	88.6
Altaiskii *krai*	18.7	21.4	20.8	25.6
Novosibirskaya *oblast'*	17.8	15.9	5.1	48.5
Omskaya *oblast'*	14.2	21.1	15.5	54.7
Tomskaya *oblast'*	17.1	32.7	20.9	100.0
Tyumenskaya *oblast'*	4.4	4.0	19.1	100.0
Krasnoyarskii *krai*	11.9	9.7	5.3	55.4
Chitinskaya *oblast'*	22.0	42.1	50.5	30.4
Magadanskaya *oblast'*	33.8	100.0	100.0	100.0

Note: Data for Tyumenskaya *oblast'* exclude the oil-rich Khanty-Mansiiskii and Yamalo-Nenetskii autonomous *okruga*.
Source: Solyannikova (1993, p.82)

Table A.6 Percentage distribution of expenditures among subnational budget categories, 1958

Subnational unit	FNE	SCM
Expenditures of republics (ASSR) and of territory, *oblast'* and *okrug* budgets	33.4	60.0
Expenditures of city budgets of republics	38.4	58.7
Expenditures of *raion* budgets of republics	9.5	84.1
Expenditures of workers' settlements of republics	13.7	81.7
Expenditures of rural budgets of republics	2.5	82.0

Note: FNE = Financing the national economy
SCM = Social and cultural measures.
Source: Hutchings (1983, p.47)

Table A.7 Share of expenditures by different budgetary levels, 1965–90 (in Rbn and percentage)

Budgetary Level	1965	%	1980	%	1990	%
Total budget	101.6	100.0	294.6	100.0	513.2	100.0
Union budget	43.2	42.5	157.8	53.6	240.5	46.9
Republic budgets	37.3	36.7	89.4	30.3	173.6	33.8
Regional and local budgets	21.1	20.8	47.4	16.1	99.1	19.3

Source: Solyannikova (1993, p.16)

Table A.8 Regional and local budget expenditures, 1960–75 (in Rmn and percentage)

Type of regional or local soviet	1960	%	1970	%	1975	%
Oblast', other	2 952	20.5	5 770	20.0	7 746	20.2
City	6 566	45.5	13 126	45.5	17 848	46.5
Raion	3 840	26.7	7 482	26.0	9 393	24.4
Workers' settlement	301	2.1	652	2.3	878	2.3
Village	747	5.2	1 800	6.2	2 531	6.6
Total (% as percentage of USSR state budget)	14 406	19.7	28 830	18.7	38 396	17.9

Note: 'Other' includes ASSR, *krai* and *okrug* units.
Source: Lewis (1983, p.63)

Table A.9 The structure of industry in Siberia, 1960–70 (in per cent of gross output)

Industrial Branch	West Siberia		East Siberia		Far East	
	1960	1970	1960	1970	1960	1970
Fuel industries	21.10	23.70	15.13	16.86	11.00	7.74
Electric power	3.50	3.60	4.85	7.69	1.50	2.77
Iron and steel	8.10	5.20	0.85	0.95	0.80	0.95
Nonferrous metals	2.60	1.90	11.40	17.66	7.40	10.37
Chemical industries	4.80	9.40	2.76	4.63	0.70	1.22
Wood products, pulp and paper	7.20	4.70	20.73	13.84	13.20	11.63
Building materials	3.70	3.50	7.73	5.01	6.40	7.25
Machine-building	18.30	28.20	10.06	16.20	16.80	21.88
Light industries	11.70	8.60	9.10	11.53	5.40	5.29
Food industries (including fishing and fish processing)	22.50	14.80	22.24	13.35	38.30	33.67
All industries	100.00	100.00	100.00	100.00	100.00	100.00

Source: Dienes (1982, p.232)

Table A.10 Labour intensity of industrial branches in the European RSFSR and Siberia in 1977

Industrial branches	Labour intensity of production (man-year per R10 000 of gross output)		Index of labour intensity in Siberia relative to European RSFSR (Europ.RSFSR=100)
	European RSFSR (including Urals)	Siberia (including Far East)	
Fuel industries	0.35	0.34	97.1
Electric power	0.39	0.44	112.8
Iron and steel	0.42	0.47	111.9
Nonferrous metals	0.31	0.39	125.8
Chemicals and petrochemicals	0.45	0.47	104.4
Machine-building and metalworking	1.04	1.01	97.1
Wood products, pulp and paper	1.19	1.12	94.1
Building materials	1.00	0.89	89.0
Light industries	0.55	0.66	120.0
Food industries	0.29	0.33	113.8

Source: Mozhin (1980, p.214)

Table A.11 Indices of living conditions in Siberia (including Far East) and share of ministries and departments in their financing, 1971–5

Infrastructure and service indicators	Average level of supply relative to European USSR (mean for European USSR = 100)	Share of ministries in financing service (% of budget channelled through ministries)
Pupils per classroom	114.8	8.2
Personnel in retail establishment per 100 population	127.5	27.4
Number of hospital beds per 1000 population	113.4	30.1
Sitting place in dining halls and cafeterias	95.4	43.2
Kindergarten and nursery places per 100 pre-school age children	92.5	64.5
Mean level of urban housing space per population	87.3	71.3

Source: Mozhin (1980, p.154)

Figure A.1 Federal and provincial committees and associations dealing with regional policy in Russia, 1994–early 1995

1. Federal Level:

Executive Power:

- Office for issues of subjects of federation in President's administration (head: German Aksenov)
- Office for work with territories in President's administration (head: Nikolai Medvedev)
- Ministry for issues of nationalities and interregional policy (minister: Nikolai Egorov)
- Section *Regionalistika* of the analytical centre of the President's apparatus (head: Leonid Smirnyagin)

Legislative Power:

- Committee for issues of the federation, the federation treaty and regional policy of the federation council (head: Vasili Tarasenko)
- Committee for issues of the federation and regional policy of the State Duma (head: Vladimir Ryzhkov)
- Deputies' group 'new regional policy' in the State Duma (head: Vladimir Medvedev)
- Committee on local self-government of the State Duma (head: Anatolii Sliva)

National Parties:

- Party of Russian Unity and Accord (PRES) (leader: Sergei Shakhrai)
- Congress of Russian Communities (leader: Yurii Skokov)
- Left-centrist Movement 'Regions of Russia' (leader: Ivan Rybkin)

2. Provincial and Interregional Level:

Executive Power:

- Union of heads of republics
- Union of Russian governors (head: Anatolii Tyazhlov)

Legislative Power:

- Regional associations: 'Siberian agreement', Central Russia, Black Earth regions, North-West regions, Ural, Caucasus Nations, Far East and others

Source: various issues of Russian central press

Table A.12 National origin of executives of enterprises in industry, agriculture, transport, communication and construction in autonomous territories of the RSFSR, 1 January 1989 (in per cent)

Autonomous Territory	Percentage of Titular Nation	Percentage of Titular Nation's Executives	Index of Executives
Buryatiya	24.0	36.7	1.53
Tatariya	48.6	64.1	1.32
Mordoviya	32.5	37.9	1.17
Yakutiya	33.4	38.2	1.14
Bashkiriya	21.9	24.2	1.11
Kalmykiya	45.4	48.1	1.06
Checheno-Ingushetiya	70.7	71.5	1.01
Dagestan	83.4	83.8	1.00
Udmurtiya	30.9	30.8	1.00
Russian total	81.5	77.3	0.95
Kareliya	10.0	9.0	0.90
Chuvashiya	67.8	59.2	0.87
Komi	23.3	18.3	0.79
Tyva	64.3	39.6	0.62
Mari	43.3	26.4	0.61

Note: The 'index of executives' was calculated by dividing the percentage share of the titular nationalities' executives through the percentage share of the titular nationality of the total population.
Source: Perepelkin (1992, p.105–6)

Table A.13 Index of relation between Russians and Tatars in different spheres of the economy and the public sector in Kazan', 1974–5 and 1983

Economic and Public Sectors	1974–5	1983
Industry	0.99	1.12
Construction	0.66	0.58
Transport and Communication	1.54	0.97
Retail Trade and Public Catering	0.62	0.87
Science, Education, Health and Culture	1.22	1.17
State Administration	0.88	0.82

Note: The 'index of relation' was calculated by deviding the percentage share of Russians employed in a particular sector through that of Tatars.
Source: Perepelkin (1992, p.106)

Table A.14 Number of former nomenklatura members as heads of local administrations in a few Russian regions, March 1994

Oblast'	Total Number of Heads of Administration	Former Leading Party Officials	% of Total
Rostovskaya	58	28	48.3
Voronezhskaya	33	25	75.7
Belgorodskaya	27	21	77.8
Irkutskaya	38	16	42.1
Novosibirskaya	37	14	37.8
Sverdlovskaya	24	12	50.0

Source: RV, 3 March 1994, p.2

Table A.15 Sharing rates for revenues and expenditures between the centre and the regions in 1992–mid-1994 (in per cent)

	Federal Budget			Regional Budgets		
	mid-1992	1 Aug 93	1 Aug 94	mid-1992	1 Aug 93	1 Aug 94
Total Revenues	n.a.	50.0	48.0	n.a.	50.0	52.0
Profits Tax	40.7	35.0	35.0	59.3	65.0	65.0
Personal Income Tax	0.0	0.0	1.0	100.0	100.0	99.0
VAT	80.0	64.0	66.0	20.0	36.0	34.0
Excise Duties	n.a.	56.0	57.0	n.a.	44.0	43.0
Income from Foreign Economic Activities	n.a.	96.0	99.0	n.a.	4.0	1.0
Total Expenditures	n.a.	52.0	51.0	n.a.	48.0	49.0
Economy	n.a.	32.0	33.0	n.a.	68.0	67.0
Social Infrastructure and Culture	n.a.	20.0	20.0	n.a.	80.0	80.0
Administration	n.a.	77.0	79.0	n.a.	23.0	21.0
National Defence	n.a.	100.0	100.0	n.a.	0.0	0.0

Note: Percentage figures under mid-1992 were also valid for the third and the fourth quarters of 1992.

Source: Compiled from Wallich (1994, p.53) and FI, 29 September 1994, p.4

Table A.16 Planned federal investment programmes for 1995 (in Rbn and percentage figures)

Sphere of Investment	Absolute Amount	Percentage of Total
Total	18 766.57	100.0
Fuel and Energy	391.17	2.1
Food and Medicine	661.23	3.5
Conversion of VPK	763.60	4.1
Space Shuttle Programme	857.40	4.6
Transport and Communication	334.52	1.8
Housing Construction	5 004.30	26.7
Science	1 456.48	7.8
Social Infrastructure	5 149.66	27.4
New Entrepreneurship	75.63	0.4
Consumer Goods and Services	8.03	0.04
Primary Spheres of Industry	1 671.42	8.9
Environment	67.37	0.4
Compensations for Accidents and Natural Disasters	2 325.76	12.4

Note: Percentage figures add up to 100.1 per cent because of rounding.
Source: KD, 21 December 1994, p.2

Table A.17 Comparison of privatisation results and the concentration of banking capital and insurance payments by macroregion, July–September 1994

Macroregion	Privatisation (1 August 1994)	Banking Capital (% of total, 1 July 1994)	Insurance (% of total, 1 September 1994)
Russian total	0.864	100.00	100.00
Volgo-Vyatskii	1.680	1.60	n.a.
North-West	1.246	3.59	n.a.
St Petersburg	n.a.	n.a.	4.73
Central-Black Earth	1.241	0.83	n.a.
North Caucasus	1.182	3.93	n.a.
Krasnodarskii *krai*	n.a.	n.a.	2.65
Western Siberia	1.043	5.66	n.a.
Tyumenskaya *oblast'*	n.a.	n.a.	2.88
Central	0.944	63.39	n.a.
Moscow city and *obl.*	n.a.	61.06	28.97
Povolzhskii	0.915	4.86	n.a.
Eastern Siberia	0.806	2.05	n.a.
Far East	0.680	5.59	n.a.
North	0.549	2.03	n.a.
Ural	0.481	6.47	n.a.
Sverdlovskaya *oblast'*	n.a.	n.a.	4.26
Chelyabinskaya *obl.*	n.a.	n.a.	3.00
Pribaltiiskii	0.458	n.a.	n.a.
Other	–	–	56.39

Note: Privatisation results were calculated by dividing the number of privatised enterprises which submitted applications by the number of enterprises which were subject to privatisation under the state programme. The concentration of insurance payments was only available by city and only those with more than 2.00 per cent were included in this table.

Source: Compiled from DM, special issue *Region*, no.1, September 1994, p.5; KD, 19 November 1994, p.6 and EkiZh, no.48, November 1994, p.15

Table A.18 Leading Russian regions by foreign investment, first half of 1994 (in $mn)

Region	Foreign Investment
Moscow city	42.0
Arkhangelskaya *oblast'*	41.0
Tomskaya *oblast'*	16.3
Novosibirskaya *oblast'*	5.0
Moscow *oblast'*	4.2
Irkutskaya *oblast'*	3.3
St Petersburg	3.1
Sakhalinskaya *oblast'*	2.6
Kareliya Republic	2.15
Vladimirskaya *oblast'*	2.13

Source: KD, 12 November 1994, p.2

Table A.19 Price differentials for services in various cities and urban settlements in Altaiskii *Krai*, 9 August 1994 (in R)

Indicator	Barnaul	Biisk	Rubtsovsk	Gornyak	Slavgorod	Kamen' n.O.
Public bus	121	100	100	40	100	100
Long-distance telephone call (unit per min)	233	200	320	200	160	200
Municipal rents for housing (per square m)	38	50	38	25	35	37
Hot water supply (per unit)	1 095	979	1 279	n.a.	775	147
Kindergarten place (monthly)	728	1 105	651	455	469	350
Dentist check	1 615	900	300	n.a.	1 120	n.a.

Source: AP, 17 August 1994, p.2

Table A.20 Retail price differentials in various West Siberian cities, 9 August 1994 (in R per kg or l)

Indicator	Barnaul	Novosibirsk	Krasnoyarsk	Tomsk	Kemerovo	Omsk
Beef	2 633	2 991	3 610	3 500	4 400	1 900
Vegetable oil	1 550	2 185	2 059	1 700	2 000	1 850
Milk	498	470	585	715	470	305
Cheese	4 875	5 239	5 353	5 117	6 540	4 400
Sugar	1 050	989	1 138	834	n.a.	1 260
Bread	560	667	693	750	843	341
Vodka	4 660	5 064	5 270	6 535	5 827	4 467
Petrol	93	324	250	324	230	255
Coal (per t)	9 090	7 872	5 475	2 028	1 004	810
Firewood (per t)	15 880	14 500	3 538	800	1 500	426
Electricity (per kWh)	12	17	15	36	9	25

Source: AP, 17 August 1994, p.2

Table A.21 Comparison of Russian domestic and world market prices for energy resources, May 1994 (in R per t)

Energy Resource	Domestic price	World market price	Relation domestic/ world market price
Oil (incl.VAT)	75.6	199.5	0.38
Diesel fuel	220.0	260.8	0.84
Fuel oil	83.4	149.6	0.56
Petrol	350.0	267.6	1.31
Gas (per '000 cbm)	57.7	153.4	0.38

Source: KD, 8 July 1994, p.2

Table A.22 Natural increase of total Altaiskii *Krai* population compared with the one living in the officially recognised area subject to radiation from the Semipalatinsk testing facility, 1955–92 (per '000 people)

Indicator		1950	1959	1970	1979	1989	1992*
Birth rate	A	31.8	28.8	15.0	17.4	14.4	10.9
	B	35.8	29.8	15.9	18.6	16.1	11.3
Death rate	A	11.5	7.2	8.4	10.7	10.7	11.6
	B	12.1	8.1	9.1	11.9	12.3	12.2
Natural Increase	A	20.3	21.6	6.6	6.7	3.7	–0.7
	B	23.7	21.7	6.8	6.7	3.8	–0.9

Note: A = Total AK population;
B = Population living in the officially recognised area subject to radiation from Semipalatinsk testing facility.
*Data only for first nine months of 1992 available.

Source: Rodionova (1993, p.73)

Table A.23 Unemployment rates by macroregions of the Russian Federation, December 1993–December 1994

Macroregion	Dec 1993	Dec 1994
RF total	1.2	2.5
North	1.8	3.4
North West	1.6	2.8
Central	1.8	3.7
Volga-Vyatka	1.8	3.7
Central Chernozem	0.7	1.7
Povolzhskii	1.0	2.4
North Caucasus	1.5	2.7
Urals	1.0	2.4
West Siberia	0.7	1.8
East Siberia	1.1	2.3
Far East	1.0	2.1

Source: RET, 3(4) 1994, p.89

Table A.24 Increase of CPI by macroregions in the Russian Federation, 1992–4 (December 1992 = 100)

Macro-region	Dec 1992	Dec 1993	Dec 1994
RF total	100	898	2 927
North	100	847	2 517
North West	100	921	2 982
incl St Petersburg	100	916	3 126
Central	100	818	2 877
incl Moscow city	100	906	3 767
Volga-Vyatka	100	1 015	3 299
Central Chernozem	100	855	2 818
Povolzhskii	100	951	2 964
North Caucasus	100	766	2 351
Urals	100	823	2 732
West Siberia	100	923	3 138
East Siberia	100	976	3 351
Far East	100	983	3 306

Source: RET, 3(4) 1994, p.40

Table A.25 Consumer prices for municipal services in selected regions of Western Siberia and the Russian Far East, 1 July 1994

Region	Gas (R per person)	Hot water (R per person)	Electricity in city (R kWh)	Coal (R t)	Firewood (R cbm)	Petrol (R l)
Western Siberia						
Altaiskii *krai*	n.a.	856	12	9 070	7 107	245
Krasnoyarskii *krai*	177	353	573	7 773	4 304	288
Irkutskaya *oblast'*	n.a.	19	4	n.a.	n.a.	275
Kemerovoskaya *oblast'*	16	432	600	n.a.	n.a.	n.a.
Novosibirskaya *oblast'*	20	591	6	713	10 167	215
Omskaya *oblast'*	158	633	25	n.a.	426	215
Tomskaya *oblast'*	17	180	6	2 028	800	205
Tyumenskaya *oblast'*	90	623	855	24 213	5 288	252
Far East						
Primorskii *krai*	n.a.	64	5	345	n.a.	437
Khabarovskii *krai*	n.a.	20	5	420	364	381
Amurskaya *oblast'*	n.a.	425	30	22 650	20 317	440
Kamchatskaya *oblast'*	n.a.	38	40	n.a.	n.a.	n.a.
Magadanskaya *oblast'*	n.a.	2 500	30	10 500	6 300	520
Sakhalinskaya *oblast'*	n.a.	614	40	35 196	12 774	615
Republic Sakha/Yakutiya	864	1 701	36	5 000	4 200	440
Evreiskaya auton *oblast'*	n.a.	27	6	361	n.a.	381

Note: Prices for household gas and hot water were charged as a lump sum per person in each household.

Source: Compiled from Goskomstat Rossii (Primorskii *krai* Office), *Nekotorye pokazateli, kharakterizuyushchie khod ekonomicheskikh reform, po Primorskomu krayu v sravnenii s drugimi regionami Sibiri i Dal'nego Vostoka na 1 iyulya 1994 goda*, Vladivostok: 1994, p.20–2

Table A.26 Main income sources of the consolidated budgets of the Altaiskii and Primorskii *kraya* in 1994 (in Rmn and % of total)

Income Source	AK	%	PK	%
Total	1 690 262	100.0	2 186 682	100.0
Profits tax	218 522	12.9	551 117	25.2
VAT	268 011	15.9	203 664	9.3
Personal income tax	189 584	11.2	392 657	18.0
Excise duties	41 701	2.5	34 752	1.6
Other	154 927	9.1	264 872	12.1
Total guaranteed income	872 745	51.6	1 447 062	66.2
Subsidies	158 750	9.4	77 386	3.5
Federal budget	559 756	33.1	569 928	26.1
Federal loans	30 206	1.8	53 500	2.4
Credits	68 801	4.1	–	–
Federal programmes	–	–	38 806	1.8

Note: Absolute figures for AK add only to R 1 690 258mn.

Source: Compiled from Komitet po finansam, nalogovoi i kreditnoi politike administratsii Altaiskogo kraya, *Spravka ob ispolnenii byudzheta 1994 goda v Altaiskom krae* (mimeo) and interview with the deputy head of the budget office of the PK administration, L. Popova, in November 1995

Table A.27 Consolidated budget of Novosibirsk *oblast'*, 1992–4 (in Rmn and % of total)

Income Sources	1992	%	1993	%	1994	%
Total	40 376.0	100.0	571 229.0	100.0	2 192 012.0	100.0
Profits tax	9 546.6	23.6	124 833.0	21.8	408 758.0	18.6
VAT	6 712.1	16.6	82 239.0	14.4	401 881.0	18.3
Personal income tax	6 674.6	16.5	66 975.0	11.7	274 685.0	12.5
Excise duties	1 752.6	4.3	11 250.0	2.0	50 214.0	2.3
Other	4 434.2	11.0	29 861.0	5.2	326 640.0	14.9
Total guaranteed income	29 120.1	72.1	315 158.0	55.2	1 462 178.0	66.7
Subsidies	1 171.7	2.9	53 658.0	9.4	314 104.0	14.3
Federal budget	6 827.7	16.9	187 643.0	32.8	332 058.0	15.1
Federal loans	3 256.5	8.1	12 770.0	2.2	3 239.0	0.1
Credits	–	–	2 000.0	0.4	–	–
Federal fund for financial support of regions	–	–	–	–	80 433.0	3.7
Spheres of expenditure						
Total	49 721.0	100.0	669 298.5	100.0	2 769 679.9	100.0
Current expenditure	33 240.9	66.8	483 865.0	72.3	1 946 545.0	70.3
of which:						
Wages	6 338.7	12.7	79 084.0	11.8	327 593.0	11.8
Social benefits	1 890.9	3.8	8 512.0	1.3	75 098.0	2.7
Equipment/furniture	6 733.9	13.5	65 267.0	9.7	424 112.0	15.3
Mutual settlements	5 648.2	11.4	156 606.0	23.4	123 846.0	4.5
Price compensation	4 861.9	9.8	19 761.0	3.0	156 113.0	5.6
Subsidies	3 228.9	6.5	87 549.0	13.1	624 170.0	22.5
Loans	1 282.2	2.6	25 004.0	3.7	12 996.0	0.5
Other	3 256.2	6.5	42 082.0	6.3	202 617.0	7.3
Capital investment	4 906.6	9.9	51 319.0	7.7	221 152.0	8.0
Health service	5 404.4	10.9	63 835.5	9.5	272 339.9	9.8
Education	6 169.1	12.4	70 279.0	10.5	329 643.0	11.9
Budget deficit	9 345.0	18.8	98 069.5	14.6	577 667.9	20.9

Note: Percentage figures do not add up to 100.0 per cent because of rounding.
Source: Internal report by committee of financial and tax policy of the Novosibirsk *oblast'* administration, April 1995

Table A.28 Regional export quotas for the Primorskii *krai*, 1991–4 (in absolute terms as they were handed down to the PK administration)

Export product	1991	1992	1993	1994
Fish products ('000 t)	69.0	175.0	95.3	68.0
Lumber and wood products ('000 cbm)	545.0	1 000.0	80.0	140.0
Non-ferrous metals ('000 t)	18.0	–	–	–
Cement ('000 t)	5.9	–	–	–
Mineral fertilizers ('000 t)	–	50.0	25.0	–
Soybeans ('000 t)	–	–	–	10.0

Note: Data do not include those quotas which were directly distributed to export producers in the region. These figures were hardly available.
Source: Compiled from different internal papers of the PK administrations

Table A.29 Ranking of Altaiskii and Primorskii *kraya* within the Russian Federation by different indicators, 1994

Indicator	Altaiskii *krai*	Primorskii *krai*
Territory	19	20
Population	19	23
Per capita produced national income (1993)	59	24
Industrial output	34	29
Gross agricultural output	8	42
Employment in national economy	20	23
Capital investment	30	20
Profits in national economy	44	27

Source: Compiled from Goskomstat Rossii, *Sravnitel'nye pokazateli ekonomicheskogo polozheniya regionov Rossiiskoi Federatsii*, Moscow:1995

Notes

NOTES TO CHAPTER 1

1. 'Local' refers to urban or rural districts which are administratively subordinated to regions and are called in Russian *raion*. The terms 'territorial' and 'spatial' are interchangably used for both subnational, administrative levels.
2. The Federation Treaty was published in *Vostok*, April 1992, no.2 and was reprinted and translated in the Western literature in Götz and Halbach (1993, p.184–6).
3. This was first published in *Rossiiskaya gazeta* on 17 February 1994. For further discussion and analysis of the way Tatarstan was forced to back-down in its claim for state sovereignty see: Teague (1994, p.19–27).
4. At a conference in Moscow on 23 September 1994, where politicians such as Yu. Luzhkov (Moscow's mayor), N. Travkin (Democratic Russia) and G. Popov (Russian Movement for Democratic Reforms) as well as academics such as L. Abalkin and A. Granberg participated, it was proposed to fuse subnational administrative divisions into 10–12 larger units (DM, 27 September 1994, p.2).
5. This is not necessarily true for ordinary people. Hough concluded from a 1993 pre-election survey among 33 869 respondants in 31 standard provinces (not republics!) that there is 'a level of tolerance towards the autonomous republics consistent with democratic federalism' (1994, p.13), although one could also read his results in a different way – since 40 per cent of the respondants disapproved proclamations of sovereignty compared with a mere 21 per cent approval (*ibid.*, p.14).
6. Novikov (1994, p.8–10) found in a number of regional statutes whole paragraphs, which were lifted from the Russian Constitution. This could easily be an example of regional elites (admittedly, illiterate in law, as stated) claiming the primacy of regional legislation over that of the RF, for which the PK is probably the best example (which is referred to).
7. Thomas and Kroll (1993, p.455) noted that Central Bank credits to state enterprises ran to an estimated 22 per cent of GDP in 1992, which could be part of Yavlinskii's equation – being spend on behalf of the government. Easterly and Vieira da Cunha (1994, p.461) arrived at the same estimate.
8. For their convocation in Yaroslavl' in September 1994 and their joint lobbying efforts see: *Izvestiya*, 20 September 1994, p.4.
9. Przeworski (1991, p.59) stressed in his analysis of the transition to democracy in Southern Europe and Latin America also the role of trade unions and political parties, which can, in the current situation in Russia be neglected.
10. Such kind of fiscal policy was the most important instrument of regional development in the UK in the 1980s (Temple, 1994, p.228).
11. Regional institutions for privatisation include the committee for property administration of the executive body and the property fund originally

affiliated to the former regional soviets. Both were apparently devised to balance and check on each other's activity, but institutional divisions and competences remained blurred and often ended up in a showdown between executive and legislative power. Mandatory targets for privatisation set by central authorities for each industrial sector were stopped (Radygin, 1994, p.67).

12. For four other approaches in East European countries see: Stark (1992).
13. A study of housing privatisation in seven Russian cities using a sample of about 5000 households showed that inter-city differences as such are not significant (Struyk and Daniel, 1995, p.206).
14. 'Political constitution' is here defined in a broader sense as rules that allocate policy-making powers and establish relationships of accountability (cf. Roeder, 1993, p.23).
15. Przeworski (1991, p.35) noted two other features:

    1) centralised allocation of physical resources and administrative price setting were more prevalent in Eastern Europe than in capitalist countries;
    2) income distribution is incomparably more unequal in Latin America than in Eastern Europe.

16. Stark (1992, p.17–20) called this a 'designer capitalism' and based his scepticism on three reasons:

    1) the failure of socialism rested precisely in the attempt to organise all economic processes according to a grand design;
    2) systems designers and international advisory commissions who fly into the region with little knowledge of its history tend to approach the problem of 'the transition' exclusively through their own general models;
    3) blueprint designers take the 'collapse of communism' to indicate the existence of an institutional void, but it is the differing paths of extrication from state socialism that shape the possibilities of transformation in the subsequent stage.

17. This comprises the first tier of policy makers in the Politburo and Central Committee and the second tier of the selectorate in the bureaucracy. However, Roeder's definition of 'bureaucracy' was very vague and amorphous. Such theories of 'new institutionalism' have a very exclusionary projection and seem to neglect shifting social synthesis and networks in everyday life.
18. Offe (1994, p.239) distinguished between modernisation, 'genesis environment' and 'path dependency' theories, the latter two of which we consider as postmodernist, whatever difficulties this term might evoke.
19. Janos (1994) provides intriguing evidence of the economic underdevelopment of six East European countries (Czechoslovakia, Hungary, Poland, Yugoslavia, Bulgaria and Romania), when he calculated the ratio of the aggregate national product per capita with six West European countries (not identified!), which declined, according to his estimate, from 48:100 between

East and West in 1910 to 32.9:100 in 1980 and 25:100 in 1992. As a consequence, Janos argued, East European countries have no other chance to overcome backwardness than by adjusting their economic, political and legal institutions to models presented by the more advanced West.

20. In *Izvestiya* (2 July 1994, p.5) the institution of the President's administration was scrutinised and it was argued that it is characterised by an old, inherited structure and has similar functions to the former general secretary's apparatus, with the only difference being that Yeltsin's administration is a faster growing bureaucratic apparatus.
21. *Izvestiya* published in July 1994 a series of articles under the headline 'Whom Belongs Power in Russia?', which is certainly a striking example for this discourse.
22. This was contrasted to the so-called 'shock-therapy' approach adopted by the Russian government in 1992 to push through its IMF sponsored stabilisation programme. The essential difference of the latter is that monetary and budgetary instruments are given priority over institutional restructuring in the sequencing of reforms. However, Moscow's reformers quickly implemented an ambitious privatisation programme and felt the urgent need to adopt new laws on corporate governance and banking. For an explanation of the evolutionary paradigm, see also: van Ees and Garretsen (1994, p.1–13).
23. Clarke *et al.* (1994, p.212) questioned every kind of quantitative data and considered them as merely soft data. There is certainly a point in this notion considering the statistical turmoil in Russia in 1992, but later statistical reporting improved substantially. In most of the cases, attempts were made to avoid using just one source and weigh different data with each other.
24. Interviewees either did not agree to be recorded or – the main reason – situational circumstances (noise, short time, frequent interruptions) made it impossible.
25. Since March 1994 the governor of the PK, E. Nazdratenko, frequently suspended *Utro Rossii* because of its critical reporting on his business activities and the violation of human rights, resulting in severe setbacks for our research .
26. For an excellent discussion of limitations with Russian foreign trade data see: Hanson (1994a, p.31–2).
27. While under the Soviet planning system output figures were overstated to report plan-fulfillment, they are now understated to avoid taxation.
28. Hough's 1993 pre-election survey (see note 5) paid $3000 to each Russian scholar of the 71 investigated regions for their participation in the election study (1994, p.2). A television team from the BBC, which was filming in Vladivostok in September–October 1994, paid each 'fixer' of a meeting $50, not to mention the interview itself (author's conversation with the producer Jeremy Bristow).
29. Interview with the deputy head of the committee for employment and migration of the AK administration, N. Kargina, on 19 April 1994.
30. Interview with the deputy head of the committee of foreign economic and regional relations of the PK administration, V. Tikhomirov, on 14 September 1994.
31. According to Professor Grigorii Khanin from the Novosibirsk State University, who tried to recalculate official Soviet statistics in previous

years, this figure could simply be wrong in the primary source (interview on 7 April 1995).

32. The Far Eastern Basin was the only aqua-territory of the RF, where fishing did not decline substantially (from 2 749 960 t in 1992 to 2 682 000 t in 1993), which meant, in fact, a relative increase in the share of the Far Eastern Basin in Russia's total fishing from 52.7 per cent in 1992 to 63.2 per cent in 1993 (EkiZh, no.11, March 1994, p.4).

NOTES TO CHAPTER 2

1. This regional pattern may have been intensified by the Soviet system, but it was not created by it; it pre-dated the Russian Revolution in 1917.
2. In 1921, Soviet Russia's State Planning Committee (*Gosplan*) set up a special commission to establish a network of economic regions, based on the following conditions, which later became part of the Soviet locational principles:

   1) good transportation connections with other regions;
   2) emphasis on those types of economic activities for which the region was best suited in terms of natural and social costs;
   3) an integrated economic system operating on the principle of maximum labour efficiency (Lonsdale, 1965, p.467–8).

3. Instead of the term 'unity', modern social theory would probably use that of 'entropy', interpreting the movement towards complex development as one to a disorder of equal distribution.
4. For an extensive discussion on this issue see: Bahry (1987).
5. The most prominent representatives of this approach were Friedrich and Brzezinski (1965).
6. Taubman (1973, p.18) described this using three elements:

   1) 'problem-directed search' – looking for an answer close at hand;
   2) 'satisficing' – accepting the first answer that looks good enough instead of insisting on the best;
   3) 'standard operating procedures' – routines that guarantee application of old answers to new problems.

7. Examining the six basic features of totalitarian dictatorships (official ideology, single mass party led by one dictator, terroristic police control, monopoly control of mass communication, monopoly control of effective armed combat and centrally controlled economy), as they were originally defined by Friedrich and Brzezinski (1965, p.9–10), Rutland argued that 'the Soviet system still bore certain distinctive features (such as the state-controlled economy, the role played by the CPSU and the legacy of the terror) which served to separate it out from the common-or-garden authoritarian regime' (1993, p.11).
8. Western studies discussed accurate material and provided information mostly at the local level (city, *raion*). Relying on this Western discourse, we

will refer in this section to local budgets, while turning our attention to the regional level (*oblasti, kraya*) later in our case studies. 'Subnational administrative unit' refers here also to both local and regional level.

9. Ross (1987, p.76–8) provided the figure of 30.5 per cent secured income and 53.5 per cent regulated income in 1975, while Hahn (1988, p.129–32) estimated the first part between 36 and 41 per cent and the second one between 57 and 61 per cent of the total. But both show clearly that up to two-thirds of all local income came from the federal budget, while only one-third was locally based.
10. Ross (1987, p.155) gave the figure of 35 per cent of control by local soviets in the RSFSR in 1979, although it is not clear what he meant by 'general housing in stock'. This ranged, according to Rutland (1993, p.104), from 87 per cent in Leningrad down to 16 per cent in Voroshilovgrad. The latter gave, actually, the average estimate of 40 per cent for city soviets' control of housing which comes close to Dienes' figure.
11. From the regime's viewpoint, single-candidate elections operated with increasing efficiency. As Zaslavsky and Brym (1983, p.73) found, the number of candidates defeated in local elections had fallen by a factor of more than three during the 1960s and 1970s, while the number of seats had increased by some 40 per cent.
12. This concept was originally elaborated as a planning method encompassing an economic and spatial aggregate which was to be developed in accordance with a specified plan to solve an economic problem of national importance and was to be concentrated in a relatively limited and geographically compact area with a resource base suitable for solving its objectives. The essence of this concept was the locational association of technological linkages (Lonsdale, 1965, p.466) generated by a specific production cycle. The most advanced analysis in the Western discussion was de Souza (1989). The most prominant Soviet scholar on this issue was Bandman, who used complicated mathematical formulae to defend his concept until the late Soviet period (Bandman, 1990).

NOTES TO CHAPTER 3

1. The analysis in this chapter draws on Western and Russian academic discussions on Russian regional development in 1990–4, as well as extensive reading of the Russian central press on regional issues for the period of early 1994 until July 1995. Earlier ideas were expressed in Kirkow (1995c, p.1004–1020) and Kirkow (1996, p.13–29).
2. This issue was discussed more extensively in Teague (1995, p.4) and Hanson (1994a, p.9). Another contentious issue is the influence of religions other than the Russian orthodox church. A report in *Nezavisimaya gazeta* (8 December 1994, p.3) claims that an increasing number of Russian people are currently converting to Islam. According to the author of this article, the *oblasti* of Penza had five per cent, Ul'yanovsk 11.5 per cent and Astrakhan more than 20 per cent of Muslims as a share of the total population in late 1994. All three regions are predominantly populated by ethnic Russians, but

are bordering or in geographical proximity to Muslim regions of the RF. If this tendency continues, it could seriously undermine Russian statehood in which the Russian orthodox church is considered to be one of the main pillars.

3. The military suppression of Chechnya's drive for independence in December 1994–July 1995 became a bloody chapter of the recent Russian history, which further divided the Russian public in terms of support for democratic reform. While Elizabeth Teague (1993, p.10) found a north-south divide with provinces north of the Fifty-Fifth Parallel being generally more supportive for Yeltsin after his showdown with the Supreme Soviet in October 1993, Nikolai Petrov (NG, 20 January 1995, p.3) discerned a different pattern in which regions approved the war in Chechnya the more they were situated geographically away from the rebellious republic, including some strongholds in Central Russia. Due to limited information on the creation of new intragovernmental relations between Moscow and Chechnya at the time of writing, we will mainly focus on the other option which was applied to Tatarstan.
4. In fact, this triggered a perilous development of signing other bilateral agreements with a number of republics (Bashkortostan, Dagestan, Kabardino-Balkariya, North Osetiya) in 1994, while new agreements were reportedly prepared with the republics of Sakha (Yakutiya), Buryatiya and Tyva as well as standard provinces such as the *oblasti* of Kaliningrad, Murmansk, Orenburg and Krasnodar *krai* (Pozdnyakov, 1995, p.6), in which these regions claimed a similar preferential treatment to that of Tatarstan. While the former head of the President's administration, Sergei Filatov, gave this practice a positive assessment (RV, 31 August 1994, p.1), it was also faced with an increasing opposition, in particular by the Federation Council (KD, 13 September 1994, p.2). See, for strong criticism of this practice by the then head of the Committee for Issues of the Federation, the Federation Treaty and Regional Policy of the Federation Council, Vasil Tarasenko, *Delovoi mir* (supplementary *Region*, no.1, September 1994, p.3).
5. As discussed in Chapter 1, regional leaders refused to transfer federal taxes and printed money surrogates to avoid hard budget constraints which undermined macroeconomic stabilisation.
6. This bears hardly any relation to reality. Forty-one per cent of the leading positions were reportedly occupied by ethnic Russians in early 1994 compared with their 42 per cent share of the total population according to the 1989 census, correspondingly: Karachaevtsy 23%:31%, Cherkesy 9%:10%, Abaziny were in office in seven per cent of the leading positions, but their share of the total population was not available (*Segodnya*, 14 January 1995, p.3 and Teague, 1995, p.17).
7. One could, of course, ask whether it is worth keeping people there today under economic cost-efficiency criteria. In many cases, they were prisoners before and used as cheap labour for logging and mining.
8. Shakhrai, who is also the leader of PRES with its main thrust on regional development and territorial integrity, discussed these issues in his 'basic thesis' on federalism and new regional policy. In the tradition of dialectical materialism, he called for the 'equalisation of regional opportunities',

leaving open whether he wants more regional efficiency or equity (RG, 4 February 1995, p.4).

9. This is also true for a number of standard regions like Perm *oblast'* (*Segodnya*, 7 October 1994, p.2) and Sverdlovsk oblast', where officials even claimed elements of statehood (KD, 10 November 1994, p.3).
10. The latter applies also to Kalmykiya (RG, 30 June 1995, p.4).
11. The author of this article, Arbakhan Magomedov, considers the essential difference between both prototypes of regional elites in the fact that there was a vertical mobilisation of the ruling elite in Ul'yanovsk compared with a horizontal one in Nizhnii Novgorod (*Segodnya*, 31 December 1994, p.10). This comes, respectively, close to Putnam's model (1993, p.101 and p. 175) of elitist policy and vertical patron-client networks in southern Italy compared with horizontal networks of civic engagements and cooperation in northern Italy. However, it is also worth pointing out that Boris Nemtsov in Nizhnii Novgorod kept many former party and state officials as deputies and *raiony* heads of administration.
12. For other discussions of this topic in the Russian central press, see: RV, 25 May 1995, p.2; RV, 6 June 1995, p.2; RG, 6 June 1995, p.2 and RV, 22 June 1995, p.2.
13. The OTD organised under Polezhaev a network of shops which enjoyed tax allowances and lower rents. A preferential treatment applies also to bread factories. As a result, 92 per cent of total regional revenues in 1994 came reportedly from the defence industry compared with merely two per cent from small-scale industry and services (DM, 23–29 January 1995, p.17). After Moscow shifted down the responsibilities for social infrastructure and capital investment in 1992, the deterioration of social services seems to encourage local corporatism and preferential treatment for local industries. For price controls by the Omsk administration and Polezhaev's favouring of the agrarian lobby, see: *Segodnya*, 8 February 1995, p.9.
14. There is a review of the General Proceeding's actions against regional and local councils and administrations in 1993–4 in *Rossiiskaya Federatsiya* (no.8, 1995). It includes cases of misuse of official positions in Nizhnii Novgorod (at *raion* level).
15. Other examples reported in the Russian central press include Astrakhan (*Segodnya*, 22 October 1994, p.3), Moscow city (KD, 3 November 1994, p.2) and Voronezh (*Izvestiya*, 6 December 1994, p.5). For the authoritarian style of the governor of Amurskaya *oblast'*, V.Polevanov, who declared later the denationalisation of vital spheres of industry when he became the head of the federal GKI, his arbitrary distribution of credits, the misuse of extrabudgetary funds, patron-client relations and family dynasty in power, see: RV, 1 November 1994, p.2.
16. For a more extensive discussion of the challenge by the governor of the PK, Evgenii Nazdratenko, who sought a democratic mandate to claim more independence from Moscow, see Chapter 5. Yeltsin's decree 'On Measures for the Strengthening of a Unified System of Executive Power in the Russian Federation' on 3 October 1994 was, in fact, a direct reply to Nazdratenko's challenge.
17. Executive members of leading energy and construction companies (*Bashkirenergo*, *Bashuralenergostroi*) were reportedly kidnapped and

arrested. The oil pipeline network from Western Siberia running through Bashkiriya to European Russia was tapped by the republic leadership for use in the region, while selling, at the same time, lower quality Bashkir oil (RG, 11 February 1995, p.3).

18. Some of them, though, showed higher political ambitions and intruded openly into the sphere of competence of regional officials, for example, the President's representatives in Rostov *oblast'*, Vladimir Zubkov, who was sacked by Yeltsin on 16 December 1994 (RV, 20 January 1995, p.2), and in Orenburg *oblast'*, Vladislav Shapovalenko (RV, 5 April 1995, p.2). On the positions of Yeltsin's representative in Tyumen *oblast'*, see: RV, 1 March 1995, p.2.
19. In Kaliningrad *oblast'*, 8000 people worked reportedly in federal structures in mid-1994 (*Segodnya*, 25 August 1994, p.2). But this figure presumably excludes total army personnel. While total population in this province amounted to 900 000 people in early 1995, about 200 000 soldiers were stationed in the region at that time (FI, 23 February 1995, p.VIII). In Tomsk, 40 different federal structures operated in autumn 1994 and 49 in Lipetsk (DM, September 1994, p.2).
20. For a discussion of conflicts between the President's administration and 'Siberian Agreement', see: Hughes (1994, p.1133–61). For a meeting of the Prime Minister, Viktor Chernomyrdin, with representatives of 'Siberian Agreement' and the latters' demands including the management of 50 per cent of state-owned shares of Siberian oil companies, the retention of 50 per cent of revenues from export and additional state compensations after quotas and licences for oil exports were abolished, see: KD, 26 July 1995, p.2.
21. It was reported that 170 political organisations and 20 small parties were active in Tambov *oblast'* in late 1994 which severely complicated the finding of a political consensus for ultimate decision making (RV, 7 September 1994, p.2). In Amurskaya *oblast'*, 130 political parties and social movements were active in early 1995 (RV, 24 March 1995, p.2).
22. In Samara, the regional leader of 'Democratic Russia's Choice', German Shtatskii, and the President's representative in the province, Yurii Borodulin, were involved in a scandal being accused of embezzling R4.2bn from the extrabudgetary fund for medical insurance. About 200 people received reportedly R50 000 to become members of this party (NG, 25 February 1995, p.1–2).
23. Regional branches of 'Our Home Russia' were reportedly set up in Krasnoyarskii *krai* (*Izvestiya*, 4 May 1995, p.2), Krasnodarskii *krai* (*Segodnya*, 7 June 1995, p.2), Tatarstan (*Segodnya*, 8 June 1995, p.3), Bashkiriya (*Segodnya*, 28 June 1995, p.2), Voronezhskaya *oblast'* (*Segodnya*, 5 July 1995, p.3) and Novgorodskaya *oblast'* (*Segodnya*, 12 July 1995, p.3).
24. For the political positions of the leadership of the 'Congress of Russian Communities' and its nationalist stance, see: KD, 25 May 1995, p.3.
25. Most of the local heads of administration were former nomenklatura members as shown in the appendix (Table A.14). For gerrymandering in Arkhangelsk *oblast'*, see: RV, 3 March 1994, p.2. Twenty seats in the new parliament in Komi republic were reserved for local administrative units

and it was widely expected that the heads of local administration would get these seats (RV, 26 October 1994, p.2).

26. In Moscow *oblast'*, the turnout in some voting districts for the election to the regional Duma did not reach 10 per cent (RV, 23 February 1995, p.2).

27. However, Andrews and Vacroux (1994, p.64–5) showed that members of the military, the militia and the KGB received many more votes than average and that candidates who were employed by the Communist Party neither benefited nor suffered as a result of their profession.

28. See for the LDPR in Novgorod (*Segodnya*, 17 November 1994, p.3), Kaliningrad (*Izvestiya*, 18 November 1994, p.5), Krasnodar (RG, 24 November 1994, p.1) and Bryansk (*Izvestiya*, 10 December 1994, p.2) and for the KPRF in Bryansk (RV, 21 February 1995, p.2).

29. The member of the President's Council, Leonid Smirnyagin, mentioned 57 provinces by mid-February 1995, while, according to him, legislation on local self-government was still not adopted in 12 regions at that time (RV, 16 February 1995, p.2).

30. For a more extensive discussion on how these 'coping mechanisms' can undermine stabilisation, see: Wallich (1994, p.80).

31. For comparison it is worth mentioning neighbouring Leningradskaya *oblast'*, which planned for 1995 a budget deficit of 26 per cent (KD, 21 December 1994, p.3). It does not have strong commercial banks like St Petersburg, although it could offer more land for sale.

32. McLure (1994, p.186) estimated that taxes based on production, including the implicit tax that resulted from price controls on domestically sold oil, took more than 90 per cent of the world market value of oil sold on the domestic market in 1994, even before a profits tax was levied.

33. This compares with Lavrov's estimate (1994, p.6) that about 10–12 regions (mainly standard provinces) provided 60 per cent of total tax revenues in 1993, as outlined in Chapter 1. This was also the case in 1994 (Lavrov, 1995, p.5). According to Shirobokova (1995, p.18), 13 provinces provided 50 per cent of total tax revenues in 1994. Moscow city's share of total federal revenues increased from 13 per cent in 1993 to 19.5 per cent in 1994 (FI, 16 February 1995, p.II).

34. Companies operating in Ingushetiya are reported to pay no local taxes, only 20 per cent of the federal taxes and 50 per cent of regular export and import tariffs (Bell, 1994, p.14). In Kalmykiya, companies pay quarterly $600, while being exempted from all other taxes (KD, 10 February 1995, p.8).

35. A report in *Finansovye izvestiya* (29 September 1994, p.IV) claimed that there were 27 central and 70 different locally raised taxes in Russia in autumn 1994 compared with 10 federal and four state or local taxes in the USA.

36. These consist of 19 basic consumer items. The regional differences in costs of consumer baskets were reported to be 1:4.1 in late July 1994 (RG, 3 August 1994, p.3). It increased rapidly to 1:5 by the end of August 1994 (DM, special issue *Region*, no.1, September 1994, p.4), but fell to 1:3.9 in February 1995 (RV, 11 March 1995), presumably due to late 1994 wage payments.

37. At the conference on local self-government in February 1995, Chernomyrdin had praised these modifications as a major breakthrough

towards fiscal decentralisation (RG, 21 February 1995, p.2). However, VAT retention rates were much higher in many regions before; the provincial rate of profits taxes was up to 13 per cent in 1994. Personal income taxes are assigned 100 per cent to regional authorities in many other federal states.

38. Parts of the federal budget with a clear regional objective were estimated to amount to 25 per cent of the total budget in 1995 including seven per cent for the 'Fund for the Financial Support of Regions' and another 14 per cent for subsidies for Moscow city, subsidies for closed towns, the maintenance of social infrastructure and food supply of the Far North. Subsidies for industrial sectors include coal industry, agriculture, compensations for the Chernobyl' and Chelyabinsk accidents and nuclear fall-out of the Semipalatinsk testing facility as well as the fuel, road and ecological funds (DM, 12–18 December 1994, p.23).
39. Official budgetary income in the Komi republic amounted to R2.2trn in 1994 compared with a total of extrabudgetary funds of R1.3trn in that year (DM, 21 April 1995, p.5). A similar relation is expected for 1995.
40. It was reported that treasury offices were set up in 69 regions by the end of August 1994 (DM, 30 August 1994, p.5).
41. This compares with 83 per cent central capital investment as a share of total investment in 1991 (Karavaev, 1995, p.137).
42. Sakha's President, Mikhail Nikolaev, turned out to be the strongest advocate of federal support for the Far North in public. He published a whole series of articles in several central newspapers with more or less the same content. See, for example, RV, 15 July 1994, p.3; DM, 30 September 1994, p.4; NG, 20 October 1994, p.5 and 24 November 1994, p.3.
43. The first comprehensive discussion in Western academic journals on FIG in Russia was provided in *Communist Economies and Economic Transformation*, vol.7, no.1, 1995.
44. The above-mentioned extrabudgetary fund for the stabilisation of the economy in Ul'yanosvk region consisted of a 65 per cent price differential between state controlled and free-market prices which became, in fact, a local tax, but it also included sanctions and a one per cent local turnover tax (DM, special issue *Region*, no.1, September 1994, p.4).
45. A comparison of prices for privatised housing makes the whole picture more complicated, since one has to take local specifics into account, in particular in big cities like Moscow with a high concentration of federal ministries and representative offices of foreign companies. Traditional Ul'yanosvk city with a price of up to $27 100 for a three-room flat in July 1994 did not differ much relative to reformist Nizhnii Novgorod city ($36 000), if compared with Moscow city ($120 000) or even Samara city ($59 200) in that month. One could, of course, speculate whether the price in Ul'yanovsk city was a result of a small free market in the presence of executive price control, while that in Nizhnii Novgorod could have been one of more general price competition (DM, special issue *Region*, no.1, September 1994, p.6).
46. For a more extensive discussion of the early Russian concept of FEZs in 1988–92, see: Kirkow (1993, p.229–43).
47. The development of the FEZ concept in Kaliningrad was analysed, for the period 1991–3, in: Dörrenbächer (1994) and for 1994, in: Reymann (1995). For other articles in the Russian central press in the course of preparing a

new decree on the special status of Kaliningrad *oblast'* in autumn 1994, see: *Segodnya*, 27 October 1994, p.3; *Izvestiya*, 18 November 1994, p.5 and KD, 24 November 1994, p.4. Details of the preferential regime, which was proposed by the Kaliningrad regional administration, were discussed in: *Segodnya*, 26 November 1994, p.2.

48. Bill-of-exchange-schemes operated reportedly in 20 Russian regions in late 1994 (*Segodnya*, 3 November 1994, p.2). See for their introduction in Krasnodarskii *krai* (DM, 5 November 1994, p.5) and in Novgorod *oblast'* (*Segodnya*, 10 November 1994, p.3) and for both bill-of-exchange-schemes and the issue of municipal bonds in Moscow city (KD, 26 October 1994, p.2) and in St Petersburg (*Segodnya*, 11 February 1995, p.3). The issue of municipal bonds in Perm' was discussed in several issues of *Kommersant-daily*, for example 5 August 1994, p.6; 25 August 1994, p.6; 1 September 1994, p.6 and 27 October 1994, p.6.
49. For the introduction of municipal housing loans in St Petersburg, see: *Segodnya*, 15 October 1994, p.2 and KD, 15 October 1994, p.6 and in Moscow city, see: KD, 20 October 1994, p.2.
50. Provinces were receiving more than 75 per cent of all public revenues from oil and gas in the second half of the 1980s, 80 per cent of which went to Alberta alone (Simeon and Robinson, 1990, p.244).
51. The 1980 referendum resulted in a 59.5 per cent no-vote against 40.5 per cent approval of sovereignty. Support for the *Parti Québécois* came increasingly from the more conservative small town rather than the urban constituencies (Simeon and Robinson, 1990, p.253–5). The no-vote in the autumn 1995 referendum had an even smaller margin. Linguistic diversity was also a sensitive issue in many countries. In Spain, an estimated one quarter of the total population do not speak Castillian as their first language (Williams, 1994, p.86).
52. Canadian provincial revenues rose from 8.7 per cent of GNP in 1960 to 18 per cent in 1976. Moreover, the provincial share of government spending on goods and services rose from 18.6 per cent in 1955 to 43 per cent in 1975 (Young *et al.*, 1988, p.140–3) and further to more than 50 per cent by the end of the 1980s (Courchene, 1988, p.182).
53. In 1980, resource revenues accounted for less than three per cent of gross general revenue in all provinces except British Columbia (12.5%), Saskatchewan (28.6%) and Alberta (51.4%), see: Young *et al.* (1988, p.160, note 65).
54. This includes the following intragovernmental agreements:

- the Atlantic Accord 1985 to meet Newfoundland's claim for jurisdiction over offshore oil and gas;
- the western Accord 1985, according to which a host of taxes associated with the New Energy Policy, including the Petroleum and Gas Revenue Tax (PGRT) and the Petroleum Compensation Charge (PCC), were to be eliminated or quickly phased out;
- an agreement among Ottawa, Alberta, Saskatchewan and British Columbia to deregulate natural gas prices in November 1985;
- pressure grew on Ottawa to help rescue western grain farmers in 1987 (Simeon and Robinson, 1990, p.307–9).

55. In September 1976, Canadian provincial government personnel amounted to 519 000 people, federal government, civil service and armed forces to 557 000 and municipal government 256 000, as a result of which nearly one out of every nine members of the Canadian workforce was employed by the two senior levels of government at that time (Cairns, 1977, p.5).
56. A lot of intragovernmental problems discussed here with reference to the RF apply also to other former socialist countries. For a comparison of regional reforms between Russia, Poland and Bulgaria in the period 1990–4, see: Kirkow (1995, p.120–33). For the Chinese approach of introducing a four-tier system of intragovernmental relations, see: Ferdinand (1987, p.11).

NOTES TO CHAPTER 4

1. First ideas on this topic were expressed in Kirkow (1994, p.367–84) and Kirkow (1994a, p.1163–87).
2. First differentiations within these informal platforms started between leftist, reform Marxist and right groupings, setting up structures like '25th October' or 'Red Informals'. The following information was provided by one of the leading activists of 'Democratic Russia' in the province, E. Zvezdkin, a lecturer in biochemistry at the medical institute in Barnaul (interview on 21 April 1995).
3. These are members of the NTS, an organisation which was created by Russian emigrants in the 1930s and operated, as it was claimed, illegally in the former USSR (interview with the leader of the Altai NTS, A. Shvedov, on 24 April 1995). Its ideology is based on a curious mix of solidarity, Christianity, Russian patriotism and imperialism, liberty for the individual and a free market system, but it has a clear commitment towards creating a civic society and opposing state intervention in private and local life (*Politicheskaya platforma NTS*). For more details, see discussion below.
4. University lecturers tried to get their students involved in the democratic movement. On the anniversary of Stalin's death in 1988, they encouraged their students to come forward with anti-Soviet posters and slogans (interview Zvezdkin).
5. Interview with Emeshin on 18 April 1995.
6. Interview with Shvedov.
7. Zhil'tsov is today the head of a department of the Ministry for Fuel and Electric Power Industry in Moscow according to the then head of the FEZ administration of the AK, V. Kolesova (interview on 7 April 1994). Kolesova is today the deputy governor and head of the committee for legislation of the AK administration.
8. Interview with Sidorov on 12 April 1993.
9. Interview with the then head of the Altai department of the Siberian branch of the Russian Academy of Sciences, A. Loginov, on 16 April 1994. Loginov is today the director of the Altai branch of the Siberian Energy Bank.
10. Interview with Shuba on 19 April 1994.
11. See: AP, 23 September 1993, p.2; 25 September 1993, p.1 and 27 November 1993, p.1–2.

12. Openyshev expressed in an interview for *Altaiskaya pravda* (29 November 1994, p.1–2) a strong anti-reformist view, effectively supporting the attempt by the new regional parliament to undermine the vertical of executive power through elections of local heads of administration.
13. Bessarabov described his function in the State Duma in the most populist way: 'We all are lobbyists for the region' (AP, 1 June 1994, p.1).
14. Efremov claimed in June 1994 that he managed to get R13bn in form of federal payments for grain delivered from the AK the year before (AP, 1 June 1994, p.1). In contrast, Surikov claimed for his part the total of federal payments for the harvest in 1993 (AP, 16 June 1994, p.2).
15. *Kto est' kto na Altae*, Barnaul, 1994, p.44.
16. Taking an interview from him is a special adventure. He seems to know in advance what the questions could be, for which he has ready-made, populist answers, which are initially logical and persuasive (interview on 19 April 1994).
17. This corresponds with issues raised at his reception with the general public, which were discussed extensively in the local press: wages and pensions, executive power and its alleged indifference, Chechnya, pyramid schemes like MMM, agriculture, housing, women and the military (AP, 19 April 1995, p.1–3). This gives also an understanding of his perception of his potential electorate.
18. Interview with Safronov on 25 April 1995.
19. Interview with Emeshin.
20. It is worth pointing out the strange character of government in Moscow that this tactic illustrates. A member of a government should be following an agreed government line and then, if necessary, trying to ensure that members of parliament can be talked into supporting that line. Not the other way around.
21. Raifikesht had apparently applied for a new job as the cultural attaché in the Russian embassy in Germany, which he did not get in the end (interview with Loginov).
22. Interview with Korshunov on 21 April 1994.
23. *Ibid.*
24. At a meeting with the Russian Prime Minister, Viktor Chernomyrdin, he lobbied strongly for the military enterprise *Barnaultransmash*, whose director, V. Kargapolov, is also the head of the 'Director's Council', a regional industrial lobby (AP, 27 April 1994, p.1).
25. This was admitted by Sidorov, the head of the economics committee, during an interview taken by this author on 22 April 1995. Their function is more and more changing towards the provision of services.
26. This was the main message in *Programma vtorogo etapa reformirovaniya ekonomiki Altaiskogo kraya* (1994, mimeo, p.4–5), which was prepared by the committee for property administration. After privatisation entered into its second stage, when shares could be traded for money, this committee was naturally searching for new functions and suggested the fusion of its structure with the committee for industry. It ended up, however, with setting up new quangos like the 'Fund for Post-Privatisation Support of Enterprises'. According to the new 'Law on Privatisation in the Altaiskii *Kraї*' (see discussion below), this fund receives 51 per cent of the proceeds

of privatisation of regional state property (interview with the deputy head of this fund, T. Bobrovskaya, on 18 April 1995).

27. Interview with Sidorov on 19 April 1994. For projects for marble extraction in the Altai, see: FI, 26 January 1995, p.II.
28. Interview with Sidorov on 22 April 1995. According to the programme on grain production, wheat production in the AK should be doubled by the year 2000. For the recognition as a depressed region they lobbied particularly well in the Ministry of Geology and hoped to get more state orders from the centre.
29. There was a recent scandal over this fund, in which the former head of the provincial committee for property administration, Sergei Potapov, was involved, who was accused of having embezzled 20 000 privatisation vouchers, which were allocated to this fund (KD, 17 June 1995, p.20).
30. One example would be the programme on bus production in Siberia, which was agreed between enterprises in Kemerovo, Novosibirsk and the AK (interview with Sidorov on 22 April 1995). This pragmatic approach was also confirmed by the deputy head of the foreign economic department of the AK administration, V. Sukach (interview on 19 April 1995).
31. Interview with the then deputy head of the committee for legislation of the AK soviet, Sarychev, on 22 April 1993.
32. For example, the 'small council' decided on the amount of profits taxes to be paid by regional enterprises only by the end of March 1994, which led to substantial payment arrears (AP, 5 July 1994, p.2).
33. This was in line with the outcome in other Russian regions. In Novgorod city in none of the eight voting districts was the turnout more than 25 per cent, while in Novgorod *oblast'* eight re-elections had to take place all together (*Moskovskie novosti*, 27 March–3 April 1994, p.7). While the total turnout in Russia was just above 35 per cent, that in AK was 36.8 per cent (AP, 15 March 1994, p.1). A more comprehensive analysis of the 1994 regional elections, including a discussion on the 'ruralisation' of Russian regional politics, can be found in: Petrov (1994b, p.8–12).
34. The smallest voting district was that of the rural Pavlovskii *raion* with 28 200 eligible voters compared with the largest one of the city of Novoaltaisk of 50 300. The big cities of Barnaul, Biisk and Rubtsovsk had an average of 43–44 000 eligible voters per existing voting district compared with those of most of the rural areas of 30–35 000 (AP, 12 January 1994, p.1). This was a clear breach of the election regulation, which defined the deviation to be between five and 10 per cent (AP, 1 February 1994, p.1). Democratic forces appealed in the regional court against this arbitrary division of voting districts, which gave the communist-agrarian nomenklatura a clear advantage due to the large number of rural areas, but it was rejected (interview with Shvedov).
35. This he denied later when this author interviewed him on 19 April 1994.
36. Interview with the deputy chairman of the AK parliament, V. Safronov, on 19 April 1994. The number of active supporters of the communist-agrarian faction increased to 28 deputies after by-elections took place in four districts in February 1995 (interview with Safronov on 25 April 1995).
37. Interview with Emeshin.

38. Boldyrev is a typical representative of the old nomenklatura, who worked before as the first party secretary and chairman of the local soviet in Shelabolikhinskii *raion* and became later the general director of a joint stock company (AP, 16 June 1994, p.1).
39. *Otchet komiteta po upravleniyu imushchestvom Altaiskogo kraya za 1994 god*, Barnaul, 1995, p.16–17 (mimeo).
40. Interview with the head of the federal treasury office in the AK, S. Gusev, on 21 April 1995.
41. Interview with the chief-economist of the pension fund in the AK, L. Shavrunova, on 26 April 1995.
42. Interview with Kargapolov on 19 April 1995.
43. Interview on 22 April 1995.
44. Interview with Tverdokhlebov on 14 April 1994.
45. Interview with the general director of *Altaienergo*, V. Zubkov, on 11 April 1994.
46. He reiterated this intention in an interview in April 1995 when he just came back from the national congress of the Agrarian Party (AP, 20 April 1995, p.1). For a discussion on the nomenklatura background of this party and its competitor, the Peasants Party, which relies mainly on new entrepreneurs in agricultural production and farmers, see: *Izvestiya*, 20 April 1995, p.2.
47. The voter's movement 'For Genuine People's Power, Civic Peace and the Interests of Working People' consisted of representatives from the Communist Party, the Agrarian Party, the Agrarian Union, the trade union of APK workers, the veteran's union, the women's committee, the communist youth union, the movement 'Working Altai' and the teachers movement 'Education and Future' (interview with Safronov on 25 April 1995).
48. New entrepreneurs intended to give financial help to organise the party structure of Altai's Choice in the whole region for the run-up to the next elections at the federal and provincial level in 1995–6 (interview with V. Zlatkin, the director of 'Avantage' on 6 April 1994) and to prepare a similar project to that of G. Yavlinskii in Nizhnii Novgorod for the AK (interview with V. Pokornyak, the director of 'Altan' on 15 April 1994 and 20 April 1995), which did not materialise in the end.
49. Interview with Emeshin on 18 April 1995, who is one of the leading democratic activists in the region, having a medical and computer scientist background, and who set up the private company *Meditsinskaya Profilaktika*.
50. This was confirmed by another leading democratic activist, Zvezdkin, who considered the democratic movement as 'bureaucratised' and admitted that they have no real leverage on political decision making (interview on 21 April 1995).
51. *Politicheskii kur'er partii Demokraticheskii Vybor Rossii*, no.2, 1995, p.3.
52. Interview on 24 April 1995.
53. *Programma vtorogo etapa reformirovaniya ekonomiki Altaiskogo kraya (mikrouroven')*, Barnaul, 1994, p.1–2 (mimeo).
54. Interview with the managing director of *Barnaultransmash*, N. Loginov, on 6 April 1994. By the end of 1994, about 30 per cent of the workforce had reportedly been made redundant (AP, 7 December 1994, p.2).
55. Interview with the general director of *Barnaultransmash*, V. Kargapolov, on 18 April 1994. For an even further extension of this social infrastructure

in 1994, see: AP, 8 December 1994, p.3. In mid-1994, one-third of the housing stock in the city of Barnaul belonged still to branch ministries, while the city budget had a 74 per cent deficit and a further debt of R63bn, which was almost half of the total income at that time (AP, 14 May 1994, p.8 and 31 May 1994, p.1).

56. *Otchet komiteta po upravleniyu imushchestvom Altaiskogo kraya za 1994 goda*, Barnaul, 1994, p.8 (mimeo).
57. Interview with the head of the AK branch of the Russian Central Bank, V. Zemskov, on 7 April 1994.
58. Interview on 22 April 1995.
59. These figures were publicly announced by governor Korshunov, but they exceeded the amount spent for agriculture as indicated in the official statistics for budgetary expenditure in 1993 (see Table 6 in: Kirkow, 1994a, p.1176). Thus, it either appeared under a different heading or it was taken from extrabudgetary funds.
60. These figures were given by the then head of the committee for agriculture of the AK administration, A. Zatler. Korshunov reported a month later that they got R190bn from the centre and another R149bn as soft credits, which far exceeded the estimated amount of R200bn needed for the harvest in 1994. According to him, they also got R34bn for grain supply to the regional fund and R13bn to the federal fund from the centre (AP, 18 October 1994, p.1), which was presumably the above mentioned federal loan.
61. *Spravka ob ispolnenii byudzheta 1994 goda v Altaiskom krae*, Barnaul, 1995 (mimeo).
62. For a more detailed discussion on the falling share of guaranteed income in the AK budget, see Chapter 6.
63. *Sostoyanie zanyatosti na rynke truda kraya v 1994 godu*, Komitet administratsii Altaiskogo kraya po zanyatosti naseleniya, Barnaul, 1995, p.7–13 (mimeo).
64. Interview with the deputy head of the committee for employment and migration of the AK administration, N. Kargina, on 19 April 1994.
65. *Sostoyanie zanyatosti na rynke truda kraya v 1994 godu*, Komitet administratsii Altaiskogo kraya po zanyatosti naseleniya, Barnaul, 1995, p.13 (mimeo).
66. Grigor'ev (1993, p.59) found the highest death rates and a particularly high infant mortality for the considered period in 1950–1, that is following the biggest nuclear test in 1949.
67. According to Ryzhkov, a total of R219.2bn from the Semipalatinsk programme was promised for the region in 1995 (*Svobodnyi kurs*, 13–20 April 1995, p.3).
68. Interview with Safronov on 25 April 1995.
69. The new Russian Constitution left it open to be decided by authorities in each region in which way to elect the governor. As discussed in the previous chapter, President Yeltsin had decreed in October 1994 to delay the elections of governors until new Presidential elections would take place in mid-1996, but this was ignored by the AK parliament, which scheduled the elections for March 1996 (interview with Shuba on 27 April 1995).
70. *Ibid.*

NOTES TO CHAPTER 5

1. Earlier ideas on this topic were expressed in Kirkow (1993, p.754–70), Kirkow (1995a, p.923–47), Kirkow (1995b, p.325–70) and Kirkow and Hanson (1994, p.63–88). The help and inspiring discussions with Jeremy Bristow – the producer of the BBC film 'Lord of the East' – who generously provided records of interviews and shared information with this author while his television team was filming in Vladivostok in September 1994, are gratefully acknowledged.
2. For that reason, we focus in this section on the alliance of regional politicians with the industrial management and the military, while turning later to the rather modest influence of parties and social movements. For an examination of the role of trade unions and parties in privatisation in the PK, see: Vacroux (1994, p.39).
3. This information was provided by Damir Gainutdinov, a journalist of the local newspaper *Utro Rossii*, when this author interviewed him on 17 September 1993.
4. BBC interview with V. Shkrabov on 28 September 1994.
5. Nazdratenko claimed in an open letter to *Rossiiskaya gazeta* (20 October 1994, p.3) that he had to change the personnel of his predecessor completely because of corruption. He frequently tried to justify his authoritarian rule by the necessity to fight crime.
6. This stands for 'Primorskii Shareholding Company of Commodity Producers'.
7. Interview with the deputy head of the budget office of the PK administration, V. Rybakova, on 7 September 1994.
8. This was confirmed by Shkrabov during his BBC interview: 'Nazdratenko did not conquer power, he was promoted to power'.
9. Interview with the deputy head of the committee for economy and planning of the PK administration, G. Sorokin, on 17 September 1993.
10. Interview with the deputy head of the committee for fishing industry of the PK administration, Yu. Ponomarev, on 9 September 1994.
11. Interview with the deputy director of investment holding *Dal'moreprodukt*, O. Chichkalova, on 19 September 1994.
12. For some of them, both workplace background and party affiliation were indicated on the candidate list. However, the latter played, during the pre-election campaign, only a minor role and most of them were proposed by 'voters' groups' (UR, 12 March 1994, p.2).
13. Ipatov was sacked by the Minister of the Interior, Viktor Erin, in February 1995 for abuse of power and 'bad handling' of the investigations against Cherepkov (KD, 7 June 1995, p.14).
14. Interview with P. Nazarov on 20 September 1994.
15. Interview with the head of the federal treasury office in the PK, N. Sadomskii, on 21 September 1994.
16. Executives of commercial banks in the PK sensed the potential threat of large Moscow-based banks operating in their region under the shelter of the provincial administration. After *ONEKSIM bank* acquired the controlling package of shares of the local bank *Primor'e* in March 1995, leading officials of the Far Eastern Banking Association declared their intention to

fuse all 24 member banks into two or three large banks to be able to compete with the Moscow-based banks (KD, 3 March 1995, p.6).

17. *Informatsiya o realizatsii regional'nykh eksportnykh kvot, vydelennykh Primorskomu krayu v 1992 godu*, Otdel analiza i prognozirovaniya vneshnikh svyazei upravleniya ekonomiki i planirovaniya administratsii Primorskogo kraya, Vladivostok, 1993, p.2–3 (mimeo)
18. Interview with V. Butakov on 24 September 1993.
19. Interview with the managing director of the mining company *Primorskugol'*, I. Kopko, on 13 September 1994. *Primorskugol'* increased its prices to R24 000 per t of coal in September 1994. This compares with the price of R100 000 per t of coal from the Kuzbass at that time (including transport tariffs to Vladivostok).
20. *Kommersant-daily* (30 July 1994, p.3) reported a subsidy of R134bn for that time, which included price compensations for tariffs on freight transport of coal and fuel oil.
21. The third important issue was that of Nazdratenko's attempt at scheduling the election of the governor of the PK for 7 October 1994, a device to secure a democratic mandate to concentrate more authoritarian power in his hands, since the success of his manipulated re-election was without any doubt. This challenge to the centre will be discussed below.
22. The Southern Kurile islands suffered an out-migration of 931 people in 1993, but no figures for their total population were given in this report (*Segodnya*, 6 September 1994, p.3).
23. According to a state programme until 2000, the Kurile islands should receive an annual amount of R100bn (in 1994 prices) in subsidies, but they got merely R5bn by September 1994 (Venevtsev and Demkin, 1994, p.4).
24. For the PK and Sakhalin *oblast'*, necessary foodstuff, medicine, clothes and other products were imported from South-East Asian countries worth $100mn (RG, 13 October 1994, p.1).
25. *Rezhim khozyaistvovaniya dlya ekonomicheskoi stabilizatsii i razvitiya Primorskogo kraya*, Kraevaya administratsiya Primorskogo kraya, Vladivostok, 1994, p.12 (mimeo)
26. Interview with V. Tikhomirov on 14 September 1994.
27. It is worth noting that Ustinov's economic programme, which was summarised in *Kommersant-daily* (19 August 1994, p.3), did not differ substantially from Nazdratenko's project. He also demanded a special economic status and relied on the support of the traditional industrial lobby.
28. This author was told that Ustinov received 10 000 signatures from Viktor Cherepkov, the first democratically elected mayor of Vladivostok, who was brutally forced out of office by Nazdratenko in March 1994 (see below), to enhance Ustinov's chances (interview with Cherepkov's former advisor, I. Sanachev, on 19 September 1994).
29. The latter issue is discussed, in more detail, in Chapter 6 in the context of the analysis of economic reform.
30. Figures on Chinese illegal migration into Russia published by Russian sources are highly contradictory. *Kommersant-daily* (5 November 1994, p.4) claimed that 5mn Chinese people lived in Eastern Siberia and the Russian Far East in late 1994, while *Segodnya* (3 March 1995, p.6) reported 2mn for Russia as a whole.

31. It is interesting to note that Nazdratenko voted, as a former deputy of the Russian Supreme Soviet, for the ratification of this treaty in 1991 (RV, 16 March 1995, p.2).
32. Interview with I. Sanachev.
33. For first results of this experiment see: Yavlinskii (1992).
34. Interview with I. Sanachev.
35. *Ibid.*
36. However, these were still highly controlled prices compared with production costs of R100 per kWh in October 1994 (KD, 14 October 1994, p.11). In mid-1995, energy prices were R64 per kWh for household electricity and R287 for industrial enterprises. However, a number of enterprises paid a special rate of only R113 per kWh. The Ministry of Fuel and Energy Production reportedly issued a new soft credit of R300bn for preparation of the winter 1995–6 season in the PK (UR, 3 June 1995, p.1). Customers in the PK paid only 9.5 per cent of real electricity costs in 1994 (UR, 11 July 1995, p.2).
37. Interview with I. Sanachev.
38. At the time of writing, it is still not clear whether Nazdratenko has any ambitions for higher political office in Moscow. He was apparently offered the job of the head of the federal Committee for Precious Metals, which would be the rank of a minister (KD, 29 October 1994, p.3), but he refused (UR, 29 October 1994, p.1).

NOTES TO CHAPTER 6

1. Earlier ideas on this topic were expressed in Kirkow (1994b, p.144–61) and Kirkow (1996b).
2. While regional committees for property administration originally developed a bias to over inflate privatisation results, since they were pressed by the centre with mandatory targets and were offered preferential funding for completing privatisation assignments (Bornstein, 1994, p.440), provincial *Goskomstat* offices may not have received adequate information due to insider control. However, since mandatory targets were increasingly ignored by regional authorities, figures reported by both institutions came much closer in the course of 1994 (interview with colleagues of the economics institute in Akademgorodok in April 1995). General percentage figures for privatisation can hardly be taken as an indicator, since they refer only to those enterprises released for privatisation, which can be proportionally much less in a region with a high concentration of defence-related or energy production enterprises. Moreover, numerous exemptions and 'golden share' options for the government led to a vast variety of legal forms, which could at best be described as a 'commercialisation' (Rutland, 1994, p.1124).

   In terms of fiscal arrangements, one has to distinguish between *vydeleny* (allotted) and *perechisleny* (transferred) central subsidies, which can differ considerably in terms of the amount of money actually received and the time lag, resulting, in real terms, to much less due to high inflation. The inefficient Russian banking system allows commercial banks to capitalise on budgetary transfers before passing on the money to the proper recipient. Furthermore, Russian firms tend to under report output in order to minimise taxation and enhance their chance to get financial assistance (Rutland, 1994a, p.12), and caution is also necessary with data for paid income due to tax evasion by employees.

Finally, while one third of the PK retail trade turnover was estimated to be in 'non-registered', hence unreported form (UR, 28 July 1994, p.2), the same applied reportedly to 47 per cent in the AK (AP, 7 February 1995, p.1). There is also an increasing amount of 'shuttle trade', which was estimated for Russia as a whole at $6.2bn in 1993 and $7.5bn in 1994 (RET, 3(4) 1994, p.73).

3. According to the former deputy Minister of Finance and director of the Union of Industrialists and Entrepreneurs' Expert Institute, Sergei Aleksashenko, who is acting now as the deputy head of the Russian Central Bank, the central *Goskomstat* adds, for each region, to the numbers supplied by its regional offices (a) VPK data and (b) estimates of unregistered, informal economic activity (interview by Philip Hanson on 5 July 1995). How it can estimate (b) from Moscow, remains an open question.
4. More detailed explorations on difficulties with Russian statistics will be provided in the analysis of this chapter.
5. It is worth pointing out that both sets of regional data refer to points in time after the end of the first stage of privatisation (mid-1994), at which the whole process changed in nature, and there was a slowdown while the policies for the 'money' stage of privatisation were being disputed.
6. There were no data available for privatised medium- and large-sized enterprises by industrial sectors for Russia as a whole. *Russian Economic Trends* (vol.3, no.4, 1994, p.94) provided only a total figure of 15 052 privatised enterprises after voucher privatisation came to an end in July 1994.
7. The 'Far Eastern Shipping Company' employed 15 000 people by the end of 1994 (UR, 15 October 1994, p.1). Its officially declared profits of R150bn in 1993 amounted to almost one third of the total regional budget in that year (see Section 6.3).
8. Foreign investment amounted to 26.7 per cent of the founding capital, while the total debt of the fleet was estimated at R79bn (approximately $20mn) by the end of 1994 (*Segodnya*, 15 November 1994, p.3).
9. Interview with the managing director of *Primorskugol'*, I. Kopko, on 13 September 1994. This compares with production costs of R13 500 per t in early 1994 and R41 500 in early 1995 (FI, 18 April 1995, p.II). Thirty eight per cent of the shares were controlled by the national company *Rosugol'* and another 20 per cent by the Federal Property Fund (UR, 18 April 1995, p.2).
10. For a more extensive discussion on the price policy for coal and electricity in the PK, see Section 6.2.
11. Slider (1994, p.380) provided central GKI figures for medium- and large-scale privatisation according to which the PK ranked among the regions with the highest results of privatised enterprises, but this was before voucher privatisation was stopped by Nazdratenko. His data for small-scale privatisation in the PK by October 1993 (*ibid.*, p.384) could rather be an understatement, since the PK was indicated among those provinces with the

lowest results. This shows the difficulties with using central data, while not taking local reports and qualitative analysis into account at the same time. Slider's data for the AK are in line with our findings.

12. Competitive tenders and selling-off of leased premises, which were the most frequently used forms of small-scale privatisation in Russia, included special clauses prescribing a particular time period for maintaining the profile and workforce, but this was often ignored.
13. These results suggest that a critical mass of the number of private farms and privately used arable land seems to have been achieved in early 1995, since the percentage figures are almost identical with those for the beginning of 1994 (Kirkow 1996b, Table 8). Although there were still high fluctuations with 1780 private farms going bankrupt in the PK in 1994 (UR, 27 April 1995, p.3) and 714 in the AK between January and September 1994 (AP, 3 November 1994, p.3), the 10 per cent share of arable land privately used was maintained over the last two years. There is also a tendency for private farmers to put their cultivated land and machinery together for common agricultural production as was reported for the AK (AP, 12 July 1994, p.2).
14. It was also reported that regional officials intend to give Cossacks in the PK another 15.5mn ha of state reserve land (UR, 25 October 1994, p.3), which would make the above indicated figure of 73 300 ha of privately used land look fairly small. However, it is ironic that many private farmers in the PK employ Chinese people in order that their businesses survive (UR, 2 August 1994, p.1 and 13 April 1995, p.1).
15. The same applies to Russia as a whole. Farmers received reportedly soft state credits of a total of R112.2bn by the end of 1994, while former state structures got R8.3trn at the same time (*Izvestiya*, 23 November 1994, p.4). This is clearly in no relation to the above indicated five per cent of privately used land as a percentage share of the Russian total arable land, but this could also be evidence of a more efficient production by private farmers if compared with structures of the former APK. *Izvestiya* (23 November 1994, p.4) reported a significant fall in livestock production for the latter in 1994, while private farmers increased their output at the same time. According to *Nezavisimaya gazeta* (29 November 1994, p.4), there was a dramatic decline of gross output of the APK by more than 30 per cent in 1991–3.
16. In the Uglovskii *raion* of the AK, for example, private farmers cultivated 15 per cent of the arable land in the *raion* in 1993, while providing 41 per cent of the total grain production (AP, 21 March 1995, p.1). Even if former APK structures engaged in other spheres than grain production, this still indicates a comparatively high efficiency.
17. This means that the privatised percentage share of the initially state-owned housing in the PK is larger than this. Most rural housing and some urban housing have been owner-occupied from the state.
18. Particularly high unemployment rates were to be found in Ingushetiya (17.8%) and Ivanovo *oblast'* (10.2%) in May 1995, while Moscow city had the lowest one of the RF with 0.4 per cent at that time (DM, 29 May–4 June 1995, p.42).
19. According to Rutland (1994a, p.13), some 20 per cent of prices were still regulated at the national level (mainly energy and communication) and 30 per cent at the subnational level (food and utilities) by the end of 1994.

20. Unfortunately, no consistent data for the increase of the IPI at the regional level were available.
21. Goskomstat Rossii (Primorskii *Krai* Office), *Nekotorye pokazateli, kharakterizuyushchie khod ekonomicheskikh reform, po Primorskomu krayu v sravnenii s drugimi regionami Sibiri i Dal'nego Vostoka na 1 iyulya 1994*, Vladivostok, 1994, p.23
22. The whole Soviet and Russian practice of reporting and analysing regional 'money supply' seems odd in Western eyes. When a credit-card payment by telephone from London can get a good delivered by mail from Manchester, the notion of a regional money supply makes little sense. In the former USSR, and perhaps still in the RF, however, it does have some (limited) significance. As long as most consumer incomes and spending come and go in cash, and consumption is highly localised, MO of a region is perhaps (still) interesting.
23. The former adviser to Prime Minister Chernomyrdin and current director of the Moscow-based Institute of Economic Analysis, Andrei Illarionov, estimated the increase of money supply at 10 per cent for the first quarter of 1995 and another 20 per cent in April 1995 alone (*Segodnya*, 25 May 1995, p.2). This seems to apply to the growth rates of ruble M2, but part of this is a result of the CBR bying US-dollars to raise its currency reserves and emitting rubles in doing so. The effect of such kind of CBR actions is controversial.
24. Household prices for electricity in the PK were reported to be R6 per kWh compared with R30 in Moscow city, R47 in Sakhalin *oblast'* and R43 in Khabarovskii *krai* in 1994 (UR, 26 November 1994, p.2), which amounted to a price difference of almost 1:8 between the PK and Sakhalin.
25. In order to rely on standardised *Goskomstat* methodology, reports from the local press were used, but no adequate statistics for the Russian average data were available for the same months. However, figures are still highly contradictory. A central *Goskomstat* report indicated an average monthly income of R88 587 for the AK and R194 584 for the PK in June 1994 (Gosudarstvennyi komitet Rossiiskoi Federatsii po statistike, *Sotsial'no-ekonomicheskoe polozhenie Rossii*, January–June 1994, p.273). In contrast, the local *Goskomstat* office in the PK reported in an internal report an average monthly income of R159 400 in the AK and R362 400 in the PK for the same month (Goskomstat Rossii, Primorskii *krai* Office, *Nekotorye pokazateli, kharakterizuyushchie khod ekonomicheskikh reform, po Primorskomu krayu v sravnenii s drugimi regionami Sibiri i Dal'nego Vostoka na 1 iyulya 1994*, Vladivostok, 1994, p.5). What becomes clear is that both figures for the PK in the table are probably an understatement.
26. According to Alexei Novikov, a former consultant at the Analytical Centre of the President of the RF, official data on incomes generally are only for income received in rubles. Incomes paid in US-$ are largely unreported (interview by Philip Hanson in July 1995).
27. Interview with the head of the budget office of the AK administration, V. Aleinikov, on 8 April 1994.
28. Interview with the deputy head of the budget office of the AK administration, N. Yurdakova, on 8 April 1994.

29. The total of the federal fund for financial support of the regions in the RF 1995 budget law was R14 858.1bn (RG, 7 April 1995, p.3), which would mean a transfer of R1 129.2bn for the AK and R416bn for the PK.
30. According to information published by the Institut ekonomiki perekhodnykh problem, *Rossiiskaya ekonomika v 1994g.*, Moscow: 1995, the federal fund for regional support, at 22 per cent of VAT revenue equalled 6.1 per cent of federal budget expenditure in 1994. In the 1995 budget plan it is 27 per cent of VAT revenue and 7.0 per cent of federal expenditure. The implementation of this support is said to be very hard to unravel. Net federal-regional transfers in 1994 were 3.5 per cent of GDP, but this is a mixture of some regional support fund transfers (others were not necessarily reported) and other sorts of transfers. Sixty four regions received transfers (of some sort) in 1994, and 75 per cent of the (recorded) transfers were outside the regional support fund.
31. However, for comparison, the consolidated budget of Novosibirsk *oblast'* had a significant deficit in 1992–4 as shown in Table A.27.
32. The result of a total budgetary income of R1.69trn including a guaranteed income of only R872.7bn in 1994, as presented in Table A.26, shows that the original target was much more realistic.
33. Komitet administratsii Altaiskogo kraya po zanyatosti naseleniya, *Sostoyanie zanyatosti na rynke truda kraya v 1994 godu*, Barnaul: 1995, p.13
34. In both Central Bank soft credit and 'memorandum items' income and expenditure figures are the same, suggesting an automatic balancing of the books for presentational purposes. The procedure in Table 6.11 may be quite legitimate, but it means the figures were not telling us much. It is possible, for example, that a surplus in the official budget in year t is carried over to an off-budget fund in year t+1 and the income and expenditure figures for year t+1 then only show the extent to which the resulting balance was drawn down.
35. As noted in Chapter 5, the PK pension fund provided R25bn in July 1994 for Nazdratenko's populist measures in his pre-election campaign. The AK pension fund transferred R840.2mn in 1994 to the regional employment fund to meet earlier retirement costs (Komitet administratsii Altaiskogo kraya po zanyatosti naseleniya, *Sostoyanie zanyatosti na rynke truda kraya v 1994 godu*, Barnaul: 1995, p.12).
36. Interview with the chief-economist of the AK pension fund, L. Shavrunova, on 26 April 1995.
37. Total revenues of the RF pension fund amounted to R38 987.1bn in 1994 (KD, 12 May 1995, p.3), which means that the AK had 1.7 per cent of the total. The corresponding figures for the social insurance fund were R7 869.5bn and 1.1 per cent, and for the medical insurance fund R299.8bn and 13.7 per cent. Bearing in mind the above mentioned corruption scandals in the AK medical insurance fund, this was still an unusually high percentage share for a region with 1.8 per cent of the RF total population and is probably linked with the Semipalatinsk programme.
38. Interview with the deputy head of the PK state tax inspection, E. Ponomarchuk, on 12 September 1994.
39. Interview with the head of the PK social insurance fund, G. Perkovskii, on 14 September 1994.

40. Interview with the head of the PK pension fund, P. Nazarov, on 20 September 1994.
41. One example for methodological problems with the statistics in the PK relates to the sale of outdated naval vessels from the Pacific Fleet for an estimated $9mn (*Izvestiya*, 7 December 1994, p.4), 60 per cent of which were reportedly to be used for housing construction for military personnel (*Segodnya*, 22 November 1994, p.13), but it is difficult to define the source of financing for capital investment as used in Table 6.12 (see also KD, 28 March 1995, p.9).
42. However, an increase of output in chemical industries and a stabilisation in construction materials industries was expected in 1995 (FI, 23 May 1995, p.II). For a more extensive discussion on structural changes by industrial sector in Russia for the period 1985–94, see FI, 25 May 1995, p.IV.
43. The share of AK exports to Kazakhstan rose reportedly from 25 per cent of the total in 1993 to 32 per cent in 1994 (Departament vneshneekonomicheskoi deyatel'nosti administratsii Altaiskogo kraya, *Obshchie itogi po eksportu i importu*, Barnaul: 1995, p.5, mimeo), but this could look fairly different if hard currency payments were applied in each case. PK exports to non-CIS countries amounted to $99.4mn in the first quarter of 1995 compared with only $0.7mn with CIS-countries (UR, 27 April 1995, p.3), which makes trade with the latter category statistically almost negligible. Statistics on total Russian exports and imports (including CIS-countries) also varied widely. A report in *Ekonomika i zhizn'* (no.17, April 1995, p.35) on the balance of payment of the RF in 1994 indicated exports of $66 668mn and imports of $51 184mn, but it was not made clear how foreign trade with CIS-countries was calculated. Figures used in Table 6.13 were compiled from an analysis of *Russian Economic Trends* which used official *Goskomstat* PPP exchange rates to convert ruble CIS trade into US-dollars. As the authors outlined, this method may overestimate CIS trade in dollars, as ruble prices in intra-CIS trade grow faster than Russian domestic prices, but using the market exchange rate would lead to an even greater underestimation of CIS trade in dollar terms because of the large undervaluation of the ruble (RET, 3(4) 1994, p.81). For an excellent discussion of these issues, see: Michalopoulus and Tarr (1994, p.9–19).
44. Interview with the deputy head of the committee of foreign economic and regional relations of the PK administration, V. Tikhomirov, on 15 September 1993.
45. Authorities in the PK managed to keep 10 per cent of state customs duties in their territory in 1993 and expected this to increase up to 35 per cent in 1994 (interview with V. Tikhomirov on 14 September 1994).

Bibliography

RUSSIAN LANGUAGE MONOGRAPHS

M. Bandman, *et al.*, *Territorial'no-proizvodstvennye kompleksy. Prognozirovanie protsessa formirovaniya s ispol'zovaniem setei Petri* (Novosibirsk, 1990)

E. Gaidar, *Gosudarstvo i evolyutsiya* (Moscow, 1995)

A. Granberg (ed.), *Ekonomika Sibiri v razreze shirotnykh zon*, (Novosibirsk, 1985)

S. Grigor'ev and Yu. Rastov, *Prichiny passivnosti izbiratelei: urok na segodnya i zavtra* (Barnaul, 1994, mimeo)

N. Kolosovskii, *Teoriya ekonomicheskogo raionirovaniya* (Moscow, 1969)

A. Loginov, *et al.*, *Analiz khoda ekonomicheskoi reformy v Altaiskom krae* (Barnaul, 1993, mimeo)

A. Loginov and T. Sazonova (eds), *Formirovanie rynochnykh otnoshenii i strukturnaya politika v Altaiskom krae* (Novosibirsk, 1992)

A. Loginov and A. Trotskovskii, *Ekonomicheskie aspekty problemy likvidatsii posledstvii mnogoletnego vozdeistviya yadernykh ispytanii na Semipalatinskom poligone na territoriyu Altaiskogo kraya* (Barnaul, 1992, mimeo)

A. Loginov and T. Sazonova (eds), *Problemy likvidatsii na territorii Altaiskogo kraya posledstvii yadernykh ispytanii na Semipalatinskom poligone* (Novosibirsk, 1993)

P. Minakir, *Sintez otraslevykh i territorial'nykh planovykh reshenii* (Moscow, 1988)

V. Mozhin (ed.), *Ekonomicheskoe razvitie Sibiri i Dal'nego Vostoka* (Moscow, 1980)

B. Osipov (ed.), *Ekonomicheskii potentsial i problemy razvitiya Primorskogo kraya* (Vladivostok, 1992)

N. Petrov and A. Treivish, *Riski regional'noi dezintegratsii Rossii* (Moscow, 1994, mimeo)

S. Potapov and T. Bobrovskaya, *Itogi i perspektivy privatizatsii v Altaiskom krae* (Barnaul, 1994, mimeo)

A. Radygin, *Reforma sobstvennosti v Rossii: na puti iz proshlogo v budushchee* (Moscow, 1994)

V. Savalei (ed.), *Ekonomika Primorskogo kraya i ryada otraslei Dal'nego Vostoka v period reform 1992–93gg.* (Vladivostok, 1994)

A. Sidorov, *et al.* (eds), *Ekonomicheskaya reforma: otsenka sostoyaniya ekonomiki Altaiskogo kraya i blizhaishie perspektivy ee razvitiya* (Barnaul, 1994)

S. Solyannikova, *Byudzhety territorii* (Moscow, 1993)

G. Yavlinskii, *Nizhegorodskii prolog. Ekonomika i politika v Rossii* (Nizhnii Novgorod/Moscow, 1992)

ENGLISH AND GERMAN LANGUAGE MONOGRAPHS

H. Armstrong and J. Taylor, *Regional Economics and Policy, 2nd edn* (New York/London: Harvester Weatsheaf, 1993)

D. Bahry, *Outside Moscow. Power, Politics, and Budgetary Policy in the Soviet Republics* (New York: Columbia University Press, 1987)

V.N. Bandera and Z.L. Melnyk (eds), *The Soviet Economy in Regional Perspective* (New York: Praeger Publishers, 1973)

U. Beck, *Die Erfindung des Politischen. Zu einer Theorie reflexiver Modernisierung* (Frankfurt a.M.:Suhrkamp Verlag, 1993)

C. Bell, *Der rußländische Staatshaushalt: Die Beziehungen zwischen Zentrum und Territorien* (Cologne: Berichte des Bundesinstituts für ostwissenschaftliche und internationale Studien, no.65, 1994)

B. Bobrick, *Land der Schmerzen – Land der Hoffnung. Die Geschichte Sibiriens* (Munich: Droemer Knaur, 1993)

K. Bolz and A. Polkowski, *Der Wirtschaftsraum Sankt Petersburg. Wirtschaftliche und soziale Entwicklung im Herbst 1994 und Programme für die Zukunft* (Hamburg: HWWA-Report, no.149, 1995)

A.C. Cairns, *The Governing of a Federal Society: The Canadian Case* (London: Canada House Lecture Series, no.1, 1977)

A.C. Cairns, *Quebec and Canadian Federalism* (London: Canada House Lecture Series, no.49, 1991)

R.W. Campbell (ed.), *Issues in the Transformation of Centrally Planned Economies. Essays in Honor of Gregory Grossman* (Boulder Co.: Westview Press, 1994)

J.A. Dellenbrant, *The Soviet Regional Dilemmma. Planning, People, and Natural Resources* (New York/London: M.E. Sharpe, Armonk, 1986)

H.U. Derlien, U. Gerhardt and F.W. Scharpf (eds), *Systemrationalität und Partialinteresse. Festschrift für Renate Mayntz* (Baden-Baden: Nomos Verlagsgesellschaft, 1994)

P. de Souza, *Territorial Production Complexes in the Soviet Union – With Special Focus on Siberia* (University of Gothenburg, 1989)

L. Dienes, *Soviet Asia. Economic Development and National Policy Choices* (Westview Press/Boulder and London, 1987)

H. Dörrenbächer, *Die Sonderwirtschaftszone Jantar' von Kaliningrad (Königsberg). Bilanz und Perspektiven* (Forschungsinstitut der Deutschen Gesellschaft für Auswärtige Politik e.V., Arbeitspapiere zur internationalen Politik, no.81, Bonn: 1994)

D.A. Dyker, *The Process of Investment in the Soviet Union* (Cambridge: Cambridge University Press, 1983)

P. Ferdinand, 'Centre-Provincial Relations in the Peoples Republic of China Since the Death of Mao: Financial and Political Dimensions' (Working Paper no.47, Warwick University, December 1987)

I. Filatotchev, 'Geographic Aspects of Russian Privatisation' (University of Nottingham, 1994, mimeo)

T.H. Friedgut, *Political Participation in the USSR* (Princeton: Princeton University Press, 1979)

T.H. Friedgut and J.W. Hahn (eds), *Local Power and Post-Soviet Politics* (New York/London: M.E.Sharpe, Armonk, 1994)

C.J. Friedrich and Z.K. Brzezinski, *Totalitarian Dictatorship and Autocracy* (New York/London: Praeger, 1965)

J. Gibson and P. Hanson (eds), *Transformation from Below. Local Power and the Political Economy of Post-Communist Transitions* (Cheltenham: Edward Elgar, 1996)

R. Götz and U. Halbach, *Republiken und nationale Gebietseinheiten der Russischen Föderation. Bevölkerung, Politik und Wirtschaft* (Cologne: Bundesinstitut für ostwissenschaftliche und internationale Studien, 1993)

J. Habermas, *Die nachholende Revolution* (Frankfurt a.M.: Suhrkamp Verlag, 1990)

J.W. Hahn, *Soviet Grassroots. Citizen Participation in Local Soviet Government* (London: I.B. Tauris & Co Ltd. Publishers, 1988)

P. Hanson (1994a), *Regions, Local Power and Economic Change in Russia* (London: Chatham House, 1994)

P. Hanson (1994b), *Economic Change and the Russian Provinces* (University of Birmingham, 1994, mimeo)

R.J. Hill, *Soviet Political Elites. The Case of Tiraspol* (London: Martin Robertson, 1977)

J.F. Hough, *The Soviet Prefects: The Local Party Organs in Industrial Decision-Making* (Cambridge Mass: Harvard University Press, 1969)

R. Hutchings, *The Soviet Budget* (London: Macmillan, 1983)

E.M. Jacobs (ed), *Soviet Local Politics and Government* (London: Allen & Unwin, 1983)

J. Kornai, *The Socialist System. The Political Economy of Communism* (Oxford: Clarendon Press, 1992)

I.S. Koropeckyj and G.E. Schroeder (eds), *Economics of Soviet Regions* (New York: Praeger, 1981)

C. Michalopoulos and D.G. Tarr (eds), *Trade in the New Independent States* (Washington, D.C.: The World Bank/UNDP, Studies of Economies in Transition, no.8, 1994)

K. Mildner, *Local Government Finance in Russia* (paper prepared for the annual convention of the German Association of Political Science, Potsdam, 25–28 August 1994, mimeo)

J.C. Moses, *Regional Party Leadership and Policy-Making in the USSR* (New York/London: Praeger Publishers, 1974)

A. Nove, *The Soviet Economic System, 3rd edn* (London: Allen & Unwin, 1986)

C. Offe, *Der Tunnel am Ende des Lichts. Erkundungen der politischen Transformation im Neuen Osten* (Frankfurt/New York: Campus Verlag, 1984)

R.D. Olling and M.W. Westmacott (eds), *Perspectives on Canadian Federalism* (Scarborough, Ontario: Prentice-Hall Canada Inc, 1988)

R.D. Putnam, *et al.*, *Making Democracy Work. Civic Traditions in Modern Italy* (Princeton: Princeton University Press, 1993)

S. Reymann, *Kaliningrader Gebiet. Wirtschaftsentwicklung und- politik im Herbst 1994* (Hamburg: HWWA-Report, no.150, 1995)

P.C. Roberts, *Alienation and the Soviet Economy. The Collapse of the Socialist Era* (New York/London: Holmes & Meier, 1990)

P.G. Roeder, *Red Sunset. The Failure of Soviet Politics* (Princeton: Princeton University Press, 1993)

C. Ross, *Local Government in the Soviet Union. Problems of Implementation and Control* (London Sydney: Croom Helm, 1987)

P. Rutland, *The Politics of Economic Stagnation in the Soviet Union. The Role of Local Party Organs in Economic Management* (Cambridge: Cambridge University Press, 1993)

R. Sakwa, *Russian Politics and Society* (London/New York: Routledge, 1993)

J.R. Schiffer, *Soviet Regional Economic Policy. The East-West Debate Over Pacific Siberian Development* (London: Macmillan, 1989)

K. Segbers (ed), *Rußlands Zukunft: Räume und Regionen* (Baden-Baden: Nomos Verlagsgesellschaft, 1994)

K. Segbers and S. De Spiegeleire (eds), *Post-Soviet Puzzles. Mapping the Political Economy of the Former Soviet Union* (Baden-Baden: Nomos Verlagsgesellschaft, 1995)

T. Shabad and V.L. Mote (eds), *Gateway to Siberian Resources (the BAM)* (Washington, D.C.: Scripta Publishing Co., 1977)

R. Simeon and J. Robinson, *State, Society, and the Development of Canadian Federalism* (University of Toronto Press, 1990)

G. Szoboszki (ed), *Democracy and Political Transformation: Theories and East-Central European Realities* (Budapest: Hungarian Political Science Association, 1991)

W. Taubman, *Governing Soviet Cities. Bureaucratic Politics and Urban Development in the USSR* (London/New York: Praeger Publishers, 1973)

M. Temple, *Regional Economics* (London: Macmillan, 1994)

K. von Beyme, *Systemwechsel in Osteuropa* (Frankfurt a.M.: Suhrkamp Verlag, 1994)

P. Wagstaff (ed), *Regionalism in Europe* (Oxford: Intellect Books, Europa 1(2/3), 1994)

C.I. Wallich, *Fiscal Decentralization. Intergovernmental Relations in Russia* (Washington, D.C.: The World Bank, 1992)

C.I. Wallich (ed), *Russia and the Challenge of Fiscal Federalism* (Washington, D.C.: The World Bank, 1994)

J. Webb, *Beyond Moscow: The Politics of Russia's Regions* (Washington, D.C.: Georgetown University, 1994, mimeo)

RUSSIAN LANGUAGE ARTICLES

E. Aksenova, 'Byudzhet i ekonomicheskaya samostoyatel'nost' regionov', *Mirovaya ekonomika i mezhdunarodnye otnosheniya* (1992) no.5, p. 115–28

V. Aleinikov and T. Mikhailyuk, 'Predvaritel'nye itogi ispolneniya byudzheta kraya za 1993 god', in: A. Sidorov, *et al.*(eds), *Ekonomicheskaya reforma: otsenka sostoyaniya ekonomiki Altaiskogo kraya i blizhaishie perspektivy ee razvitiya* (Barnaul, 1994, p. 41–2)

S. Alekseev, 'Grimasy antitotalitarnoi revolyutsii v Rossii, ili O poiske formuly soglasiya', *Nezavisimaya gazeta*, 19 January 1994, p. 5

D. Brodyanskii, 'Ne zhdat' chuda ot Khlestakovykh', *Utro Rossii*, 13 January 1994, p. 2

D. Gainutdinov, 'Pobedili li Primortsy?', *Utro Rossii*, 12 June 1993, p.2

A. Granberg, 'Ekonomika Sibiri–zadachi strukturnoi politiki', *Kommunist* (1987) no.2, p.31–40

A. Granberg, *et al.* (eds), 'Razvitie proizvoditel'nykh sil Sibiri. Ekonomicheskaya reforma i sotsial'no-ekonomicheskoe razvitie Sibiri', *Region: ekonomika i sotsiologiya* (1991) no.1, p.3–18

S. Grigor'ev, 'K voprosu o sostoyanii i evolyutsii estestvennogo dvizheniya naseleniya Altaiskogo kraya v zone vliyaniya Semipalatinskogo poligona v

1949–1991gg.', in: A. Loginov and T. Sazonova (eds), *Problemy likvidatsii na territorii Altaiskogo kraya posledstvii yadernykh ispytanii na Semipalatinskom poligone* (Novosibirsk, 1993, p.57–70)

I. Grishin, 'K itogam referenduma i vyborov 12 dekabrya 1993g. v Rossii', *Mirovaya ekonomika i mezhdunarodnye otnosheniya* (1994) no.4, p.51–63

K. Guseva, 'Investitsionnaya deyatel'nost' v regionakh Rossii', *Voprosy ekonomiki* (1995) no.3, p.129–34

A. Illarionov, 'Vneshnyaya torgovlya Rossii v 1992–1993 godakh', *Voprosy ekonomiki* (1994) no.6, p.74–91

V. Karavaev, 'Regional'naya investitsionnaya politika: rossiiskie problemy i mezhdunarodnyi opyt', *Voprosy ekonomiki* (1995) no.3, p.135–43

P. Kirkow (1994b), 'Ekonomicheskoe samorazvitie regionov v Rossii: predvaritel'nyi sravnitel'nyi analiz Altaiskogo i Primorskogo kraev', *Region: ekonomika i sotsiologiya* (1994) no.3, p.144–61

I. Korol'kov, 'Okhota v svobodnoi zone', *Izvestiya*, 24 June 1995, p.3

V. Kucherenko, 'Zona bedstviya. Ot kakogo zla uzhe vtoroi god stradaet Primor'e?', *Rossiiskaya gazeta*, 28 September 1994, p.1 and p.7

A. Kurakin, 'Altaiskii ekonomicheskii administrativnyi raion i problemy ego razvitiya', *Izvestiya AN SSSR. Seriya geograficheskaya* (1960) no.6, p.38–46

V. Kuznechevskii, 'Komu ne po dushe edinaya Rossiya', *Rossiiskaya gazeta*, 6 April 1995, p.1–2

A. Lavrov, 'Byudzhetnyi federalizm obraztsa 1994g.: shag vpered, dva shaga nazad', *Rossiya regionov* (Moscow: napravlenie regionalistika analiticheskogo tsentra pri Presidente RF, no.1, October 1994, p.5–8)

A. Lavrov, 'Rossiiskii byudzhetnyi federalizm: pervye shagi, pervye itogi', *Segodnya*, 7 June 1995, p.5

V. Leksin, *et al.*, 'Regional'nye byudzhetno-nalogovye sistemy', *Rossiiskii ekonomicheskii zhurnal* (1994) no.1, p.23–32

V. Leksin and A. Shvetsov (1994), 'Regional'naya politika i formirovanie zemel'nogo rynka', *Rossiiskii ekonomicheskii zhurnal* (1994) no.2, p.41–51

V. Leksin and V. Shvetsov (1994a), 'Gosudarstvennoe regulirovanie i selektivnaya podderzhka regional'nogo razvitiya', *Rossiiskii ekonomicheskii zhurnal* (1994) no.8, pp.37–48

Yu. Levada, 'V Rossii ustanovilas' "demokratiya bezporyadka"', *Segodnya*, 15 April 1995, p.3

L. Maevskaya, 'Regional'naya investitsionnaya politika', *EKO* (1994) no.6, p.72–81

A. Magomedov, 'Politicheskie elity rossiiskoi provintsii', *Mirovaya ekonomika i mezhdunarodnye otnosheniya* (1994) no.4, p.72–9

A. Melkov and R. Gotfrid, 'Razvitie ekonomiki kraya v federal'nykh i kraevykh programmakh', in: A. Sidorov, *et al.*, *op. cit.*, 1994, p.51–2

A. Mel'nik and L.Rodionova, 'Zanyatost' i rynok truda', in: A. Sidorov, *et al.*, *op. cit.*, 1994, p.29–30

V.T. Mishchenko and V.V. Mishchenko, 'Ekonomicheskaya otsenka vliyaniya yadernykh ispytanii na protsess vozproizvodstva prirodnykh resursov', in: A. Loginov and T. Sazonova (eds), *op. cit.*, 1993, p.44–56

A. Novikov (1994), 'Komu nuzhny ustavy regionov?', *Rossiya regionov* (Moscow: napravlenie regionalistika analiticheskogo tsentra pri Presidente RF, no.1, October 1994, p.8–10)

A. Novikov (1994a), 'Monopolizatsiya natsional'noi ekonomiki v regional'nom razreze', *Rossiya regionov* (Moscow: napravlenie regionalistika analiticheskogo tsentra pri Presidente RF, no.2, November 1994, p.5–7)

N. Ostrovskaya, 'Primorskii PAKT', *Izvestiya*, 1 December 1993, p.5

V. Panskov, 'Reforma mestnykh finansov predel'no aktual'na', *Rossiiskii ekonomicheskii zhurnal* (1994) no.9, p.21–5

L. Perepelkin: 'Istoki mezhetnicheskogo konflikta v Tatarii', *Mir Rossii* (1992) vol.1, no.1, p.91–112

N. Petrov (1994), 'Khronika provintsial'noi zhizni', *Rossiya regionov* (Moscow: napravlenie regionalistika analiticheskogo tsentra pri Presidente RF, no.2, November 1994, p.1–4)

N. Petrov (1994a), 'Regional'nye vybory '94: itogi i uroki', *ibid.*, p.8–12

A. Pozdnyakov, 'Regional'naya politika: problemy stanovleniya i metody realizatsii', *Segodnya*, 8 July 1995, p.6

Yu. Rastov, 'Sotsial'noe rassloenie i dinamika napryazhennosti v Altaiskom krae v techenie 1992 goda', *Aktual'nye problemy sotsiologii, psikhologii i sotsial'noi raboty* (Barnaul, vol.2, 1993, p.17–28)

L. Rodionova, 'Vliyanie yadernykh ispytanii na protsess vozproizvodstva naseleniya i trudovykh resursov', in: A. Loginov and T. Sazonova (eds), *op. cit.*, 1993, p.71–83

A. Sarychev, 'V zhestkikh usloviyakh. Deputatskii klub kraevogo Soveta: opyt chetyrekh let raboty', *Altaiskaya pravda*, 12 March 1994, p.2

V. Savalei, 'Primor'e: poisk ekonomicheskoi nishi', *Problemy Dal'nego Vostoka* (1991) no.5, p.71–7

V. Savalei (1994), 'Realii perevernutego mira', *Utro Rossii*, 11 February 1994, p.1–2

V. Savalei (1994a), 'Razvitie ekonomicheskoi reformy v Primorskom krae', in: V. Savalei (ed), *Ekonomika Primorskogo kraya i ryada otraslei Dal'nego Vostoka v period reform 1992– 93gg.* (Vladivostok, 1994, p.3–21)

I. Savvateeva, 'Evgenii Nazdratenko kak zerkalo rossiiskikh reform', *Izvestiya*, 1 December 1994, p.5

T. Sazonov, 'Posledstviya yadernykh ispytanii i ekonomika Altaiskogo kraya: vzaimosvyaz' problem', in: A. Loginov and T. Sazonova (eds), *op. cit.*, 1993, p.17–33

G. Semenov, 'Ratsionalizatsiya vzaimootnoshenii mezhdu federal'nym i regional'nymi byudzhetami: puti obnovleniya nalogovo-byudzhetnogo mekhanizma', *Voprosy ekonomiki* (1994) no.9, p.38–51

A. Sergienko, 'Sotsial'naya differentsiatsiya territorii kraya i problemy ee regulirovaniya', in: A. Loginov and T. Sazonova (eds), *Formirovanie rynochnykh otnoshenii i strukturnaya politika v Altaiskom krae* (Novosibirsk, 1992, p.48–66)

V. Shirobokova, 'Nalogovye neravenstva regionov', *Delovoi mir*, 8–14 May 1995, p.18

A. Shvedov, 'Politicheskaya situatsiya v Altaiskom krae', *Za Rossiyu* (1994) no.8–9, p.2

A. Sidorov, *et al.*, 'Kratkie itogi raboty khozyaistva kraya za 1992–1993 gody', in: A. Sidorov, *et al.*(eds), *op. cit.*, 1994, p.4–5

T. Smirnova, 'Syuzhet dlya dramy', *Utro Rossii*, 23 November 1993, p.1–2

A. Surikov, 'Razmyshleniya s nadezhdoi na budushchee', *Altaiskaya pravda*, 2 November 1993, p.1–2

V. Venevtsev and D. Demkin, 'Zachem "vozdelyvat'" Kuril'skuyu gryadu', *Vladivostok*, 15 September 1994, p.4

G. Yavlinskii, 'Inaya reforma. Vozmozhna drugaya strategiya perekhodnogo perioda', *Nezavisimaya gazeta*, 10 February 1994, p.4

ENGLISH AND GERMAN LANGUAGE ARTICLES

J. Andrews and A. Vacroux, 'Political Change in Leningrad: The Elections of 1990', in: T.H. Friedgut and J.W. Hahn (eds), *Local Power and Post-Soviet Politics* (New York/London: M.E. Sharpe, Armonk, 1994, p.43–72)

R. Bahl, 'Revenues and Revenue Assignment: Intergovernmental Fiscal Relations in the Russian Federation', in: C.I. Wallich (ed), *Russia and the Challenge of Fiscal Federalism* (Washington, D.C.: The World Bank, 1994, p.129–80)

P. Barker, 'The Development of the Major Shared-cost Programs in Canada', in: R.D. Olling and M.W. Westmacott (eds), *Perspectives on Canadian Federalism* (Scarborough, Ontario: Prentice-Hall Canada Inc, 1988)

D. Berkowitz, 'Local Support for Market Reform: Implications of a Consumption Bias', in: T.H. Friedgut and J.W. Hahn (eds), *op. cit.*, 1994, p.192–207

S.A. Billon, 'Centralisation of Authority and Regional Management', in: V.N. Bandera and Z.L. Melnyk (eds), *The Soviet Economy in Regional Perspective* (New York: Praeger Publishers, 1973)

M. Bornstein, 'Russia's Mass Privatisation Programme', *Communist Economies & Economic Transformation* (1994) vol.6, no.4, p.419–57

M.J. Bradshaw and P. Hanson, 'Regions, Local Power and Reform in Russia', in: R.W. Campbell (ed), *Issues in the Transformation of Centrally Planned Economies. Essays in Honor of Gregory Grossman* (Boulder Co: Westview Press, 1994)

L. Bruszt, 'Transformative Politics: Social Costs and Social Peace in Eastern Europe', *East European Politics and Society* (Winter 1992) vol.6, no.1, pp.5–72

A. Bull, 'Regionalism in Italy', in: P. Wagstaff (ed), *Regionalism in Europe* (Oxford: Intellect Books, Europa 1 (2/3), 1994, p.69–83)

A. Butt Philip, 'Regionalism in the United Kingdom', in: P. Wagstaff (ed), *op. cit.*, 1994, p.99–115

D.T. Cattell, 'Local Government and the Sovnarkhoz in the USSR, 1957–62', *Soviet Studies* (1964) vol.15, no.4, p.430–42

L.G. Churchward, 'Public Participation in the USSR', in: E.M. Jacobs (ed), *Soviet Local Politics and Government* (London: Allen & Unwin, 1983)

S. Clarke, *et al.*, 'The Privatisation of Industrial Enterprises in Russia: Four Case-studies', *Europe-Asia Studies* (1994) vol.46, no.2, p.179–214

M. Cline, 'Nizhnii Novgorod: A Regional View of the Russian Elections', *RFE/RL Research Report*, vol.3, no.4, 28 January 1994, p.48–54

T.J. Courchene (1988), 'Equalization Payments and the Division of Powers', in: R.D. Olling and M.W. Westmacott (eds), *op. cit.*, 1988

T.J. Courchene (1988a), 'Economic Management and the Distribution of Powers', in: R.D. Olling and M.W. Westmacott (eds), *op. cit.*, 1988

M. Delyagin and L. Freinkman, 'Extrabudgetary Funds in Russian Public Finance', *RFE/RL Research Report*, vol.2, no.48, 3 December 1993, p.49–54

P. de Souza, 'Siberian Futures? Economic Perspectives', *Sibirica. A Journal of North Pacific Studies* (Winter 1990–1) vol.1, no.2, p.170–83

L. Dienes, 'The Development of Siberian Regions: Economic Profiles, Income Flows and Strategies for Growth', *Soviet Geography: Review and Translation* (April 1982) vol.XXIII, no.4, p.205–44

L. Dienes (1987a), 'Regional Planning and the Development of Soviet Asia', *Soviet Geography: Review and Translation*, vol.XXVIII, no.5, p.287–314

L. Dienes, 'Perestroyka and the Slavic Regions', *Soviet Economy* (1989) vol.5, no.3, p.251–75

L. Dienes, 'Siberia: Perestroyka and Economic Development', *Soviet Geography* (1991) vol.XXXII, no.7, p.445–57

O. Dmitrieva, 'Die regionale Entwicklung im Zeitraum der Wirtschaftsreform', in: K. Segbers (ed), *Rußlands Zukunft: Räume und Regionen* (Baden-Baden: Nomos Verlagsgesellschaft, 1994, p.99–117)

W. Easterly and P. Vieira da Cunha, 'Financing the Storm: Macroeconomic Crisis in Russia', *Economics of Transition* (1994) vol.2, no.4, p.443–65

Q. Fan and M.E. Schaffer, 'Government Financial Transfers and Enterprise Adjustment in Russia, With Comparisons to Central and Eastern Europe', *Economics of Transition* (1994) vol.2, no.2, p.151–88

D.V. Friedheim, 'Bringing Society Back into Democratic Transition Theory after 1989: Pact Making and Regime Collapse', *East European Politics and Societies* (Fall 1993) vol.7, no.3, p.482–512

R. Frydman and A. Rapaczynski, 'Insiders and the State: Overview of Responses to Agency Problems in East European Privatizations', *Economics of Transition* (1993) vol.1, no.1, p.39–59

A.G. Gagnon and J. Garcea, 'Quebec and the Pursuit of Special Status', in: R.D. Olling and M.W. Westmacott (eds), *op. cit.*, 1988

J.W. Gillula, 'The Growth and Structure of Fixed Capital', in: I.S. Koropeckyj and G.E. Schroeder (eds), *Economics of Soviet Regions* (New York: Praeger, 1981)

A. Granberg, 'The Restructuring of the Soviet Economy and Propects for Siberia's Development', *International Regional Science Review* (1989) vol.12, no.3, p.291–304

J.W. Hahn, 'Reforming Post-Soviet Russia: The Attitudes of Local Politicians', in: T.H. Friedgut and J.W. Hahn (eds), *op. cit.*, 1994, p.208–38

F.E.I. Hamilton, 'Spatial Dimensions of Soviet Economic Decision Making', in: V.N. Bandera and Z.L. Melnyk (eds), *op. cit.*, 1973

P. Hanson, 'Local Power and Market Reform in Russia', *Communist Economies & Economic Transformation* (1993) vol.5, no.1, p.45–60

P. Hanson (1994), 'The Center versus the Periphery in Russian Economic Policy', *RFE/RL Research Report*, vol.3, no.17, April 1994, p.23–8

B. Harasymiw, 'Party "Leadership" of the Local Soviets', in: E.M. Jacobs (ed.), *op. cit.*, 1983

P. Henze, 'The Demography of the RSFSR', in: K.Segbers (ed.), *op. cit.*, 1994, p.13–25

R.J. Hill, 'The Development of Soviet Local Government Since Stalin's Death', in: E.M. Jacobs (ed), *op. cit.*, 1983

V. Holubnychy, 'Spatial Efficiency in the Soviet Economy', in: V.N. Bandera and Z.L. Melnyk (eds), *op. cit.*, 1973

J.F. Hough, 'The Russian Election of 1993: Public Attitudes Toward Economic Reform and Democratization', *Post-Soviet Affairs* (1994) vol.10, no.1, p.1–37

T.O. Hueglin, 'Federalism in Comparative Perspective', in: R.D. Olling and M.W. Westmacott (eds), *op. cit.*, 1988

J. Hughes, 'Regionalism in Russia: The Rise and Fall of Siberian Agreement', *Europe-Asia Studies* (1994) vol.46, no.7, p.1133–61

E.M. Jacobs (1983), 'Introduction: The Organizational Framework of Soviet Local Government', in: E.M. Jacobs (ed), *op. cit.*, 1983

E.M. Jacobs (1983a), 'Norms of Representation and the Composition of Local Soviets', in: E.M. Jacobs (ed), *op. cit.*, 1983

A.C. Janos, 'Continuity and Change in Eastern Europe: Strategies of Post-Communist Politics', *East European Politics and Societies* (Winter 1994) vol.8, no.1, p.1–31

P. Kirkow (1993), 'Das Konzept "Freier Wirtschaftszonen" in Rußland. Seine Entwicklung von 1988 bis Herbst 1992', *Osteuropa* (1993) no.3, p.229–43

P. Kirkow (1993a), 'Regionale Politik und wirtschaftliche Ausdifferenzierung. Eine Fallstudie über Rußlands fernöstlichen Primorskij Kraj', *Osteuropa* (1993) no.8, p.754–70

P. Kirkow (1994), 'Das Altaj-Gebiet zwischen Autonomiebestrebung und wirtschaftlicher Ausdifferenzierung. Eine Fallstudie', *Osteuropa* (1994) no.4, p.367–84

P. Kirkow (1994a), 'Regional Politics and Market Reform in Russia: The Case of the Altai', *Europe-Asia Studies* (1994) vol.46, no.7, p.1163–87

P. Kirkow (1995), 'Regionale Besonderheiten systemischer Transformation in Rußland, Polen und Bulgarien. Eine Dreiländerstudie', *Osteuropa* (1995) no.2, p.120–33

P. Kirkow (1995a), 'Regional Warlordism in Russia: The Case of Primorskii *Krai*', *Europe-Asia Studies* (1995) vol.47, no.6, p.923–47

P. Kirkow (1995b), 'Russia's Palermo in the Far East: Politics and Economics in Primorskii *Krai*', in: K. Segbers and S. De Spiegeleire (eds), *Post-Soviet Puzzles. Mapping the Political Economy of the Former Soviet Union* (Baden-Baden: Nomos Verlagsgesellschaft, vol.II, 1995, p.325–370)

P. Kirkow (1995c), 'Roulette zwischen Zentrum und Regionen. Rußlands asymmetrischer Föderalismus', *Osteuropa* (1995) no.11, p.1004–1020

P. Kirkow, 'Roulette zwischen Zentrum und Regionen (II). Rußlands wirtschaftlicher Umbruch', *Osteuropa* (1996) no.1, p.13–29

P. Kirkow (1996a), 'The Siberian and Far Eastern Challenge for New Centre-Periphery Relations in Russia: A Comparison Between Altaiskii and Primorskii Kraya', in: J. Gibson and P. Hanson (eds), *Transformation from Below. Local Power and the Political Economy of Post-Communist Transitions* (Cheltenham: Edward Elgar, 1996)

P. Kirkow and P. Hanson, 'The Potential for Autonomous Regional Development in Russia: The Case of Primorskiy Kray', *Post- Soviet Geography* (1994) vol.35, no.2, p.63–88

I.S. Koropeckyj, 'Growth and Productivity', in: I.S. Koropeckyj and G.E. Schroeder (eds), *op. cit.*, 1981

A. Kuznetsov, 'Economic Reforms in Russia: Enterprise Behaviour as an Impediment to Change', *Europe-Asia Studies* (1994) vol.46, no.6, p.955–70

C.W. Lewis, 'The Economic Functions of Local Soviets', in: E.M. Jacobs (ed.), *op. cit.*, 1983

J.I. Litvack, 'Regional Demands and Fiscal Federalism', in: C.I. Wallich (ed), *op. cit.*, 1994, p.218–40

R.E. Lonsdale, 'The Concept of the Territorial-Production Complex', *Slavic Review* (1965) no.3, p.479–96

J. Martinez-Vazquez, 'Expenditures and Expenditure Assignment', in: C.I. Wallich (ed.), *op. cit.*, 1994, p.96–128

M. McAuley, 'Politics, Economics, and Elite Realignment in Russia: A Regional Perspective', *Soviet Economy* (1992) vol.8, no.1, p.46–88

C.E. McLure, Jr, 'The Sharing of Taxes on Natural Resources and the Future of the Russian Federation', in: C.I. Wallich (ed), *op. cit.*, 1994, p.181–217

Z. Mieczkowski, 'The 1962–1963 Reforms in Soviet Economic Regionalization', *Slavic Review* (1965) no.3, p.479–96

K. Mildner, 'Lokale Finanzen und kommunale Selbstverwaltung in Rußland', *Osteuropa* (1995) no.8, p.1–20

J. Miller, 'The Decentralization of Industry', *Soviet Studies* (1957–8) vol.9, no.1, p.65–83

B. Mitchneck, 'The Changing Role of the Local Budget in Russian Cities: The Case of Yaroslavl', in: T.H. Friedgut and J.W. Hahn (eds), *op. cit.*, 1994, p.73–95

J.C. Moses, 'Saratov and Volgograd, 1990–92: A Tale of Two Russian Provinces', in: T.H. Friedgut and J.W. Hahn (eds), *op cit*, 1994, p.96–137

P. Murrell, 'Conservative Political Philosophy and the Strategy of Economic Transition', *East European Politics and Societies* (Winter 1992) vol.6, no.1, p.3–16

W.E. Oates, 'Fiscal Decentralization and Economic Development', *National Tax Journal* (1992) vol.XLVI, no.2, p.237–43

'Panel on Siberia: Economic and Territorial Issues', *Soviet Geography* (June 1991) vol.XXXII, no.6, p.363–432

A. Przeworski, 'Political Dynamics of Economic Reforms: East and South', in: G. Szoboszki (ed), *Democracy and Political Transformation: Theories and East-Central Realities*, Budapest: Hungarian Political Science Association, 1991, p.21–74

P. Rutland (1994), 'Privatisation in Russia: One Step Forward: Two Steps Back?', *Europe-Asia Studies* (1994) vol.46, no.7, p.1109–31

P. Rutland (1994a), 'A Twisted Path Toward a Market Economy', *Transition*, OMRI, 1994 in review, part II, p.12–18

T. Shabad, 'Siberian Resource Development in the Soviet Period', in: T. Shabad and V.L. Mote (eds), *Gateway to Siberian Resources (the BAM)*, Washington, D.C.: Scripta Publishing Co, 1977

D.J.B. Shaw, 'Regional Planning in the USSR', *Soviet Geography: Review and Translation* (1986) vol.XXVII, no.7, p.469–84

D. Slider, 'Privatization in Russia's Regions', *Post-Soviet Affairs* (1994) vol.10, no.4, p.367–96

T. Stammen, 'Federalism in Germany', in: P. Wagstaff (ed), *op. cit.*, 1994, p.51–67

D. Stark, 'Path Dependency and Privatization Strategies in East Central Europe', *East European Politics and Societies* (Winter 1992) vol.6, no.1, p.17–54

G. Stevenson, 'The Division of Powers', in: R.D. Olling and M.W. Westmacott (eds), *op. cit.*, 1988

R.J. Struyk and J. Daniell, 'Housing Privatization in Urban Russia', *Economics of Transition* (1995) vol.3, no.2, p.197–214

P. Sutela, 'Insider Privatisation in Russia: Speculations on Systemic Change', *Europe-Asia Studies* (1994) vol.46, no.3, p.417–35

E. Teague, 'North-South Divide: Yeltsin and Russia's Provincial Leaders', *RFE/RL Research Report*, vol.2, no.47, 26 November 1993, pp.7–23

E. Teague, 'Russia and Tatarstan Sign Power-sharing Treaty', *RFE/RL Research Report*, vol.3, no.14, 8 April 1994, p.19– 27

E. Teague, 'Russia and the Regions: The Uses of Ambiguity', in: J.Gibson & P. Hanson, *op. cit.*, 1996

S. Thomas and H. Kroll, 'The Political Economy of Privatization in Russia', *Communist Economies & Economic Transformation* (1993) vol.5, no.4, p.445–59

V. Tolz, 'Problems in Building Democratic Institutions in Russia', *RFE/RL Research Report*, vol.3, no.9, 4 March 1994, p.1–7

M.B. Trofimenko, 'Legal Aspects of Economic Centralisation', in: V.N. Bandera and Z.L. Melnyk (eds), *op. cit.*, 1973

A. Vacroux, 'Privatization in the Regions: Primorsky Krai', in: *Russia: Creating Private Enterprises and Efficient Markets*, Washington, D.C.: The World Bank, The Private Sector Development Department, 1994, p.35–44

H. van Ees and H. Garretsen, 'The Theoretical Foundation of the Reforms in Eastern Europe: Big Bang versus Gradualism and the Limitations of Neo-classical Theory', *Economic Systems* (March 1994) vol.18, no.1, p.1–13

H.-J. Wagener, 'Rules of Location and the Concept of Rationality: The Case of the USSR', in: V.N. Bandera and Z.L. Melnyk (eds), *op. cit.*, 1973

A. Williams, 'Regionalism in Iberia', in: P. Wagstaff (ed), *op. cit.*, 1994, p.85–97

J. Wishnevsky, 'Problems of Russian Regional Leadership', *RFE/RL Research Report*, vol.3, no.19, 13 May 1994, p.6–13

H. Wollmann, 'Jelzins Reformpolitik im Dickicht des institutionellen Umbruchs und des Machtkampfes in Rußland', in: H.U. Derlien, U. Gerhardt and F.W. Scharpf (eds), *Systemrationalität und Partialinteresse. Festschrift für Renate Mayntz*, Baden-Baden: Nomos Verlagsgesellschaft, 1994, p.329–53

J.F. Young, 'Institutions, Elites, and Local Politics in Russia: The Case of Omsk', in: T.H. Friedgut and J.W. Hahn (eds), *op. cit.*, 1994, p.138–61

R.A. Young, *et al.*, 'The Concept of Province-building: A Critique', in: R.D. Olling and M.W. Westmacott (eds), *op. cit.*, 1988

V. Zaslavsky and R.J. Brym, 'The Structure of Power and the Functions of Soviet Local Elections', in: E.M. Jacobs (ed), *op. cit.*, 1983

RUSSIAN STATISTICAL SOURCES

Goskomstat RSFSR, *Narodnoe khozyaistvo Primorskogo kraya v 1990 godu*, Vladivostok, 1991

Goskomstat Rossii, *Osnovnye pokazateli sotsial'no-ekonomicheskogo razvitiya i khoda ekonomicheskoi reformy v Rossiiskoi Federatsii za 1993 god*, Moscow, 1994

Glossary

Agropromsoyuz	Regional administration of the former Soviet Union's *Gosagroprom* created under Gorbachev
AK	Altaiskii *krai*
Altaiagropromsnab	AK committee for supply of agro-industrial materials
Altaiavtodor	AK motorway construction company
Altaidizel'	AK diesel engine company
Altaienergo	AK energy company
Altaienergouglesnab	AK energy and coal supply company
Altaikoksokhimstroi	AK chemical coke construction company
Altaimolprom	AK milk industrial processing company
Altainefteprodukt	AK oil processing company
Altaipromstroi	AK industrial construction company
Altaisel'khozbank	AK bank for agricultural producers
Altaisel'mash	AK agricultural machinery company
Altaiskotoprom	AK industrial livestock processing company
Altaistroi	AK construction company
Altaistroizakazchik	AK construction order company
Altaizernoprodukt	AK grain production company
APK	Agro-industrial complex
ASSR	Autonomous Soviet Socialist Republic
Astrakhan'gazprom	Astrakhan' *oblast'* subsidiary of *Gazprom*
Bashkirenergo	Energy company in Bashkir republic
Bashneft'	Oil company in Bashkir republic

Bashuralenergostroi	Energy construction company in Bashkir republic and Urals
BBC	British Broadcasting Corporation
CBR	Central Bank of Russia
Chuvashenergo	Energy company in Chuvash republic
CIS	Commonwealth of Independent States
CMEA	Council for Mutual Economic Assistance
CPI	Consumer price index
CPSU	Communist Party of the Soviet Union
Dal'energo	Russian Far Eastern energy company
Dal'moreprodukt	Russian Far Eastern sea product company
EES Rossii	'Russian Unified Energy System', the national energy company
Federation Council	Upper house of the Russian parliament
FEZ	Free economic zone
FIG	Financial-industrial group
FYP	Five-Year Plan
Gazprom	Russian leading gas company
GDP	Gross domestic product
GKI	Federal Committee for Property Administration
GNP	Gross national product
Gosagroprom	State Agro-industrial Committee created under Gorbachev
Gosek	Soviet State Economic Commission during the *sovnarkhozy* period
Goskontrol	Soviet Committee of State Auditing
Goskomstat	Federal Committee for Statistics
Gosplan	Soviet State Planning Committee

IMF	International Monetary Fund
IPI	Industrial price index
kolkhoz	Collective farm, plural *kolkhozy*
KPRF	Communist Party of the Russian Federation
krai	Subnational administrative-territorial unit, plural *kraya*
Länder	Federal provinces in Germany
LDPR	Liberal-democratic Party of Russia
Magadanenergo	Energy company in Magadan *oblast'*
Minfin	Russian Ministry of Finance
MO	Money supply in cash
NMP	Net material product
NTS	People's Labour Union
obkom	Provincial CPSU committee, plural *obkomy*
oblast'	Subnational administrative-territorial unit, plural *oblasti*
okrug	Subnational administrative-territorial unit, plural *okruga*
OTD	Trade house in Omsk *oblast'*
PAKT	Primorskii Shareholding Company of Commodity Producers
Perestroika	Policy of reconstruction under Gorbachev
PK	Primorskii *krai*
PKTV	Primorskii commercial TV company
PPP	Purchasing power parity
PRES	Party of Russian Unity and Accord
Primorkhleboprodukt	PK bread products company
Primorrybprom	PK fish processing company

Primorskuglesbyt	PK coal selling company
Primorskugol'	PK coal company
Promstroibank	Bank for Industrial Construction
Radiopribor	PK-based defence-related enterprise
raion	Local administrative-territorial unit, plural *raiony*
RF	Russian Federation
Roskomrybolovstvo	Russian Committee for Fishing Industry
Rosugol'	Russian national coal company
RSFSR	Russian Soviet Federal Socialist Republic
Sibenergosnab	Siberian energy supply company
sovkhoz	State farm, plural *sovkhozy*
sovnarkhoz	Regional Economic Council, plural *sovnarkhozy*
starosta	Elderly man, head of local self-government
State Duma	Lower house of the Russian parliament
TEK	Fuel and energy complex
TPC	Territorial Production Complex
UK	United Kingdom of Great Britain and Northern Ireland
USSR	Union of Soviet Socialist Republics
VAT	Value added tax
VE	Victory over Europe
Vostokrybkholodflota	PK-based fishing fleet
VPK	Military-industrial complex
zemvstvo	Pre-revolutionary territorial subdivision

Note: Russian words which are commonly used in English language articles such as soviet, nomenklatura or intelligentsia are not particularly emphasized.

Index

Figures in italic, tables in bold